Justice Chambers
1987

Black and African Theologies

The Bishop Henry McNeal Turner Studies
in North American Black Religion

Vol 1. *For My People*
    by James H. Cone

Editor:

James H. Cone,
Union Theological Seminary, New York

Associate Editors:

Charles H. Long,
University of North Carolina, Chapel Hill

C. Shelby Rooks,
United Church Board of Homeland Ministries

Gayraud S. Wilmore,
New York Theological Seminary

The purpose of this series is to encourage the development of biblical, historical, theological, and pastoral works that analyze the role of the churches and other religious movements in the liberation struggles of blacks in the United States and the Third World. What is the relationship between black religion and black peoples' fight for justice in the U.S.? What is the relationship between the black struggle for justice in the U.S. and the liberation struggles of the poor in Asia, Africa, Latin America, and the Caribbean? A critical investigation of these and related questions will define the focus of this series.

The series is named after Bishop Henry McNeal Turner (1834–1915), whose life and work symbolize the black struggle for liberation in the U.S. and the Third World. Bishop Turner was a churchman, a political figure, a missionary, a pan-Africanist—a champion of black freedom and the cultural creativity of black peoples under God.

*The Bishop Henry McNeal Turner Studies
in North American Black Religion, Vol. II*

Josiah U. Young

Black and African Theologies

Siblings or Distant Cousins?

ORBIS BOOKS
Maryknoll, New York 10545

The Catholic Foreign Mission Society of America (Maryknoll) recruits and trains people for overseas missionary service. Through Orbis Books Maryknoll aims to foster the international dialogue that is essential to mission. The books published, however, reflect the opinions of their authors and are not meant to represent the official position of the society.

Manuscript editor: William E. Jerman

Library of Congress Cataloging-in-Publication Data

Young, Josiah U. (Josiah Ulysses)
  Black and African theologies.

  (The Bishop Henry McNeal Turner studies in North American Black religion; vol. 2)
  Bibliography : p.
  Includes index.
  1. Black theology.   2. Theology, Doctrinal—Africa, Sub-Saharan.   I. Title.   II. Series.
BT82.7.Y68   1985   200'.96   85–32090
ISBN 0–88344–252–3 (pbk.)

To my wife Pamela Monroe

Contents

Preface

This book is more than a product of long years of education. It is also a result of my long search for wholeness and identity. Wholeness, it seems to me, is achieved in a relationship with God that in faith allows one to be comfortable with the ramifications of contingency. My own self-identity has been heightened through intense probing into African and Afro-American experiences. It seems logical, then, that my study focus upon theologies that extract and articulate notions of God from experiences and idioms intrinsic to Africa and the African diaspora.

Afro-American and African theologies have much to teach us. Attesting to a God of liberation and indigenization, they rightly seek to send the cancer of white supremacy into remission. From them we learn that liberation from oppression and preservation of authentic culture are critical to the integrity of the church. What is more, they teach us that struggles against systemic racism and quests to modify and develop indigenous cultures are sanctified in the image of God, in the humanity of God, and in the Spirit of God. (If we are created in God's image, then certainly all cultures bear the impress of the orders of preservation; if Jesus is Reconciler, then we are to live unburdened by gross bigotry; if the Spirit is to redeem us, then She must work against oppression.)

Humanity is broken if humans oppress one another; and our identity as *homo sapiens* is vitiated if we fail to see God's image incarnate in aspects of the cultures of others. We are not Christian if we crucify our neighbors; we miss a critical christological insight if we mandate that Christianity conform to European cultural patterns. We learn in Acts 10:15 that all of us are acceptable to Christ largely as we are. Remember, none of us, really, are unclean. Neither precious memories and rhythms that remind us of our ancestors nor a dogged commitment to extinguish a sickening chauvinism are lost in Christ. Rather, he fructifies them.

Affirmation here of a certain fruition in Christ serves two purposes in relation to Afro-American and African theologies. The first purpose is to stress that a certain wholeness in God is intrinsic to celebrations of African and Afro-American identities. The second purpose is to reveal that God *may* speak prophetically to us today through oppressed blacks—through their refusal to accept oppression, through their critical development of their cultures.

Many persons to whom I am grateful for critical support must be acknowledged.

Encouraging me as a master of divinity student, guiding me as a doctoral student, Professor James Cone has been my mentor at Union Theological Seminary. Moreover, this book is a product of Dr. Cone's vision. He suggested I write on this topic at the very beginning of my doctoral program. He knew the topic would delight and inspire me.

Professor Christopher Morse offered suggestions that helped clarify issues related to the liberal and neo-orthodox theologies of Europe. Immeasurably helpful have been critical readings of the text by Professors Roger Shinn, Robert Handy, and Kosuke Koyama. Also helpful were Professors James Washington and Cornel West. Professor Gayraud Wilmore granted me an interview and offered valuable insight into meetings between Afro-American and African theologians.

My fellow doctoral scholars asked hard, sharp questions with which I must continue to wrestle. I especially thank Kelly Brown, Alonzo Johnson, Dennis Wiley, Dwight Hopkins, and Sherrill Holland for their penetrating critiques and sincere support.

My good friend Kenneth Jackson has been an inspiration. His knowledge of and love for Africans and his strong support of my work have been such a help. He understands those who appreciate the "blues" and has initiated me into the complexities of the new jazz. Those rhythms have really kept me going—"we all must have our kindred spirits." Walter Stafford, a black scholar and friend, read the manuscript and has been very encouraging.

Because my trip to South Africa provided valuable insight for this study, additional thanks are due Professor Koyama and Reverend Dr. Isaac Bivens for securing for me funds to travel there in 1982. Critical insight into the South African situation was provided by the South Africans I met during my visit there. I cannot name them all. Special thanks go to Dr. James Moulder; Dr. Allan Boesak; certain young persons of Langa; faculty and students at the Federal Theological Seminary; Professor Simon Mimela and his family; former political prisoners and detainees; and the Reverend Dr. Beyers Naudé. Special thanks go to the family and congregation of the Reverend Dr. Elia Tema. And to Elia I say thank you for our long and inspiring conversations on black and African theologies. In New York City Dr. Peter Molutsi graciously talked with me at length about his experiences as an African freedom fighter. Particularly fascinating were his insights into the life and thought of Kwame Nkrumah.

Indispensably critical to the completion of this study has been Carol Pusano. Ms. Pusano typed this study masterfully, efficiently, and swiftly. Cheerfully and graciously she picked up the many edits and revisions. I cannot express the depth of my gratitude to her.

My thanks are also due Ms. Betty Bolden. A remarkably efficient librarian, Ms. Bolden has often been of invaluable assistance to me in my search for materials.

I must honor my beloved parents, Josiah and Jacqueline. Without their love and sacrifices, I could not have come this far. My dear siblings—Debbie, Lorri, and Geoffrey—have been my cheerleaders in all this, showing deep love and respect for their "big brother." Kevin Harris, my first cousin, has been very supportive, patiently listening to my ideas for years. I have learned much from him. Intellectually and spiritually, he is my "double."

Betty and Eddie Monroe, my in-laws, have been wonderfully supportive, never once making a disparaging remark as I forsook full-time employment to focus exclusively on my studies. My sister-in-law Marilyn has been a jewel of support. She frequently buys little books for me and one of them was valuable for the early progress of my work. Eddie Monroe, my brother-in-law, has been a best friend and a source of encouragement. Another supportive in-law has been Martha Wynn.

Above all on earth I thank my darling wife Pamela Monroe. The depth of her love and support for me is ineffable. She critically, painstakingly, and lovingly read the first draft. Because of her efforts, revisions suggested by my advisors were minor.

Acronyms

AACC	All Africa Conference of Churches
AME	African Methodist Episcopal
CMS	Christian Missionary Society
EATWOT	Ecumenical Association of Third World Theologians
NCBC	National Conference of Black Churchmen
SNCC	Student Non-Violent Coordinating Committee
SSBR	Society for the Study of Black Religion
UTS	Union Theological Seminary
WCC	World Council of Churches

Introduction

Black North American theologians are of African descent and thus share with African theologians the racial characteristics of blackness. Within the contexts of their histories of domination by the people of Europe, moreover, both groups have accepted the Christian faith from white missionaries. They found additional similarity in their rejections of elements of the liberal and neo-orthodox theologies of Europe.[1]

Both have emerged in contexts of white oppression. They are agreed that the oppression of blacks is inconsistent with the gospel. What is more, Afro-American and African theologies emerged in the late 1960s—during the after-math of the civil rights movement and decolonization. These movements affirmed blacks' rejection of white supremacist rule, and specifically set the contexts for both theologies.

As products of the black church of the United States, Afro-American theologians are related to African theologians in the historical role black North American clergy played in African christianization. Among both groups of theologians, elements of the Pan-African views of those clergymen are still evident.[2] Certain black theologians claim, moreover, that black theology should rely more upon aspects of African traditional religion to sharpen the distinctions between black theology and liberal and neo-orthodox theologies.[3] Should more black theologians adopt the much contested view that traditional Africa has yielded a monolithic worldview relevant for black theology, then both theologies would be influenced by African traditional thought.

Black theology, however, is a theology of liberation. African theology, on the other hand, is a theology of indigenization or, more specifically, africaniza-tion.[4] In spite of their similarities, the two theologies differ radically in theolog-ical focus.

African theology represents efforts of black Africans to make the Christian theology inherited from Europe continuous with African traditional religious thought. An additional goal of African theologians is to indigenize the mis-sionary church with an African clergy and liturgies, African in music, lan-guage, and movement. Very much related to African theology are the independent churches, which have achieved a certain syncretism between African traditional religion and mission Christianity without an effort to synthesize this mixture into an academic, systematic theology. For my pur-poses, African theology refers neither to the Coptic nor Ethiopian Orthodox theologies, nor to the theologies of the North African scholars of the patristic

1

period. African theology is not African traditional religion, although the latter has an important relationship to the work of African theologians. Lastly, African theology is distinct from the reflections of African Muslims and black South African *liberation* theologians. In sum, the major task of African theologians is to expose continuities and discontinuities between African traditional religion and Christian faith. Favoring a theological agenda grounded explicitly in a cultural problem, African theologians give little attention to political problems of postcolonial Africa.

Black theology in the United States is, by contrast, sharply political, condemning the institutions and attitudes that exacerbate black suffering. As the well-known black theologian James Cone defines it: "Black theology is a theology of liberation because it . . . arises from an identification with oppressed blacks of America, seeking to interpret the gospel of Christ in the light of the black condition" (*Liberation*, 23).

Although black South African theologians are creators of a black theology, I use the term primarily in reference to the black North American theology of liberation. Black theology here, then, is a post–civil rights discourse—a development out of the black power movement and the theological reflections of members of the radical black clergy who sensed a prophetic revelation within black power rhetoric. It first appeared on the academic scene with the publication of James Cone's *Black Theology and Black Power* in 1969. A more systematic exposition appeared in 1970 with Cone's *A Black Theology of Liberation*. Inasmuch as black theological discourse has received contributions from other scholars—J. D. Roberts, Cecil Cone, Gayraud Wilmore, Major Jones, Charles Long, William Jones, Jacquelyn Grant et al.—I shall attempt to reflect the plurality of black theological discourse since 1969.

Dissimilarity between the two streams of theology invites reexamination of their similarities. It seems the more I analyze their sameness, the more their differences come irrepressibly to the fore.

For instance, although Afro-American theologians have African roots, they have been less influenced by African cultures than are Africans indigenous to that continent.

Afro-Americans' ignorance of their ancestry is one of the ramifications of chattel slavery. Slavery forcibly and brutally weakened the cultural legacy of the Africans traded into slavery. Although slaves passed vestiges of African culture to their descendants, this culture does not influence blacks in the United States to the degree it does other blacks in the Americas (DuBois, *Negro*, 113). African cultural legacy in the United States is fused with elements of European culture.[5] Unlike, then, African theologians initiated into the complexities of their traditional religions, black North American theologians are unable to gain adequate knowledge of African traditional religion solely by way of black folk religion in the United States. Those wishing to understand in depth the African roots of black religion must come under the tutelage of Africans who have insight into African traditional religion. That the two groups of theologians are racially similar hardly makes them the same.

Reexamining the rejection by both theologies of elements of the liberal and neo-orthodox theologies of Europe, I find these rejections at different points and with different nuances. For Afro-American theologians, European theology failed to make the problem of black suffering crucial to theological reflection. In the North American context, black theologians ask: "How can theologians influenced by the liberal and neo-orthodox schools of Europe do theology without reference to the historical oppression of blacks?"[6] African theologians, on the other hand, reject the liberal and neo-orthodox tendencies to equate African traditional religion with animistic barbarism, and traditional African institutions generally with cultural inferiority (see Idowu, *African Traditional Religion*).

Why are two theologies, emerging simultaneously in rebellion to white domination, so heterogeneous in theological focus? After all, if enslavement of blacks in the West is half the history of European exploitation of Africans, is not the other half European colonization of Africa after 1885? Although the answer seems to be yes, both theologies spring from *different* histories of African peoples. There is the history of an African people of the United States and that of the majority of Africans who remained on the continent or returned there in the nineteenth century. Still, these histories reveal points of substantial contact through individuals who show an essential parity in thought.

Thus far, the paradoxical relationship of black theology to African theology has been noted. Because the two are similar *and* dissimilar, quick judgments as to their precise relationship must be resisted. The two are neither wholly the same nor wholly different.

I find it understandable, then, that dissent exists among black North American and African theologians regarding the nature of their relationship. South African theologian Desmond Tutu, for instance, argues that the two groups of theologians are soul mates, and North American theologian James Cone appears sympathetic to that view. The Kenyan, John Mbiti, however, with the Sierra Leonean, E. W. Fashole-Luke, asserts that the two have little in common.

This study upholds the view that there is ground for a future alignment between black theologians of the United States and Africa. Inasmuch as black theologians in both places share similarities, black liberation themes might join with themes of African indigenization in a theology relevant to Africa and its diaspora. Together they might render valuable service to the poor and thus to the gospel. That, it seems to me, is why such a study is important. Before that possibility is entertained, however, a more fundamental question begs for an answer: Are black and African theologies siblings or at best only distant cousins? "Siblings" functions metaphorically to denote the possibility for a future intimate association between black and African theologians. Derived from Desmond Tutu's use of the term "soul mates," "siblings" here represents the view that ancestral, political, and religious connections between blacks in North America and Africa are strong enough for their theologians to eventually adopt a common theological perspective. I use "distant cousins" in modification of Bishop Tutu's use of the term "antagonist," which is derived from the views of African theologians such as John Mbiti and E. W. Fashole-Luke. For these theologians, Afro-American and African theologies are radically dissimilar and have no prospect for a future symbiosis. From their perspective, ancestral, political, and religious connections between blacks in North America and Africa are negligible.

An answer to the question—siblings or distant cousins?—requires an indepth examination of the two theologies in relation to one another. I shall now give an account of the method employed for this task.

Black and African theologies are intrinsically related to Afro-American and African churches, which broadly represent the historical experience of blacks in the United States and Africa. A conclusion on the relationship of the two theologies, then, requires a broad understanding of pertinent epochs within the black experience in Africa and the United States. Such an understanding will help account for the nature and scope of black and African theologies, and give a certain insight into the reasons for their similarities and differences.

In chapter 1, therefore, I examine historical antecedents of both theologies from the nineteenth to the twentieth centuries. In each period studied, the ramifications of chattel slavery and colonization are noted *only* in relation to the development of both theologies. Thus, historical analysis here will be neither exhaustive nor strictly comprehensive. I am concerned, moreover, only with *the history to which both groups of theologians relate themselves*. Critical appraisal of the way in which those theologians do so is beyond my concern, as is an apologetic against the view that Afro-American liberation theologians tend to be ahistorical.[7] In addition, focus upon certain writers, movements, and events is highly selective. In short, I highlight examples of antecedents of black and African theologies in order to show the emergence of both from a particular history.

Chapter 1 ends in the period spanning the years from 1969 and the present, years in which both theologies have grown significantly. In order to begin to assess this growth and appreciate substantially their differences in perspective, chapter 2 critically examines black theology, focusing on the various ways black theologians accent the theme of liberation. Chapter 3 examines African theology as a theology of indigenization. Because African traditional religion is essential to the process of theological africanization, the broad contours of this religion are discussed, and then the ways in which African theologians are attempting to relate African traditional religions to Christian doctrines.[8]

If, then, the basis of comparison in chapter 1 is historical, in chapters 2 and 3 it is textual: the writings of black theologians in the United States and Africa are examined back to back in order to interpret both theologies in relation to and distinction from one another. Against this background, chapter 4 assesses arguments that the two are fundamentally different, and arguments that they are significantly similar.

Results synthesized from the first four chapters provide information needed in chapter 5 to offer an answer to the question: Are black and African theologies siblings or distant cousins?, and to explore the ground for Pan-African theology.

This study emerges from a strong desire to examine black and African theologies "objectively." My own ideological enthusiasms have been repressed in an effort to discover the most fertile ground for a future symbiosis between the two groups of theologians, if any exists. Had my motivation been to promote a certain point of view, my efforts could not lead to a balanced understanding of the relationship of black theology to African theology. And I believe that only a balanced, "objective" study can elucidate both sides of the issue, and offer an evenhanded solution.

Objectivity, however, is not easy to achieve. No one, it seems, is perfectly objective: we are limited by our experience. Thus, although this study was written with the hope that the facts will speak for themselves, I am African-American and unable to speak for Africans except through secondary sources. Hence this study, especially chapter 5, reflects a black North American perspective.

CHAPTER I

The Historical Background:
Preludes to Black and African Theologies

Is not God a God of Justice to all . . . creatures? Do you say [God] is? Then if he gives peace and tranquility to tyrants, and permits them to keep our fathers and mothers, ourselves and our children in eternal ignorance and wretchedness, to support them and their families, would [God] be to us a God of Justice? I ask, O Ye Christians!!!

David Walker
1829

What, then, is God's word of righteousness to the poor and helpless? "I became poor in Christ in order that [humans] may not be poor. I am in the ghetto where rats and diseases threaten the very existence of my people, and they have not forgotten my promise to them. My righteousness will vindicate your suffering. . . . "

James Cone
1969

If judicious use be made of native ideas, the minds of the heathen will be better reached than by attempting to introduce new ones quite foreign to their way of thinking.

Samuel Crowther
circa 1867

7

We . . . advocate the assimilation of African religious thought forms, in an attempt to make Christian converts accept the Gospel message and turn away from their pagan concepts and forms of worship.

Harry Sawyerr
1968

THE ANTEBELLUM PERIOD AND THE PERIOD
OF MISSIONARY ADVANCE

Afro-American theologians claim their work is a continuation of a Christian tradition that emerged within the context of slavery. Many of them may be descended from enslaved Africans brought to the North American colonies. Certainly, black theologians identify with a black Christianity that resisted the inhumane institution of chattel slavery.

African theologians, on the other hand, trace their work to a Christian tradition begun by Europeans and Africans in the nineteenth century. Christianization of Africans in the nineteenth century was accomplished in a context less politically harsh than that under which blacks in the United States were christianized. The latter context concerns me first. I focus upon the relationship between black theology and (1) slave religion, (2) the independent black churches, and (3) courageous black Christians.

Christianization of North American Slaves

With resistance on the part of slavers and slaves, slow christianization of slaves was in process by the late seventeenth century. Slaves were proselytized by missionaries who were aided by laws that saw no incompatibility between Christianity and slavery. During the course of two great revivals—the Great Awakenings—black and white Protestant clergymen found slaves more receptive to an Arminian, emotional, evangelical preaching. By the nineteenth century, Christianity had spread substantially among the slaves.[1]

Being still significantly African peoples, however, slaves revealed elements of a religious behavior more African, in a traditional sense, than Protestant. Black theologian Major Jones believes that slaves fused their African background with what they "accepted of . . . Christianity" (*Ethics*, 196). Indeed, slaves africanized their new faith with ring shouts and spirituals. Ring shouts and spirituals had a falsetto timbre hard to pinpoint on the diatonic scale and a rhythmic, dynamic, spirit-filled approach to the holy—characteristics of African spirituality.[2] The presence, moreover, of conjurers and esteemed black preachers suggests that the traditional African roles of priest-diviner, herbalist, and sorcerer were retained to a degree in slave religion. Evidence of voodoo in slave quarters is another indication of the African roots of slave religion

(Wilmore, chapters 1, 9; Genovese, *Jordan*, book 2; Blassingame, chap. 3; Raboteau, chap. 2). Knowledge of these africanisms has led black theologian J. Deotis Roberts to assert: "[The slaves] did not get . . . religious enthusiasm from the Great Awakening . . . [but] already had it" (*Political Theology*, 55–56).

The significance of slave religion for Afro-American theologians is expressed as well in James Cone's statement: "In one sense black theology is as old . . . as the first [African's refusal] to accept slavery as consistent with religion" (Wilmore and Cone, 353). Implied here is that the slaves' retention of traces of their traditional religion empowered them to resist their suffering and oppression.[3] Elements of their old religions, combined with specific liberation motifs from the Old Testament, embued slave religion with revolutionary potential. Although by the nineteenth century slaves worshiped in white churches, plantation chapels, or independent black churches, they also met secretly, in a way evocative of their African origins. Black theologians have been inspired by this fact and note the slaves' secret meetings as evidence of the revolutionary impulse within slave religion. Often called "hush harbors," "praise meetings" (Blassingame, 130–40; Raboteau, 212–19), or "brush arbors," commentators refer to these meetings as part of a so-called "invisible institution" (Frazier, 23–25).

A proto-theology of liberation was expressed in many of these meetings. "The slaves' religious principles," explains James Blassingame, "were colored by . . . [a] longing for freedom . . . . Heaviest emphasis . . . was on change in their earthly situation and divine retribution for the cruelty of their masters" (ibid., 133).[4] By reference to those secret meetings, certain black theologians counter the claim that slave religion was in every case otherworldly, and show that much of it was focused upon liberation, advocating resistance to slavery.[5]

The relationship of slave religion to slave revolts supports their argument. Nat Turner's revolt, for instance, drew its inspiration from slave religion (Wilmore, 62–73). Indeed, Nat Turner, Gabriel Prosser, and Denmark Vesey have been for certain black theologians symbolic of the revolutionary spirit of black theology.[6] In general, then, slave religion and the views of black preachers unable to reconcile slavery with the gospel are remarkably similar to contemporary black theology. All rejected oppression and affirmed black liberation in theological terms.

Black theology is also continuous with the independent black churches of this period.[7] One outstanding example is the African Methodist Episcopal (AME) Church, which became independent under the passive, accommodationist leadership of Richard Allen in 1816.[8] In this church, African-Americans, slave and free, could worship without suffering the indignity of segregation. Gayraud Wilmore, a scholar of the black church, writes: "The independent church movement must be regarded as the prime expression of resistance to slavery—in every sense, the first black freedom movement" (78). Wilmore further asserts that those churches laid the foundation of the Convention Movement of the 1830s, a movement contributing greatly to black abolitionism (92). Assessing the importance of these churches for black theology, AME theologian James Cone writes that they are " . . . visible manifestations of black theology" (*Liberation*, 92). In fact, several black theologians appear to believe that these churches, with the "invisible," revolutionary "church" of the slaves, presaged today's black theology of liberation.[9]

The essential liberation focus of black theology is observed as well in individual blacks who gave it heroic expression. Stellar examples are Harriet Tubman, Sojourner Truth, Maria Stewart, and Frances W. Harper. They, in word and deed, clearly believed that God opposes the black suffering incurred as a ramification of slavery.[10]

Two other courageous black Christians were David Walker and Henry H. Garnet. Walker's *Appeal* and Garnet's *Address to the Slaves* are essays of fiery invective against slavers and urgent calls for slave revolt (Bracey et al., 67–76).[11] Both wrote with confidence that such a revolt would be God's holy war against apostates upholding slavery. According to Cecil Cone, these two pampheteers are notable precursors of the radical black theology of liberation (*Crisis*, 57–58).

Christianization of Africans

As the militant black church—visible and invisible—struggled against slavery in the United States, European missionaries were making new attempts to christianize Africa (Groves, Vol. I, chap. 9–10; July, chap. 12; Sanneh, chap. 4). North African Christianity of the patristic period had collapsed under the weight of Islam. Christianity in Nubia had succumbed to Islam. Coptic and Ethiopian churches were generally unconcerned with mission; and European missions of the fifteenth through the eighteenth centuries had faded, with few exceptions (Groves, vol. 1, chap. 3–8; Sanneh, chap. 1–3).[12] Thus, the African theology with which I am concerned is traceable to the predominantly Protestant missionary advance of the nineteenth century. It was a mission initially inspired by the cause of abolition. As African theologian John Mbiti states: " . . . missionaries who began this modern phase of Christian expansion in Africa, together with their African helpers, were devout, sincere, and dedicated men and women" (*Religions*, 303). Because the abolitionism within this new phase of European mission is important for the task of comparison, I now examine certain events and persons crucial to the establishment of missions in Africa in the nineteenth century.

By 1800, a Christian humanism had influenced the development of European abolitionism (Groves, I, 180–84). Prior to that time, with few exceptions, Western Christendom of the Enlightenment period accepted the enslavement of Africans as consistent with the gospel. As Karl Barth put it:

[Because] moral scruples, let alone Christian ones, were . . . in evidence . . . it was . . . possible to say without contradiction of the flourishing town of Liverpool that it was built upon the skulls of negroes. . . . Piety was practiced at home, reason was criticized . . . while abroad slaves were being hunted and sold.[13]

The views, however, of certain Quakers, Montesquieu, and the revivalist John Wesley, later challenged slavery, inspiring the formation of Christian organizations influenced by the abolitionist views of its members (July, 312; Groves, 179). Granville Sharp of the British Clapham Society is one outstanding example.

Sharp made the case for the illegality of slavery in England in 1772. Influenced by the writings of the Africans Olaudah Equiano and Ottobah Cugoano, Sharp spearheaded a movement to transport freed British slaves—"the Black Poor"—to Sierra Leone fourteen years later (Sanneh, 55–56).[14] There, the Sierra Leone Company was founded in 1788 with the hope that commercial development of African resources would replace the trade in African slaves. The Sierra Leone Company later developed into the urban center, Freetown, and in 1808, the year after Britain abolished the slave trade, Sierra Leone became a British colony.

Substantially influenced by the piety of its black settlers, Freetown became a center for the christianization of thousands of Africans rescued by the British antislavery patrols operating in West African coastal waters. There recaptives, as with slaves of the Americas, found points of continuity between their traditional religion and Christianity (Sanneh, 83–89). A fundamental difference between them, however, and an essential point of irony, is that Africans enslaved in North America were mostly christianized as slaves. Many Africans, however, particularly outside South Africa, in this period were christianized after being rescued from slavery. Notable among these recaptives was Bishop Samuel Crowther, a significant, early exponent of indigenization.

Freetown, with the South African Cape, was a prime place from which missionary societies gained access to the African interior. Although the deadly African mosquito, the formidable tsetse fly, numerous other disease-carrying parasites, and oppressive tropical heat hindered the missionary advance, Christianity was being firmly planted in Africa by the mid-nineteenth century.[15]

Another mission center was Liberia, whose founding in 1822 reflects the historical role that blacks from the United States played in African christianization.[16] Although many black North American missionaries who settled in Liberia oppressed the indigenous Africans of Liberia, black colonists such as Lott Carey and Daniel Coker were concerned for the welfare of their African kin.[17] Inspired by the Ethiopianism in Psalm 68:31, Carey and Coker were fiercely proud of their African ancestry. Their desire to "civilize" their "pagan" kin with Christianity and other Western values was indeed misguided, as it reveals gross ignorance of or inexcusable inattention to the civilizations of the western Sudan and the sophisticated worldviews of the Yoruba, Mende, and Dogon, for example.[18] Still, Gayraud Wilmore believes that the affinity certain black clergymen felt to Africa was expressed in " . . . a black theology of missionary emigrationism and racial destiny [that] evolved from the aggressive thrust of [slave] religion toward liberation on an African homeland" (*Religion*, 109).

Notably exemplifying that Pan-African theology of colonization and liberation were Dr. Martin Delany and Rev. Alexander Crummell (ibid., 109–16).[19] It may be fairly said, as a result, that both men have a place within the early histories of both theologies.[20] Nevertheless, elements of Crummell's paternalism toward Africans evince again that black North American views of Africa were often as unacceptable to the spirit of contemporary African theology as were the views of the British explorer Sir Richard Burton.[21]

Pride of place in African theology goes neither to Delany nor Crummell, but to the Yoruba missionary and bishop, Samuel Ajai Crowther. As with Delany and Crummell, Crowther believed that Africa "[had] neither knowledge nor skill . . . to bring out her vast resources for her own improvement" (July, 323). Unlike the two Afro-Americans, however, Crowther had an appreciation for African culture and noted continuities between African traditional religions and Christianity (Sanneh, 84).

Crowther graduated from Fourah Bay College, established in Sierra Leone by the Christian Missionary Society (CMS) in 1827 (Sanneh, 134). He was specifically trained for missionary work and the promulgation of Victorian values (July, 322). After the failure of the Niger expedition of 1841, which was designed to penetrate the Niger interior and establish Christianity and trade, and of which Crowther was a part, he received theological training and ordination in London. Thereafter, he chiefly became the embodiment of the abolitionist Thomas F. Buxton's policy of the "Bible and the plough," which inextricably bound mission to trade. Buxton held that blacks were more resistant to tropical diseases. Thus blacks were his natural selection for the implementation of a policy that would christianize Africans and train them for cash cropping. Crowther was an excellent model of Buxton's policy. Indeed, later British penetration into the Niger interior was eased by Crowther's ability to establish missions at places like Onitsha, which lay inland (July, ibid.; Groves, II, 73–78). In 1865 Crowther became bishop "of a vast diocese comprising all of West Africa [except] the already established British settlement" (July, ibid.).

In identifying forerunners of contemporary African theology, African theologians refer frequently to Crowther because of a certain sensitivity he had to the problematical relationship of Christianity to the traditions of his people. Bolaji Idowu, for instance, asserts that Crowther " . . . realized the vital importance of communicating the gospel to Africans in a language which they would understand" (in Dickson and Ellingworth, 12). According to Idowu, Crowther related the African notion that blood shed sacrificially insures environmental and moral equilibrium to the notion that "the blood of Christ . . . [cleans all] from sin" (ibid.). Crowther, then, recognized a phenomenon that was to continually shape African Christianity. As an African theologian, Ogbu U. Kalu, explains: "The history of Christianity in Africa is not only what missionaries did . . . but also what Africans thought about what was going on and how they responded" (in Appiah-Kubi and Torres, 14). In other words, Christianity in the early nineteenth century advanced only in proportion to the degree that Africans accepted it.

Lamin Sanneh writes: "African religions continued to possess a vitality which Christianity did not destroy" (83). Sanneh argues that Christianity served as a stimulus rather than as an impediment to African traditional religion (83–89). Discussion of the merits of his argument does not principally concern me. Imperative is that I note Africans' "acceptance" of Christianity as a factor crucial to the early advance of mission on that continent. Indeed, the success of missions was often due to African initiative. African theologian Harry Sawyerr put it this way: " . . . from 1854 . . . West African Christian leaders . . . initiated schemes to indigenise the Christian faith."[22]

Thus, the quest to africanize the mission church actually began in the nineteenth century. At that time, many Africans and Europeans alike desired an indigenous church. "Missionaries on the whole had little doubt that if their work was to be effective, they would have to rely . . . on Africans or, failing that, West Indians" (Sanneh, 110; July, 322). In the vanguard of this strategy were Henry Venn, Samuel Crowther, Thomas F. Buxton, and Thomas Freeman (Sanneh, 61–83).

My examination of historical antecedents of black and African theologies prior to 1865 discloses both a fundamental difference and a fundamental similarity. African theology, in its relationship to mission, has early origins in the abolitionist spirit of Britain. Black North American theology, however, has its earliest roots in chattel slavery. Might this help to account for differences between the two theologies today? Apparently yes. Intriguingly, there were in this period proto-theologies of black liberation and africanization bearing remarkable affinities to contemporary black and African theologies, and which differ from one another as radically as the later two. Clearly, great differences existed between the contexts producing slave religion and the Christian communities of Freetown. Indeed, Crowther's theology differed as radically from Nat Turner's as the Turner Plantation did from Fourah Bay.

Crowther's theology was similar, however, to Delany's and Crummell's. The three were committed to missionary enterprise in Africa and believed that "Protestant missions were the most important gift of Europe and America to Africa" (Wilmore, 110). Dissimilarity, nonetheless, remains: the African-Americans were committed to liberation, whereas Crowther was concerned with indigenization. The three, however, were no less than siblings in their passionate quest to redeem Africa. Their sense of fraternity, then, significantly marks a similarity among the historical personages with whom Afro-American and African theologians may identify.

THE POST-CIVIL WAR PERIOD AND THE PARTITIONING OF AFRICA

If European missionaries in Africa were partly motivated by the cause of abolition in the early nineteenth century, this was not generally the case just prior to 1884. And although slavery in the United States ended with the defeat of the Confederacy, the oppression of blacks abated little and again quickly became formidable. I look first at the African context.

When Europe, particularly England and France, entered the era of industrialization, commercial interests in Africa intensified. Initially, little interest was focused upon colonialization; instead interest was focused upon the importation of "oil" to lubricate Europe's growing technology.[23] Coincident with these developments was the burgeoning of white supremacist views within the missionary movement.[24] And Bishop Crowther soon experienced the unfortunate consequences.

His episcopacy in the Niger was beginning to be undermined by the CMS as early as 1877.[25] The CMS pronounced Crowther incompetent and in need of European supervision. African theologian E. W. Fashole-Luke, however, implies that Crowther's work was sabotaged by white supremacists (Anderson and Stransky, 136–37). With his demotion, the era of David Livingstone, Henry Venn, and Thomas F. Buxton came to a close. These whites, and others like them, had gained some respect from the Africans they encountered. But the new breed of missionaries was, in general, as one African theologian put it, " . . . instrumental in the enslavement of [Africans]" (Pobee, 16). Unfortunately, certain black North American missionaries had complicity as well in this "enslavement" (W. Williams, *Americans*, chap. 6–7). Even missionaries such as Livingstone, moreover, helped provide nations of the Berlin Conference with maps of the continent they would colonize.[26] Kwame Nkrumah, then, was correct when he said that European missionaries set the stage for the colonization of Africa prior to and after the Berlin Conference of 1884–85 (*Path*, 24).

Precipitated by the British-Portuguese treaty over rights to the Congo, the Berlin Conference was convened by Bismarck to effect a balance of power in the Europe in which Germany had gained ascendancy.[27] Bismark intended to bring order and equity to the European scramble for Africa. Equity, however, gave way after the conference to monopoly—notably French and British—and order was crushed under the weight of a ruthless competition for African territory in effect long before the conference had been convened.

That mission, then, was *always* linked to commerce and imperialism bears repeating, notwithstanding the beneficial contributions of European missionaries. Indeed, certain African theologians would agree with Michael Crowder that "humanitarian motives could hardly have been dominant in a [British] ruling class that tolerated conditions of industrial labour which made life on American plantations almost a paradise by comparison and which passed factory laws with such reluctance" (Crowder, 28). Although Crowder has here minimized the barbarism of many American planters, he rightly emphasizes that Britain saw abolition in the light of the economic advantages it might bring. Indeed, David Livingstone's statement—"I go to . . . Africa to make an open path for commerce and Christianity"—is a telling one. It reveals what African theologians assert repeatedly: "Missionaries came with the same ideologies that underpropped the imperialist expansion of Europe in the nineteenth century" (Appiah-Kubi and Torres, 18).

As Europe, in spite of considerable African opposition, imposed the colonial boundaries constitutive of modern Africa; as Africans suffered under the policies of colonization; and as white supremacists' views came to dominate European relationships with Africans—most missionaries sought diligently to erase African traditions. Upon colonization, missionaries no longer needed to rely on the good will of African kings to protect their missions (Crowder, 363). Advances in medicine, moreover, reduced European susceptibility to African diseases and, thus, discouraged use of African missionaries as championed by Buxton and Venn (ibid., 365). Little, then, commended Crowther's vision of africanization. Rather than use traditional concepts to explain the new faith, missionaries sought to eclipse them. As Desmond Tutu asserts: " . . . most . . . missionaries [believed the African] way of life . . . thoroughly uncivilized and . . . irredeemably heathen. So the missionary [attempted to demolish the African] past."[28] Bigotry of this sort is anathema to African theologians, even though most would acknowledge the beneficial contributions of missionaries in the areas of education and medicine.

A Pan-Africanist scholar who defended African traditions in this period was Edward Blyden. Born in the Caribbean, he was (allegedly) descended from the Ibo, and lived most of his life as a Liberian.[29] Hence African theologians consider him a West African who opposed the missionary assault on African culture. He was also one of the first to envision an African theology as a "new [form] representing the African idea . . . with the smell of Africa upon it" (Lynch, *Patriot,* 165).[30] Blyden, moreover, in response to the CMS usurpation of Crowther's authority, wanted to found an independent West African church (Sanneh, 175). As with Blyden, James H. Johnson was also sensitive to the vitality of African traditions in relation to Christianity (ibid., 74). E. W. Fashole-Luke writes that Blyden and Johnson "were in the vanguard of the development of African nationalism and resisted attempts to impose Western cultural values upon African Christians" (in Anderson and Stransky, 137).

As an outstanding advocate of black North American repatriation to Liberia, Blyden has been recognized as well by black theologians as a contributor to the historical development of black theology (Wilmore, 116–20; Cone, *God*, 189). Blyden believed that black liberation would come only when a fierce ethnocentrism—especially in blacks with little or no white ancestry—produced a passionate desire to return "home" to Africa.[31] According to Blyden, Africa was the only place where blacks could achieve liberation. He believed his views confirmed by the white supremacist ethos of the United States. Visiting the United States to promote black emigration in 1861 and 1862, he correctly predicted that the oppression of blacks would continue after the Civil War (Lynch, *Patriot* 32). Let me now, then, examine this post-Civil War period in relation to black theology.

Reconstruction, aided by independent black churches, enfranchised blacks for a period. It also provided them with education, medical care, black representation, constitutional rights, and protection from white terrorists.[32] Still, the ethos of which Blyden spoke prevailed in North America. Coincident with this racist spirit was a burgeoning capitalism rooted in the reproachful mores of the industrialist, Republican north. "Economic revolution," writes John Hope Franklin, "not Reconstruction, determined the system of public action after 1865."[33] Capitalists in control of the Republican party, therefore, supported Reconstruction with the belief that it would restore order and "hasten the exploitation of southern resources."[34] White southern opposition to Reconstruction, however, continually promoted disorder; hence northern industrialists entrenched white rule in the south for the sake of expediency. The withdrawal of the Union army by 1877 surrendered ex-slaves to the white rule still supreme in the south. Reconstruction was aborted.[35]

As Europe subjected black Africa to colonialism, blacks in the United States continued to suffer in a context more continuous than discontinuous with slavery. Black codes were enforced by white terrorists who persecuted blacks with impunity; disfranchisement became normative in the south; and racial segregation regulated southern life, giving all municipal and legal privileges to whites. As black theologian Major Jones states: "[Blacks] became fair game for the white man because [they were] no economic loss to anyone. [A dead black] was . . . one less problem for the oppressor, especially if [it was someone who protested overtly]" (*Awareness*, 29).

The outstanding person with whom black theologians identify in this period is Bishop Henry McNeal Turner. If anyone symbolizes radical theological opposition to white supremacy in the United States in this period it was Turner, the A.M.E. bishop. Like Blyden, Turner believed repatriation to Africa was the only strategy by which blacks would be liberated. They both, in addition, had a notion of divine providence in which God had ordained the African-American to suffer slavery in order to learn the technological knowledge and the true religion needed for the redemption of Africa. Western technology and Christianity, the two believed, would deliver the black continent from underdevelopment and "the darkness" of paganism.[36]

Unlike Blyden and Johnson, however, Turner was much less zealous to preserve the traditional beliefs of Africans. As with most black North American missionaries, Turner was influenced by white supremacist estimates of nonwhite worldviews and somewhat captivated by Victorian notions of social etiquette. Africans, Turner erroneously believed, needed emancipation from their pagan beliefs and heathenish ways (W. Williams, 174–75). Yet Turner, paradoxically, had fierce pride in his African identity; he claimed he was a descendant of an African prince (ibid., 96, 174–75).

His intention, then, to "civilize" Africans with Christianity and other Western values stems from his Pan-Africanism. Bearing little affinity to the forces attempting to keep Africa underdeveloped in relation to the West, the missions Turner sponsored in South Africa were undertaken in opposition to white rule. Indeed, in light of his support of the "Ethiopian" church of Mokone and

Dwane, it has been said of Turner that "he . . . helped implant the spirit of revolutionary religion in the independent churches of Africa that were taking up the struggle against colonialism in the last quarter of the nineteenth century" (Wilmore, 122–23).

"More than any other *single* individual," writes Wilmore, "Turner . . . made a black theology of liberation the core of his preaching and writing" (122). Contemporary theologians, such as James and Cecil Cone, are particularly impressed with Turner's essay "God is a Negro," written in 1898.[37] The essay was influenced by Turner's conviction that Africans " . . . believe that they resemble God, or, are created in God's image (W. Williams, 169). In applauding what he believed was the healthy ethnocentrism of Africans, Turner sought to undermine the sense of racial inferiority suffered by many Afro-Americans. By promoting the image of God as a black African, he sought to destroy the notion that black symbolizes evil, and that black features are esthetically repugnant (Bracey et al., 154–55).

Certain black theologians today, however, seem less concerned with an exposition of God's *identity* as a black person and more concerned with the notion that the blackness of God symbolizes divine *identification* with the black and oppressed.[38] Although Turner seems to imply that the blackness of God is symbolic, he does not state explicitly in his essay that blackness signifies God's identification with the oppressed.[39] But Turner is no less a forerunner of black theology, because, as Cecil Cone explains, "Turner . . . proclaim[ed] the judgment of God upon the evils of racism" (*Crisis*, 64).

Summing up, blacks in the United States and Africa during this period suffered under the domination of whites. Colonialism gave missionaries sanction to try to thoroughly undermine African culture. Reconstruction was short-lived and black North Americans as a result became, yet again, brutally oppressed. White domination of blacks continued to set the context for a theology of liberation as embodied in Turner. It influenced as well the colonial context in Africa from which recent theologies of indigenization emerged. These theologies find their prototypes in the thoughts of Johnson and Blyden. Indeed, colonialism gave new urgency to Crowther's and Venn's vision of africanization. Thus, within a wider historical context, both theologies have been influenced by a white supremacy that continued in the United States and burgeoned in Africa.

Additional similarity was found in the lives and thoughts of Edward Blyden and Henry McNeal Turner. And both have had an impact on the theological reflections of blacks in Africa and the United States. Apparently, however, few, if any, African theologians today refer to Turner's thought. Yet Blyden and Turner were as twins in their dream of a united Africa that would be free from European dominance. Coming to a stronger conclusion, reference to one may imply reference to the other.[40] It seems to me, then, that these major forerunners of both theologies, as with those of the first period, saw themselves as Africans with inextricable destinies.

WORLD WAR I AND II

White domination of blacks continued in this period. By 1914, European rule was firmly established in Africa; and blacks in the United States, migrating northward, continued to be shackled by second-class citizenship in the nation built upon their enslavement.[41] The lynchings of blacks in the United States and butchery committed by Leopold in the Congo attest to the depth of black suffering under white rule, especially during and immediately after World War I.[42]

According to one source, imperial competition over the Balkans and innovations in war technology gave birth in 1914 to World War I.[43] Many North American blacks died fighting in Europe; and in Africa, Africans lost their lives in the fight against imperial Germany. In both cases, blacks fought with the expectation that their bravery and sacrifices would result in a decrease in black suffering. They were mistaken. After the war, colonial policies were carried out in Africa with new intensity; and black veterans returned to the States only to battle white terrorists and the systemic inequity still burdening the black community.[44]

In the United States, after the death of Bishop Turner during the course of the war, few loudly voiced a prophetic theology of liberation (Wilmore, chap. 6). Thus, according to James Cone, this period is marked by an inexcusable deradicalization of the black church (*Black Power*, 105-8). Other black theologians are kinder in their assessment of the black church of this period.[45] My task is not to defend either judgment. Black clergymen like Bishop Williams and Reverdy Ramson were politically minded, but few of them appear to have spoken out with Turner's fiery intensity. It should be noted that the writings of W. E. B. DuBois and Ida Wells Barnett best represent blacks' concern with liberation (Wilmore, chap. 6, esp. p. 135).

Shortly after World War I a Pan-African movement led by Marcus Garvey was affiliated with the African Orthodox Church, in which piety was intrinsically related to political agitation. And as with Turner, this church, influenced by the views of Garvey, confessed faith in a black God.[46] Relating to Garvey's notion of a black God to Turner's, Cecil Cone writes: "Garvey, like Turner, glorified everything black and indicated that God, the angels, and Jesus were black" (*Crisis*, 65-66).

The African Orthodox Church, whose bishop had been chaplain-general of Garvey's United Negro Improvement Association, confessed faith as well in a Black Man of Sorrows—a product of Garvey's christological reflections (Burkett, 52-55, 94-98). Thus, in Garvey, black theologians find a model of a black Jesus predating the black messiahs of Albert Cleage and James Cone.[47]

The three models of a black messiah, however, are different. Cleage asserts Jesus was a black African zealot (*The Black Messiah*, 1968). Garvey, though in doubt as to Jesus' historicity, claims that blacks should adopt a christology in which Jesus "had to be conceived historically as a Black man" (Burkett, 52-

53). James Cone, on the other hand, emphasizes that blackness is more an existential symbol for Jesus' presence among the oppressed than a descriptive term for Jesus' racial identity (*God*, 133–37). With Garvey, however, Cone identifies the cross of Jesus with black suffering. Garvey, though, made this identification on the basis of the popular view that a black man bore the cross to Golgotha.[48] Nonetheless, for all three thinkers Jesus is viewed as a champion of black liberation. (Notions of a black messiah were evident as well in the pentecostal movement that grew rapidly during World War I.)[49]

In Africa during this period, radical, religious opposition to colonial rule is observed in the revolt of John Chilembwe in Malawi (Nyasaland). Greatly influenced by the black North American mission movement, Chilembwe founded an African independent church. He later led an armed revolt against the British.[50]

Revolts that emerged within the framework of traditional religion rather than Christianity are exemplified in the Maji-Maji rebellion in Tanganyika (Tanzania) (Rubin and Weinstein, 78, 84; July, 487). For the most part, however, militant movement toward independence was primarily a post-World War II phenomenon. Prior to that time, westernized African nationalists appear to have been mostly concerned with commonwealth rights rather than independence.[51]

In this period, moreover, independency—the phenomenon of African independent churches—whose beginnings can be traced back to the late nineteenth century, burgeoned.[52] The Independent Baptist Native Church, founded in 1888, partially through the efforts of Majola Agbebi, was among these early churches (Sanneh, 174; Drake, 71). In general, however, the African independent churches were not as militant as the church of Chilembwe.

According to David Barrett, independency may be defined as:

> The formation and existence within a [traditional society] . . . of any organized religious movement with a distinct name and membership . . . which claims the title Christian in [acknowledgment of] Jesus Christ as Lord, and which has either separated by secession from a mission church or an existing African independent church, or has been founded outside the mission churches as a new kind of religious entity under African initiative and leadership [Barrett, 50].

Many of these churches reveal a traditional religious ethos. Syncretism here is best observed in the correlation between healing and prayer, and the traditional preoccupation with the activity of witches, sorcerers, and evil spirits who—we are to understand—disturb community harmony. Many churches, moreover, support polygyny.[53]

Greatly influenced by the work of American pentecostal missionaries, especially in South Africa, these churches grew rapidly as the Bible was translated into the African vernacular. African theologians assert these churches " . . . are rooted in African culture and [touch] the daily life of the people"

(Appiah-Kubi and Torres, 193). But, in what way and to what extent?

Certain scholars suggest that independency emerged from political and spiritual causes. Others claim independency is primarily a religious phenomenon.[54] Resolution of this conflict in judgment rests outside the scope of my study. Indeed, thorough analysis of the independent African churches would be a study in itself. Independency is a complex subject. There are thousands of these churches in Africa, and their proliferation seems matched only by their diversity. My task is merely to explore variations in opinion in order to further assess the historical relationship of these churches to the emergence of African theology.

Bengt Sundkler favors the view that, in South Africa, these churches emerged, partly, as " . . . inner revolt[s] against the white man's missionary crusade" (*Bantu*, 19). Sundkler's discussion of the South African "Ethiopian" church reveals this kind of independency (ibid., 38–47; see also n. 55, below). Basil Davidson's examination of "Zionist" churches, such as the one founded by Enoch Mgijima, shows that Zulu contempt for white rule merged easily with a traditional spirituality (*Genius*, 275–76).[55] Davidson's discussions of the Watch Tower movement in Nyasaland (Malawi), the movement of Mwena Lesa in Zambia, and of Ruben Spartus of Uganda further confirm the view that independency is a protest against colonization (*Genius*, 280–88). "In Kenya, in addition, the Kikuyu organized a separate school system and a separate Christian Church" in opposition to the British (Rubin and Weinstein, 84). Another source asserts that independency " . . . contributed to the politicization of their followers . . . [and] formed the mass basis for African nationalism" (Geiss, 143). That view appears somewhat extreme. David Barrett attributes independency to historical, political, and economic factors that undermined traditional life. He shows religious causation as a major factor as well. But he appears to favor the view that the negative effect of European rule upon traditional life was the major cause of independency from 1885 to the end of colonialism (*Schism*, 146–50).

Harold Turner, in his study of the Aladura churches of West Africa, minimizes the significance of political causation. According to Turner, West Africa had no " . . . land problem[s], little race conflict, and a relatively trouble-free and rapid advance to political independence" (I, xiv). On this reductionistic premise, Turner asserts that independency in West Africa is of " . . . a purer type, in which [a] basic religious nature is readily discernible" (ibid.). Thus, with no reference to the *political agitation* of Garick Braide, a forerunner of the Aladura churches, Turner gives little attention to the damage done to traditional life by colonialism, and argues that the Aladura secession from the mission church was particularly motivated by the quest for spiritual independence (ibid., 5–9).[56] African spirituality is seen as the magnet that pulled the Aladura church irresistibly to a biblically based independency.

Adrian Hastings, on the other hand, asserts that independent churches were initially, in this period, examples neither of africanization nor of political opposition. His view is based on studies of major prophets such as William Wadé

Harris and Simon Kimbangu, and major movements such as Aladura, Watch Tower, and the Balokle revival (*History*, 32, 52, 67–85).[57] According to Hastings: " . . . African independent churches are clearly within the great tradition of Protestant Christianity" (*African Christianity*, 25). Hastings shows that major movements in west, east, and central Africa were greatly influenced by Western missiology. Many prophets, for instance, vociferously condemned traditional religious objects (so-called fetishes), thus accepting uncritically certain Western teaching against traditional culture (ibid., 9–12). Hastings attributes the political ramifications of these major movements to the intolerance of imperial governments. An example he cites is the case of Simon Kimbangu, in which the Belgians made Kimbangu's movement synonymous with opposition (ibid., 11–12; *History*, 85).

For the most part, African theologians on whom I focus appear to favor Turner's perspective.[58] The historical importance of independency for these theologians, therefore, appears primarily to be its relationship to indigenization. Independent churches are seen as early and current examples of the africanization of Christianity. Their political significance appears less important. Kofi Appiah-Kubi, for instance, writes that "spiritual hunger is the main cause of the emergence of the [African independent churches]" (Appiah-Kubi and Torres, 117). It seems, then, that the development of independency in this period is viewed, together with the work of Crowther, Blyden, and Johnson, as part of an evolution toward an African theology of indigenization.[59]

Also deserving of mention in this evolution is the Pan-Africanist, Reverend Majola Agbebi, whom I have already noted. At the Universal Race Congress of 1911, Reverend Agbebi said in defense of indigenization:

> The eating of human or non-human flesh differs only in kind, and human flesh is said to be the most delicious of all kinds. . . . Christianity itself is a superstructure of cannibalism. . . . In administering the Lord's Supper to converts I have often felt . . . uneasiness in repeating the formula "Take it, this is my body . . . my blood" [in Geiss, 218].

Agbebi here conveys "the tremendous tension set up by the drive for modernization, the clash between traditional and modern elements in [his] culture" (ibid.). His thoughts on the correlation between African cannibalism and the Eucharist reveal his " . . . attempt . . . to save and rehabilitate as much as possible of ancestral traditions" (ibid.).

In summary, I have examined Garvey's Black Man of Sorrows in relation to Turner's notion of a black God in order to show their continuity with a liberation tradition rooted in slave religion and the independent black churches of the United States. I concluded, moreover, that the black messiah of contemporary black theology was foreshadowed in the views of Turner and Garvey.

My discussion of African independent churches reveals a historical source for African theologians that commends their program of indigenization. These churches appear to have religious rather than political significance for the African theologians on whom I focus. Although the relationship of politics and religion is often reciprocal, and in spite of the fact that these churches grew rapidly during the high colonial period (1918–1939), they are not, according to certain African theologians, symbols of resistance to colonialism.

There are, then, obvious differences between Garvey's notion of a black messiah and the conservative prophets within independency. This insight aids an appreciation of the dissimilarities in the historical development of Afro-American and African theologies. Nonetheless, the histories of both theologies converge due to the significant creative encounters between Afro-Americans and Africans.

Majola Agbebi was a Pan-Africanist who was a champion of indigenization. More specifically, Agbebi "became a well-known spokesman for early African nationalism on an international plane. He kept up links with Afro-Americans in the U.S.A." (Geiss, 155).

Chilembwe's revolt, moreover, was inspired by the black missiology best represented in the life and thought of Henry McNeal Turner (see n. 50, above). Thus it is again clear that a Pan-Africanist Christianity has influenced the histories from which both theologies emerge.

Indeed, "John Chilembwe provides a striking example of the influence of [African] students on Afro-Americans. In less than three years, Chilembwe spoke in numerous black churches, in at least six states, under the sponsorship of the National Baptist Convention" (W. Williams, 157).

Although Chilembwe's revolt does not appear to be a major historical source for African theologians today, he certainly belongs to the history of nationalist resistance to colonial rule. As African theology itself emerges as a ramification of such resistance, an appreciation of Chilembwe's revolt bears upon the task of placing African theology in a certain historical perspective. In general, moreover, the Pan-Africanism of Turner, Blyden, Agbebi, and Garvey was to have an influence upon the nationalism of renowned Africans such as A. G. Aggrey, Nmandi Azikiwe, and Faduma Orishatukeh (William Davies). They were in the vanguard of the struggle toward African independence (ibid., chap. 8, 9).

Struggle intensified after World War II. Blacks in both places had fought gallantly against the Axis powers, but found in their postwar contexts little reprieve from the burden of white supremacy. Their condition became increasingly unbearable, and prompted a new assault on the forces rendering blacks pariahs in colonial Africa and the United States. The fight against Nazism and fascism had unleashed an impatience for liberation that gave impetus to black liberation struggles in both places.[60] African Christian nationalists, moreover—Kwame Nkrumah, Léopold Senghor, Kenneth Kaunda, Robert Sobukwe, Nelson Mandela, Patrice Lumumba, and Julius Nyerere—and black North American clergymen—Adam Clayton Powell, Jr., Malcolm X, and Martin Luther King, Jr.,—all were catalysts of black North American rebellion and African revolution. What is more, they helped impart the spirit that motivated black theologians to write of indigenization and liberation.

BLACK NORTH AMERICAN REBELLION
AND AFRICAN REVOLUTION

Black North American and African theologies emerged in this period, 1945 to 1969, as formal theological reflections of black academics. But academia was not the context that engendered them. Clearly, they were engendered by the harsh legacies of chattel slavery and colonialism, which became intolerable, erupting into movements for independence in Africa and civil rights in black North America.

Success came swifter for the Africans. In fact, the rapid decolonization of Africa embarrassed and inspired blacks in the United States, who were assured of voting rights only as of 1965.[61] Yet, the struggle of black North Americans was a seminal influence on the lives and thoughts of many leading African nationalists.

Nmandi Azikiwe, first president of Nigeria, was among the most outstanding nationalists. Still prominent in Nigerian politics today, Azikiwe (Zik) returned to Africa from the United States "with . . . first hand experience [of] . . . segregation . . . lynchings . . . [and race] riots" (July, 589). That experience, with the political writings of DuBois and Garvey, greatly influenced Azikiwe's Pan-Africanism (ibid., 589–90). Azikiwe, in addition, exerted an early and formative influence upon Kwame Nkrumah, the first president of Ghana (Nkrumah, *Ghana*, 22, 26). Like Zik, Nkrumah studied in the United States, at Lincoln University.

While in the United States, Nkrumah preached in black Baptist churches, practicing the fiery, evangelistic delivery for which he was noted in his role as the leading African political scientist and Pan-Africanist (ibid., chap. 3, 4). Nkrumah was also influenced by Marcus Garvey (ibid., 45). As the Second World War came to a close, Nkrumah was a central figure with DuBois in the Fifth Pan-African Congress, which demanded Africa's immediate independence (ibid., 54–56). According to one source, the congress " . . . set the tone that would characterize the political aspirations of the African people in the post war world" (July, 592). Also involved in the congress was Jomo Kenyatta, the first president of Kenya (Nkrumah, *Ghana*, 54–56).[62]

In Francophone West Africa, a key nationalist was Léopold Senghor, first president of Senegal. With Aimé Césaire, and in the tradition of Edward Blyden, Senghor wrote a philosophy of negritude that extolled the non-Western virtues of an allegedly pristine African culture.[63] (Negritude has been criticized, however, as an apolitical, bourgeois romanticization of African culture; see Hountondji, 18–20; Nkrumah, *Struggle*, 25–26).

Other nationalists spearheading the movement toward independence in Central, East and West Africa were Kenneth Kaunda, Julius Nyerere, Sékou Touré, and Patrice Lumumba.[64] In South Africa, the African National Congress under Albert Lithuli and the Pan-Africanist Congress under Robert Sobukwe struggled against apartheid, which became government policy in 1948.[65]

Although each of those nationalists contributed immensely to the movement for African independence, Nkrumah became the symbol of independence prior to 1966. Under his leadership Ghana, formerly the Gold Coast, became independent in 1957—the first black African state to do so. A Marxist-Leninist and a prolific writer, Nkrumah, with his notions of African personality and Nkrumaism, potently sparked the quest for independence in black Africa.[66] Soon after independence had been granted to Ghana, it came swiftly to most of Africa. (Mozambique and Angola, however, achieved independence in 1975, and Zimbabwe in 1980. Tragically and inexcusably, blacks in South Africa still suffer under one of the world's most repressive and fascist governments.)[67]

With several exceptions, then, independence came relatively easily and with little violence—by devolution rather than revolution.[68] Independence came, though the West, having lost Asia after World War II, turned greedily toward Africa for its abundance of industrial ore, gold, diamonds, and uranium.[69] Imperial powers, never too zealous to assume the costs of colonialism, and pressured by African agitation, found it expedient to grant independence after a brief period of dyarchy.[70] The colonial structure, however, remained intact in most places after independence; thus Africa, particularly Francophone, remained dependent upon the West for development. In short, the West continued to reap financial benefit from Africa. The structures of colonialism altered little in the wake of independence.[71]

The Context of African Theology

Noted at the beginning of this chapter was that African theology, per se, emerged in the context of African independence and that African Christians were in the vanguard of that movement. Mission schools produced an elite from whose ranks emerged the leaders of African nationalism. Indeed, all the leaders mentioned in this section except Touré were and are Christians. Senghor and Nkrumah had been seminarians. Kaunda's father was a clergyman and Julius Nyerere devoutly follows Catholicism. African theologians, then, would not be free to africanize theology had not Christians like Nkrumah sought first the political kingdom.[72] Thus, the relationship of African theology to the African movement toward independence seems intrinsic. I must, however, note certain important texts that foreshadow African theology but hardly resemble the political manifestos of Nkrumah.

In 1945, Belgian missionary Placide Tempels's *Bantu Philosophy* was published.[73] This work marks the beginning of a discourse that seriously studies African traditional religion in relation to Christianity. Tempels believes that knowledge of the Bantu (Baluba) religion, which he claims reveals a philosophy of "vital force," would help missionaries christianize the Baluba without destroying their culture. Although Tempels's work is paternalistic, John Mbiti asserts that " . . . it opens the way for a sympathetic study of African religions and philosophy" (*Religions*, 14).

Tempels's work was followed in 1956 by Alexis Kagame's *La philosophie bantou-rwandaise de l'être.* Kagame, a Catholic priest, was influenced by Tempels, but found *Bantu Philosophy* too general in scope. Kagame, for example, limited his notion of Bantu philosophy to the grammar of the Bantu language, Kinyamuanda. According to Paulin Hountondji, Kagame, unlike Tempels,

> is . . . wary of attributing to his fellow countrymen a philosophical *system*. . . . All he admits to is a number of invariable "philosophical principles" that give no indication of forming a system [*Philosophy*, 39].

Adrian Hastings writes that Kagame's work was " . . . an articulate African response to Tempels and the beginning of a debate on the . . . nature of African [traditional] religion and [its] proper relationship to Christianity" (*History*, 119). The impact of Tempels's and Kagame's texts on African theology is observed in their influence upon the theology of Vincent Mulago (to be discussed in chap. 3, below).

Also in 1956, a group of African and Haitian priests—including Kagame and Mulago—published *Des prêtres noirs s'interrogent*. This collection of essays exposed continuities between African traditional religion and Christianity, thus advocating the africanization of Christianity. Mulago, for instance, explored the need for the presentation of the Christian message in a mode that most closely resembles the worldview of "peoples to be won to Christ" (p. 33). Thus, he explored continuities between the Bantu emphasis on the importance of communal meals and the Eucharist (ibid., chap. 8). As with the works of Tempels and Kagame, *Des prêtres noirs* marks further the growth in attempts to africanize Christianity. That problematic was to govern subsequent reflections of African theologians such as Bolaji Idowu and Vincent Mulago.

Bolaji Idowu's *Olodumare: God In Yoruba Beliefs* and Mulago's *Un visage africaine du Christianisme* were both published in 1962. An important later text is *Biblical Revelation and African Beliefs*, edited by Kwesi Dickson and Paul Ellingworth, published in 1969.

The emergence in this period of the All Africa Conference of Churches (AACC), a Pan-African, ecumenical organization, also gave impetus to the quest for African theology. Inauguration of the AACC took place in Kampala, Uganda, in 1963. *Drumbeats from Kampala*[74] marks the historic occasion and indicates that the AACC strongly supported the quest for African theology.[75]

During the postcolonial period the phenomenon of independency grew even more remarkably. Among the more noted churches are Alice Linshina's Lumpa Church, Simeon Ondeto and Gundencia Aoko's Mario Legio, and Johane Maranke's Vapostori.[76]

As independent Africa began to experience problems, certain independent churches violently opposed African governments. A classic example is Alice Lenshina's conflict with Zambian President Kaunda. Conflict in this instance led to a small-scale civil war in 1964 (Hastings, *History*, 157). In Zaire, Placide Tempels's Jaama Movement also clashed with the government (ibid., 117–18,

244–45). At issue for many of these churches, however, was pious adherence to a fundamentalist apocalypticism rather than disappointment with the failure of development policies (see n. 76, above). Certain African theologians, therefore, still tend to regard these churches as examples of africanization having little relationship to political matters (see n. 58, above). (According to Hastings, however, John Mbiti has advocated the suppression of independent churches in Kenya. For Mbiti, they tend to promote ecclesial and political confusion.) (see *African Christianity*, 53).

The Context of Black North American Theology

James Cone writes: "The origin of black theology has three contexts" (*People*, 6). The civil rights movement is one. The other two are the publication of Joseph Washington's *Black Religion* (1964), and "the rise of the black power movement, strongly influenced by Malcolm X's philosophy of black nationalism" (Cone, ibid.). I shall first discuss the impact of the civil rights movement on the emergence of black theology.

If after Bishop Turner's death the black church was led mostly by a deradicalized clergy, the black clergy resumed leadership of the black struggle during the civil rights movement. Although the prevailing ethos of white supremacy still conditioned this struggle, new factors emerged—factors that moved the black clergy irresistibly to protest. John Hope Franklin succinctly identifies these as: (1) black migration northward and westward; (2) federal judgments against Jim Crow; (3) the catalysts Rosa Parks and E. D. Nixon, who sparked black Montgomery to rebellion; (4) Dr. King's emergence as the "priest and prophet" of civil rights; and (5) black African independence (*Slavery* [n. 32, above], 463). Thus, after at least 90 years of post-Civil War oppression in the form of Jim Crow policies, disfranchisement, white terrorism, and systemic discrimination, black indignation peaked into a black, church-led movement for municipal and voting rights, equal protection under the Constitution, and the breakdown of systemic partiality to whites (Sitkoff, *Struggle*).

Until his assassination in 1968, Martin Luther King, Jr., articulated the goals and ethic of this movement. Drawing upon the spirituality of the black church, King was regarded by many as the Moses of its people. Ascending to the mountaintop from which he envisioned the beloved community, King was North America's high priest of love and prophet of social redemption.[77] "All persons," writes James Cone, "involved in the creation of black theology were . . . involved in the civil rights movement . . . led by Martin King" (*People*, 6). Indeed, most black theologians view the civil rights movement led by Dr. King as an important watershed in the development of black theology.[78] The movement inspired the radical black clergy to form organizations such as the National Council of Black Churchmen (NCBC). Those organizations agitated for the weakening of white supremacy (Wilmore and Cone, 1–131; Cone, *People*, 11–19). Most significant was their quest for a black theology that, in the tradition of David Walker, "rejected racism and affirmed the black struggle for liberation as consistent with the gospel of Jesus" (Cone, *People*, 8). The reflections of these clergymen heralded the advent of a black theology.

The emergence of black theology was hastened by the indignant response of the radical black clergy to Joseph Washington's *Black Religion*. Although certain of Washington's insights on slave religion were regarded as valuable, radical black clergymen found his concluding judgments intolerable. Washington claimed that the black church had no theology and was thus unchristian. Because white churches had excluded blacks from true Christianity, white Christians, argued Washington, were to blame for the pseudo-Christianity of the black church. Washington argued that blacks' absorption into and tutelage by white churches would remedy the problem. Especially anathema to the creators of black theology was Washington's view that the black church's preoccupation with liberation had led to its paucity of theological reflection.

Because his views were favorably received by many white Christians, and because many whites were inclined to discredit the role of the black church in the struggle for civil rights, response to Washington was urgently critical. As James Cone explains: " . . . black theology, in part, was created . . . to refute Washington's thesis . . . that black religion is [unchristian], [has no] theology . . . , and . . . that the . . . gospel has nothing to do with the struggle for justice in society" (*People*, 9).

The ascendancy of black power rhetoric additionally hastened the appearance of a black theology. In spite of the death of civil rights workers and innocent children, and in sspite of terrorist bombings, the civil rights movement enjoyed some success. Special legislation insured blacks of enfranchisement and the end of legal discrimination. Whites, moreover, were unable to murder blacks with impunity. But there were still deep-seated problems:

> Unequal employment, housing, and educational opportunity remained beyond legal and political solutions. Poor blacks began to feel that the civil rights movement had benefited only middle-class blacks . . . [and] began to look to nationalist organizations for leadership and to turn . . . increasingly to violence [Berry and Blassingame, 385].

White supremacy proved too formidable a foe for Dr. King's love ethic, and thus his talk of love-power appeared quixotic to younger blacks. Represented best by SNCC and the Black Panthers, young blacks turned to the Pan-Africanism of Malcolm X and black power rhetoric.[79] Although Malcolm condoned *self-defense*, riots ignited in the mid-1960s in urban centers. And with King's assassination in 1968, the civil rights movement suffered a deadly blow. Minister Malcolm X's nightmare became a reality (Goldman, 107). The cry of black power replaced the hymnic "we shall overcome" and NCBC black clergymen responded in 1966 with a theological endorsement of black power printed in the *New York Times*. Also published were essays on the relationship of black power to Christianity. In 1968 Albert Cleage's *The Black Messiah* burst on the scene. Then, in 1969, coincident with the publication of James Cone's *Black Theology and Black Power*, James Forman shocked the Victorian sensibilities of white North American Christians with his disruptive "Black Manifesto."

James Cone's text definitely marks the development of black theology and puts the matter in perspective. He asserts that the radical black clergy, particularly within the NCBC, began "the conscious development of a black theology . . . which . . . separated . . . the gospel from white Christianity and identified it with the struggles of the black poor for justice" (*People*, 11). *Black Theology and Black Power* focused world attention on black theology. And, since 1969, black theology, though suffering in its early years from sexist language, has grown through the writings of black theologians. It has, moreover, gained institutional form under the auspices of the Black Theology Project.[80]

CONCLUSIONS

Black theologians identify with the struggles of black Christians against slavery and white supremacy. In identifying the earliest forerunners of indigenization, African theologians refer to a tradition that emerged in the context of British abolitionism. Although both theologies spring from histories in which blacks have been victims of white supremacy, differences between these histories are sharp.

The African experience of colonialism, with some exceptions, was less harsh than the suffering of blacks in the United States.[81] During colonization, for instance, European industrial and agricultural enterprise were confined to areas that became new urban centers. Persons in rural areas were, as a result, hardly threatened by European culture. European settlers, moreover, were as a rule unconcerned and unable to force European values upon the Africans surrounding and outnumbering them. Although missionaries undermined the traditional life of those they proselytized, significant retentions of traditional culture are found in rural areas. And the unique spirituality of the independent churches proved irresistible. Missionaries westernized elite groups of Africans, and many of these elites successfully led the African revolution. Damage done by missionaries, then, appears reversible to a degree, especially given movements toward cultural repristination.[82] Although many Africans fascinated with European values reject repristination, they seek today ground on which the traditional and colonial pasts merge to produce a neo-African Christian life. Thus, independence permits African Christians to carry out their agenda—the africanization of Christianity.

The paucity, however, of African traditions in the United States and the continual severity of black oppression encourages theological focus on political liberation. Gains toward black liberation in the United States, in addition, have come slowly and begrudgingly, with much violence. For the majority of black Africans, however, political liberation came nonviolently, by way of devolution, and swiftly—in a span of twenty years. In fact, with the exception of South Africa, white rule in Africa was short-lived—about ninety years.

The fact remains that Europeans abused Africans. Kwame Nkrumah claims that at least five million Africans died under Leopold (*Challenge*, 9). The French committed atrocities in Central Africa.[83] And, in general, colonial powers were guilty of merciless taxation, forced labor, floggings, and policies of divide and conquer. The continent as a whole, though, overcame most of those machinations, such that virulent white supremacy is a concern only to black South African theologians still under the weight of it.

White supremacy in the United States, however, still poses a formidable problem for black theologians. Moreover, American blacks have been pariahs. Africans, as a majority, especially in rural areas, hardly suffered this stigma, especially after independence. Indeed, Africans never lost touch with their ancestors, and thus with their most essential identity. And it is hard to make pariahs out of persons in touch with the traditions that celebrate their humanity.

In short, the historical contexts producing both theologies, in spite of an essential continuity in the experience of white supremacy, have been radically different for the most part. The nature of colonial rule, Africans' close contact with their lands, traditions, languages, and families, and their majority in relation to whites have produced a context for African theologians that appears to commend indigenization rather than liberation. Indeed, in every period Africans have tended to relate Christianity to what is most constitutive of their humanity—their cultures. Black Christians in the United States, however, have tended to relate their faith to the quest for first-class citizenship in a land in which they have been second-class. To criticize African theologians, then, for not being liberation theologians as are black North American theologians reveals a lack of historical perspective. (I shall argue later, however, that there is ostensibly a context—outside South Africa—for a liberation theology uniquely appropriate for black Africa.)

On the other hand, an important and ongoing link between the historical development of the two theologies has been examined. In spite of historical dissimilarities accounting for their theological differences, there are historical similarities on which certain scholars within the two groups of theologians may build.

Black North American missionaries were important contributors to the nineteenth-century missionary advance in Africa, and are seminal to the notion of Pan-Africanism that sparked the African drive for independence. Most Afro-American missionaries were grossly unsympathetic to traditional cultures, but certain of them felt intrinsically related to African peoples. Martin Delany dreamed of African redemption as fervently as did Crowther. Discussion, in addition, of Edward Blyden, James H. Johnson, and Bishop

Turner has disclosed that these three were as brothers in their love for Africa and in their hope for its redemption.

Effects of militant ideologies of black North American mission schools upon Reverend John Chilimbwe have also been noted. And the formative role of these schools on Africans such as Kwame Nkrumah has been noted as well. Hardly antagonistic to Afro-Americans, African Christians have viewed black North American Christians as soul-mates in the quest for black liberation from white supremacy. Indeed, in every period I have examined, black Christians in both continents have been conscious of their oneness as an African people.

In a more secular and wider historical context, moreover, the struggles of African and black North Americans against white supremacy have mutually enriched one another. The struggles of black North Americans generally influenced African nationalists. Conversely, the African revolution partly inspired the civil rights movement; and during the ascendancy of black power rhetoric, Patrice Lumumba, Kwame Nkrumah, and Amilcar Cabral became with Malcolm X martyrs and symbols of black revolutionary protest.

Indeed, knowledge of the historical kinship that blacks of Africa and the United States have felt for one another brought black NCBC clergymen to the AACC conference in 1969. Their desire to confer with their African "cousins" was fulfilled in several subsequent consultations between African and Afro-American theologians (see chap. 4, below). The two groups achieved a certain unanimity on "their common relationship to the experience of black suffering [and] the preaching of the gospel of liberation and resistance to white political and ecclesiastical domination" (Wilmore and Cone, 465).

Accord, however, was especially disrupted in the consultation of 1977 when the glaring fact of theological disparity came irresistibly to the fore, muddying the waters of fraternity and, at points, civility. Black North American insistence that a theology worth its salt is unequivocally of liberation brought an intolerant response. To reinterpret: "Take your liberation theme farthest south; or take it home!"[84]

That problem will be examined later. First, however, I must substantially examine what black and African theologians are saying about liberation and africanization. Only by examining the scope of each discourse can I assess arguments on their interrelationships.

CHAPTER II

Black Theologies of Liberation

Black theology declares that the Word of God is a word that liberates. It defines liberation as the core message of the Gospel. And it continues to define and refine what the Gospel's message of liberation means today.

(from a statement to The Theology
in the Americas Conference,
Detroit, 1980)

Although the histories of black and African theologies overlap and converge in the lives and thoughts of black Christians, and although both have been influenced by an experience of white supremacy, there is a radical distinction between them. A thorough examination of the content of each theology is a prerequisite for final judgments on their relationship to each other and the possibilities for cross-fertilization.

In this chapter I focus critically on black North American theology in order to acquaint African theologians with its breadth of expression. Inasmuch as Afro-American theologians, in addition, have claimed that their theology has been misrepresented by certain African theologians, this chapter will attempt to clarify misconceptions. These misconceptions are revealed in essays that African theologians have written on black theology.[1] Essays by John Mbiti, E.W. Fashole-Luke, and Harry Sawyerr, moreover, appear to have focused upon a more radical expression of black theology. The discourse of black theology, however, is multifaceted, and its different voices deserve a hearing. Indeed, if the two groups of theologians are to build upon their historical similarities, in order to collaborate theologically, African theologians must engage in a more comprehensive study of the thought of black North American theologians. I shall focus principally on four black theologians: James Cone, Major Jones, J. Deotis Roberts, and Cecil Cone. Examination of their thinking comes under four categories: (1) recourse to black history; (2) conceptual-

31

ization of God, christology, eschatology, and Christian ethics; (3) use of black cultural elements in relation to Africa; and (4) relationship to black feminism, Marxism, and the Third World. Although all four categories are interrelated and overlap, 1 and 3 are especially close: an analysis of black history discloses black cultural elements. Thus in category 3, phenomena such as music, religion, and the family have been abstracted from the broader historical context in order to appraise black theologians' efforts to integrate them into a black theology.

Methodological dependence upon these four categories is neither exhaustive nor standard for an analysis of black theology. They merely facilitate criticism and help articulate the pluralism within the discourse.

RECOURSE TO BLACK HISTORY

Today Afro-American theologians study black history seriously and in depth. James Cone, for instance, is engaged in a study of the life and thought of Malcolm X and Martin Luther King, Jr., in order to show their relevance for black theology. J. Deotis Roberts reveals an interest in uncovering the significance of the African roots of slave religion. Their commitment to these enterprises suggests that black history is making a significant contribution to the content of black theology. Earlier, however, awareness of black history was little evident in the works of James Cone and Major Jones.

James Cone

Cone's first two published books—*Black Theology and Black Power* (1969) and *A Black Theology of Liberation* (1970)—positively assessed the intrinsic relationship between radicalism and the black church of the antebellum period. But they reflect little knowledge of slave culture in relation to African traditions, and of the thought of black theologians of the antebellum period. Although that has largely been corrected now, and I am not concerned with the passé, gauging the growth of the discourse through principal authors seems important.

Hindsight suggests that Cone's lack of substantial engagement in black history led him, at first, to depend inordinately upon the thought of white theologians who wrote in European contexts that conditioned *their* problematics rather than those with which black theologians are primarily concerned. Criticism of Cone's recourse to European theologians is well known (J. Cone, *Soul*, 59–61; *People*, 82–83). The value of repeating that criticism here lies in its potential to speed the process toward a theology that searches deeply for the meaning of God *within* the context of the black experience in the United States. Indigenization here might result in a better rendering of the significance of the image of Africa for Afro-American theology, thus encouraging dialogue with certain African theologians. In general, moreover, it seems that the more black theologians probe their history, the more sources they may uncover to philosophically, systematically, and practically strengthen a *black* theology of *liberation*.

When James Cone wrote in 1969 that blacks were "completely stripped of their African heritage" (*Black Power*, 91), he unwittingly ignored that which gives black North American Christianity its uniqueness—vestiges of its African heritage. If the African heritage had been completely lost, then black North American history would be but the sad tale of pariahs in possession of a "hand-me-down" culture. As it was, retention of vestiges of African culture figured intimately, and cryptically, in patterns of resistance. Such retention also reflects black initiative in the development of an Afro-American culture.[2] Although Cone's earlier works do not demean the cultural history of blacks of the United States, they seem to reveal, nonetheless, a sense of resignation to an alleged cultural hegemony of whites over black life and thought. I am suggesting here that his resignation emerged from underappreciation of the depth of black history, and that was why he overlooked the significant role africanisms played within slave Christianity.

Foremost in slave culture for James Cone was a strong resistance to black suffering. He was attracted to this and rightly claimed his work as a continuum of slave radicalism—an early expression of black power. But in logically demonstrating that black power is the gospel, he depended upon a liberal tradition and theologians usually identified as neo-orthodox. Yet Cone is, in part, a product of a Western, liberal education; thus evidence of the influence of that tradition upon his method is to be expected. Indeed, many black theologians of the antebellum period, to whom Cone should have referred more frequently, were similarly influenced by a Western tradition. Afro-American theologians, like African theologians, cannot escape the influence of westernization upon their lives and thoughts. A problem, however, rests in determining the extent to which westernization prevents an indigenization that may substantially critique the values of the West. And Cone has attempted to critique the values of the West. But was he initially as successful in this as he could have been, and what does this inquiry mean for the future of black theologies?

Nothing is wrong, per se, with James Cone's recourse to a liberalism that "shuns compartmentalization [and] the disjuncture between reason and revelation," and posits that "truth is to be found in experience more than tradition."[3] Indeed, Cone critically used the discipline of sociology in his theology in reasoning that white supremacy in a Christian nation contradicts the gospel. The notion of truth, moreover, as embodied in the gospel, was discovered in the experience of black Christians who resisted black suffering in the name of Christ. "Liberals," in addition, "stress the ethical implications of Christianity [as] . . . a way of life to be morally enacted";[4] and Cone similarly stresses ethical action in asserting that the onus of black/white reconciliation is contingent upon the moral action of whites. In asserting that whites need to offer reparations to blacks in order to atone for their gross mistreatment of blacks, Cone chronicles that mistreatment. His appeal to history also reveals his notion of salvation history:

Black theology *focuses on black history as a source for its theological interpretation of God's work in the world because divine activity is inseparable from the history of black people.* There can be no comprehension of Black theology without realizing that its existence comes from a community which looks back on its unique past, visualizes the reality of the future, and then makes decisions about possibilities in the present [*Liberation*, 59, emphasis added].

But in using sources to substantiate his point of view, James Cone stepped too quickly outside the context of the black experience to illuminate the way in which God has been historically present within it.

Rather than rely upon an exegesis of Walker's *Appeal*, or Robert Alexander Young's *Ethiopian Manifesto* (see Wilmore, 36–37), to support the claim of God's identification with oppressed blacks, Cone relied upon the theology of Dietrich Bonhoeffer and Karl Barth. The influence of Barth was especially evident; Cone's early method fundamentally revealed a dialectical structure in which God is against oppression (sin) and for the oppressed (symbolized by the humanity of Jesus).

Using Barth's yes-and-no typology, Cone asserts that God has said yes to blackness and no to whiteness. Although his language here was determined by the socio-political context of race relations in the United States, it signifies as well a neo-orthodox, "Barthian," theological understanding of that context.[5] Righteousness is to sin as a certain blackness is to a certain whiteness. In other words, God's yes to holiness negates human sin in the form of white supremacy. Holiness, however, is not found in some neo-pelagian notion of the sinlessness of blacks, but in the historical black position that white supremacy is the antithesis of God's revelation as Christ. On the basis of that logic, Cone asserts that black power, in its negation of white supremacy, is synonymous with the gospel.[6]

Additional evidence of the influence of neo-orthodox theologians upon the thought of James Cone is observed in his early dependence upon existentialist philosophy.[7]

In attempting to provide insight into the black condition, and in urging blacks to liberate themselves, Cone referred often to Albert Camus and Jean Paul Sartre. He argued that, as blacks become aware that their oppression is *absurd* and that surrender to it invites nonbeing (death), they will be roused to assert themselves by advocating black power (being) by any means necessary. In this sense, black power means the negation of white being and the affirmation of black being (*Black Power*, 8–12). An appreciation of this tautology is, asserts Cone, required for black liberation. Thus Cone wrote in 1970: "Black Theology is the theological arm of Black Power and Black Power is the political arm of Black Theology."[8]

Using different language and influenced by different political conditions, David Walker, it seems, made similar points: that the oppression of blacks is absurd in a Christian nation; that capitulation to it is resignation to a certain kind of existential death; that God has said yes to black liberation and no to white oppression of blacks; and that blacks should seize any opportunity to liberate themselves.[9] Indeed, Cone asserted early that the "names of" courageous black Christians such as Walker, " . . . Richard Allen, Daniel Payne, and Henry Garnet, are more important in analyzing the theological implications of black liberation than Luther, Calvin, and Wesley" (*Liberation*, 73). But what about giving more attention to the written thought of those black Christians? Were only their *names* important for an assessment of the "theological implications of black liberation"? In all fairness to James Cone, however, he did give some attention to the thought of Garnet, Nathaniel Paul, and Daniel Payne in his early theology. But their thought could have been broadened by attention to the writings of other black theologians of that period. And that corpus could have been more intrinsic to the structure of Cone's first two books. In any case, the names of Allen and Garnet were used less frequently than Barth, Bonhoeffer, Tillich, and Bultmann in those early texts.

At another point, James Cone writes: "The oppressed [must] carve out the meaning of existence without appealing to alien values" (*Liberation*, 181). If, however, this is an argument for rigorous contextualization, then *dependence* upon theologies that emerged in the context of Europe would seem to contradict the premise on which a truly black theology would develop. Why did Cone not do that which he recommended? The answer, I believe, lies here: "White thinkers," wrote Cone, "make decisions about the structure and scope of theology, [thus] it is not possible for black religionists to separate themselves *immediately* from white thought" (ibid., 117). It seems that Cone's view here is symptomatic of an ideological position conditioned by a European notion of the nature of theology. If, however, "authors produce meaning out of the available system of differences,"[10] a question is raised. If Cone had scrutinized the thought of black and *very* literate clergymen such as James W. Pennington, Henry Garnett, Edward Blyden, Henry McNeal Turner, and Alexander Crummell in relation to "white thinkers," would he have depreciated the theological literacy of the black clergy of the antebellum and postbellum years by focusing more upon the thoughts of Europeans?[11] And, what relationship has his view of the inevitable conditioning of black seminarians to the paucity of indigenous sources in his early black theology? The answer, to reiterate, is that his inordinate dependence upon theologies that emerged in the context of Europe, and out of problems more endemic to that context, is a consequence of his failure to substantially investigate black history. (Or, does it reveal a judgment that available black sources are inferior, and thus useless as source material for a black theology?)

That theology must make some claim to universalness, and that theologians should be open to the particularity of a theological discourse that is different from their own, seem to be correct positions. And no case is here made for the isolation of black theology, rather for its independence. It is theoretical weakness to criticize white theologians of a liberal or neo-orthodox tradition for failure to focus critically enough upon black suffering, and then use the best representatives of those traditions to illuminate the back history of suffering. Indeed, liberal and neo-orthodox theologies did not emerge from *the problem of black suffering*. But Cone in his first two books *too easily* related Barth and Tillich to that problem. And he gave little attention to problems involved in assumptions that Barth's ecclesiology and christology, for instance, have a normative value in relation to the black experience. Karl Barth's theology may have a heuristic relationship to black theology. It would derive from discovery of affinities between the white supremacists of Nazi Germany and the United States. Indeed, such an affinity may help one learn that theologians may speak about a God who rejects vulgar forms of bigotry. But, in general, the context and idiom in which Barth wrote differ too substantially from Cone's. And Cone was not alone in forcing the thought of European theologians upon a black theology.

Major Jones

Jones seems captivated by the European theologies of hope and an incorrect assessment of black history (*Awareness*, 24). If James Cone focused upon the radicalness of the black church of the antebellum period without an adequate exegesis of the thought of its vanguard, Jones's analysis of black history is more painfully lacking in substance. Although black history is an important norm for Jones's theology, he accents the pathetic in his analysis of it.

With James Cone, J. Deotis Roberts, and Cecil Cone, Jones tells the story of blacks from slavery to the civil rights movement. But whereas the first three tend to focus more upon the radical resistance of blacks to their oppression, Jones focuses upon an alleged cultural weakness of blacks, which supposedly led to their passivity under oppression.

According to Jones, whites have " . . . refused to accept . . . [blacks] as equal[s], [hence] the black man has not heretofore had the cultural ethos wherein he could assert himself as a man." Jones traces this weakness to slavery. As with James Cone, Jones believed that enslaved Africans were " . . . stripped bare psychologically . . . and religiously" (*Awareness*, 18–19).

Nothing, however, could be further from the truth. Slaves asserted themselves in the distinctive mix of elements from their traditional religions and Christianity. In addition, other vestiges of African culture created some reprieve from the exigencies of the slave experience in the forms of recreation and resistance. That blacks have, nonetheless, suffered psychologically from their stigmatization as pariahs is true. Jones rightly says that blacks have been encouraged to internalize white definitions of themselves (ibid., 30). But he minimizes black opposition to white definitions, and fails to emphasize enough that white supremacy is historically a consequence of the *inhumanity* of a white majority rather than of blacks' resignation to their oppression.

Black awareness as an oppositional force appears to be a new phenomenon for Jones. He thinks that it will blossom only when whites fully recognize the humanity of blacks (*Awareness*, 33). Jones's position here, however, seems an unsatisfactory conclusion. Black awareness should not be contingent upon white recognition of the humanity of blacks, for that would place black self-identity outside black consciousness. Blacks, however, have historically affirmed their identity as blacks *in spite* of whites' contempt for them. Black awareness is, therefore, on the contrary, quite old. Jones's analysis, then, ignores that which is most relevant for a black theology of liberation. And although Jones writes that slaves never accepted their condition as consistent with their faith, his insight here fails to bear itself out in his interpretation of black history (ibid., 34). As a result, Jones's assessment of the historical faith of the black church also seems unsatisfactory.

Major Jones argues that the black church has always been essentially other-worldly. He writes that "its content [is] hope because slavery under the white oppressor completely destroyed [black hope] in this world" (ibid., 40). Much of slave Christianity, however, was both otherworldly and thisworldly, with the cutting edge focused upon this world (see Wilmore, chap. 1). Still, Jones asserts that slave religion embodied essentially a futuristic theology of hope, and on this basis he sees an affinity between slave Christianity and the European theology of hope.

Broadly, the theology of hope "understands hope as the expectation of a good future which rests on God's promise."[12] Foundations of hope are based on certain interpretations of the exodus, the crucifixion of Jesus, and the resurrection of Christ.[13] "The goal of hope," writes Jürgen Moltmann, "is the eternal presence of God . . . in the kingdom of glory which renews heaven and earth."[14] "Thus hope," says Moltmann, "draws believers into the life of love and frees them for solidarity with [those who suffer]."[15] Love and compassion, then, are the qualities that typify the kingdom of God.

Revealing a dependence upon Moltmann's theology, Jones writes that black preachers expressed "what . . . Moltmann means when he asserts that . . . hope is . . . a consolation in suffering, [and] . . . the protest of divine promise *against* suffering" (*Awareness*, 46). On this basis Jones argues that black preachers of the antebellum period expressed a proto-liberation theology of hope. Very otherworldly in tone, this theology expressed the belief that God is fighting against oppression (ibid.). Although Jones acknowledges that this theology had some relationship to protest, he minimizes the role of protest (ibid.). But if blacks believed earthly change unlikely, why would they protest at all? Hope for a natural death and expectation of heavenly bliss would seem sufficient.

Radical black Christians of the antebellum period, however, accepted death in the act of protest, with the expectation of earthly change. If, according to Jones, Moltmann commends a certain passivity, and if historical evidence shows, on the contrary, that much of slave Christianity was rebellious, how valid is a symbiosis between Moltmann's views on hope and the faith of antebellum black preachers? Only minimally valid, because focus upon other-worldly expressions of slave Christianity is too reductionistic.

Jones writes: "the one place the black man knew he would be equal [to whites was] . . . in Heaven" (*Awareness*, 62). He failed to realize that many black Christians *knew* they were equal to whites *on earth*, and that this empowered them to run underground railroads, to rebel against slavers, and to fight with the Union. Hardly passive, such Christians were rebellious, actively resisting the oppression of blacks. Nonetheless, the category of hope forms for Jones the theological foundation for black awareness. Thus, according to Jones, knowledge of God's protest against suffering leads to knowledge of black self-worth.

James Cone, it seems, has made a similar point but with a radical accent on praxis. Cone said in 1969 that blacks must seize their freedom by any means necessary. Jones asserts, on the other hand, that knowledge of God's identification with black suffering primarily inspired blacks to survive their oppression rather than attempt to end it.

Jones more positively relates his theology of hope to historical figures like Marcus Garvey and Martin King (*Awareness*, 111–17). In them, Jones finds messianic symbols. He writes, moreover, that blacks have "a right to appropriate . . . God in [their] own color, and to express this in art forms, language symbols, and literature (ibid., 114). But Jones has published little in this area (see section 3 of this chapter). Perhaps this is due to his fear that such interpretation of God would lead to "a cult of black awareness" (ibid., 117). After all, Major Jones believes that black awareness is undergirded by hope in God, who transcends human categories.

Tendencies to depend upon theologies rooted primarily in European contexts are less evident in the writings of J. Deotis Roberts and Cecil Cone. Roberts admits the considerable impact of neo-orthodoxy, postliberal theology, existentialism, and the theology of hope on his thought (*Liberation*, 9). But he asserts that his theology reflects, moreover, a positive appreciation for black culture and his hope that blacks "will seek a deeper knowledge and understanding of Africanisms upon [their] experience" (ibid.). Cecil Cone, in addition, criticizes both James Cone and Roberts for their failure to make black religion the central norm for black theology. To look in Cecil Cone, then, for substantial engagement with liberal and neo-orthodox theologies is fruitless.

J. Deotis Roberts

As with James Cone, Roberts relates black power to black theology. He describes the symbiosis: "Black power . . . is the basis for a gospel of power for the liberation of the oppressed. Thus . . . black theology has as its task the interpretation of the faith of our black fathers which is living still" (*Political Theology*, 72). "The task of black theology is [to focus] upon black religion as a religion of freedom. Black people must look again at what freedom has meant in their history and what it means in their present" (*Liberation*, 40).

Although Roberts' thought here bears an affinity to James Cone's, Cone's thought is more radical than Roberts's. As shown in chapter 1, above, Nat Turner, for James Cone, exemplifies the historical sacrifices blacks have made in quest of freedom. For Roberts, however, the example of Turner is not to be followed (*Liberation*, 50). Dr. King rather than Nat Turner best represents the Christian interpretation of black power, according to Roberts. Roberts asserts that King's praxis embodied a theology of love buttressed by militant, nonviolent action. Both, he asserts, were anchored in the ethos of black religion and in the institution of the black church (*Political Theology*, 153). James Cone also asserts that King's theology was substantially influenced by the black church. Cone, however, still positively relates Nat Turner to black theology.[16]

More critically related to black theology than slave rebellions, for Roberts, are the africanisms evident within black culture. Roberts says correctly that examination of the impact of an African heritage upon black history "is tied into the psychological as well as the social liberation of blacks" (*Political Theology*, 53). Somewhat reminiscent of points made in Kwame Nkrumah's widely criticized *Consciencism*, moreover, Roberts states: "To appreciate . . . our heritage does not require a total rejection of the best we can derive from exposure to the Euro-American heritage" (ibid.). Thus Roberts, like Cone, has analyzed black/white relationships in existentialist categories (*Liberation*, 46–48). A difference between them is marked by Roberts's more intense focus upon the theoretical efficacy of the African heritage for black theological reflection: "The encounter with African [traditional] religions can contribute much to [black theology]" (in Bruce and Jones, 238). Thus, Roberts *stresses* that Euro-American sources are secondary. Primary sources are uniquely *African*-American. Unlike James Cone and Major Jones, Roberts's engagement in European thought has not led him to ignore the African roots of black North Americans.

Roberts's use of terms such as "African temperament," however, and his view that Africans possess an "Oriental mind" and are "holistic thinkers" (*Political Theology*, 56; *Liberation*, 22) are suspect. These terms signify vague notions too similar to Nkrumah's notion of African personality and Léopold Senghor's negritude. Because they tend to romanticize traditional Africa, and are ahistorical, aphilosophical premises, such notions have been discredited (Hountondji, *Philosophy*). In light, however, of my quest for the ground on which Afro-Americans and Africans may work as a community of theologians, I find Roberts's interest in the African heritage of black North Americans praiseworthy.

Cecil Cone

As I have noted, Cecil Cone focuses upon black religion. Whereas Roberts asserts that black theologians must "appreciate the deep religious roots of black culture" (*Political Theology*, 59), Cecil Cone insists that the *only* appropriate source for black theology is black religion. (A more in-depth examination of his views is undertaken in section 3 of this chapter. For the moment, I note this central thesis as the basis of Cecil Cone's critique of James Cone and J. Deotis Roberts.)

Cecil Cone's analysis of black history reveals that black religion focuses on an almighty, sovereign God. Cone asserts, in addition, that black religion is essentially a continuum of African traditional religion. Because of its non-Western roots, then, study of black religion, for Cecil Cone, requires black theologians to employ a unique historical method: "The . . . historical study necessary to work out the sources and norms of black theology [does] not . . . approach the object of faith through [a] historical critical method [derived from Europe] . . . [or] the method of existential self-understanding as applied to Jesus: (*Crisis*, 20).[17] Rather, asserts Cone, the testimonies of the black religious experience should form the historical sources of black theology (ibid.).[18] Analysis of these testimonies requires a "straight forward phenomenology of the basic elements black people have known in their religious practice" (ibid.). However, I think Cone's dismissals of the historical-critical method and existentialism in reference to black religion are problematic.

Critical examination of slave testimonies, for instance, requires that they be placed in their historical context. Imperative, therefore, is assessment of the impact of a certain epoch of black history upon slave testimony itself. If these testimonies can "speak" unencumbered by the ideological bent of the investigator, the following appears true. As Cecil Cone implies, slaves, together with most Christians, saw Christ as an object. In other words, Jesus was the one on whom slaves *based* their faith. Thus, they distinguished their humanity (subject) from the humanity and divinity of Christ (object). In addition, the very closeness slaves felt to Jesus was derived from an experiential understanding of his humanity. Slaves believed Jesus a fellow sufferer. And does not that very closeness imply a certain existential understanding of the essence of his lordship? And does not the continuum of *that* understanding constitute the particular relevance of slave testimony to black theology? The difference, then, that Cecil Cone draws between his phenomenological, historical method and the one "derived from Europe" seems unclear.

If he rejects the historical-critical method because he believes slave testimonies and black theologies are not reflections in which faith existed in tension with a certain critical spirit, he may be correct. In that sense, the slaves' problem, and that of black theologians, differs from problems with which Lessing and Van Harvey have been concerned. Still, analysts of slave testimony may find a historical-critical method useful. Such a method may help black theologians better assess the way in which slaves understood their faith, and the way in which black theology is a continuum of that faith. Indeed, it was slaves' historical *experience* of suffering that led them to an *essential* understanding of Jesus Christ.[19] It seems, then, that placing slave testimony with its historical context *requires* at some point a method that dissects the *slaves'* self-understanding of Jesus.[20] Although slaves' faith in Jesus may be said in some sense to be inaccessible to the historian, I think it wise to explore the socio-economic reality of the slaves in relation to their faith. At issue here, moreover, is not the content of faith as the gospel. At issue is the unique appropriation of the gospel by slaves. Neither the assumptions, then, of the old quest of the historical Jesus nor the new quest are at issue, because slave testimony differs from the gospel. The latter is in some sense the foundation of the former. Slave testimonies, then, are not objects of faith but subjects of faith. As subjects, they are within history; and they must be examined critically in order to assess their theological significance.

I have noted that Cecil Cone employs a phenomenological analysis to uncover the "basic elements black people have known in their religious practice" (as in testimony, for example) (*Crisis*, 20). He gives little explanation as to the "whence" of his phenomenological method, but it is a fair guess that it derives from a philosophy "with . . . roots in the thought of Edmund Husserl," and given further expression in the thought of Max Scheler, Rudolf Otto, Brede Kristensen, and Mircea Eliade.[21]

Characteristic of the phenomenological approach to religion is the exposition of religious experience without recourse to a theological apriori. A description of a religious community, then, is dependent upon the idioms indigenous to that community. Thus, investigators of that community must not refer to categories outside its context.

Although this seems a good method for an analysis of black religion, a nagging question remains: Has Cecil Cone, in criticizing black theologians' use of "white" methodologies, himself been dependent on a white methodology? And is this ever completely avoidable? The relationship of westernization to literacy among African peoples has significantly limited black theologians to the use of Western languages. As a result, even the critique of the racism often inherent in that language, and the attendant quest for a black theology of liberation and indigenization, must draw upon concepts furnished by a Western tradition transmitted in written form. Still, Cecil Cone's thought is valuable; he rightly urges black theologians to be faithful to their history. The sources most appropriate for a black contextual theology of liberation are, indeed, gleaned precisely there.

CONCEPTUALIZATION OF GOD, CHRISTOLOGY, ESCHATOLOGY, AND CHRISTIAN ETHICS

As black theologians focus upon black liberation from oppression, their interpretations of certain doctrines derive from their perception of the black experience. Their interpretations of God, their christologies and eschatologies, and their notions of Christian ethics will concern me here. Attention is given as well to their use of biblical sources.

Cecil Cone

Analysis of Cecil Cone's thought is taken from his *The Identity Crisis in Black Theology*. Here, Cecil Cone devotes little attention to the systematic task of reflection upon Christian doctrines. His analysis of black religion, though, identifies the Bible as one of its central sources. He also discusses slave eschatology and christology in relation to black religion.

Cecil Cone asserts that slaves " . . . transformed Christianity and reinterpreted the scriptures in light of the black religious experience" (*Crisis*, 35). According to Cone, however, the Bible was less determinative for slaves than African traditional religion, the context of slavery, and "the personal meeting with God" (ibid.). The latter was particularly decisive for slave religion. Cone asserts that slaves' "encounter with the Almighty Sovereign God formed the basis of their interpretation of every aspect of reality" (ibid.).

As it has been argued that most African traditional societies are monotheistic, Cone asserts that enslaved Africans merely africanized the biblical God by sublating a biblical monotheism to an African monotheism. He writes that while slaves utilized the Bible as one of the sources of black religion, they did so on their own terms (ibid., 31–32). If black religion, then, has a doctrine of God, it is radically africanized and forms the essence of black religion (ibid., 26–38).

If black religion has a christology, it is centered on the *man Jesus*. Jesus has *real presence* in black religion. According to Cone, the notion that Jesus has real presence may be traced to the slaves' strong feelings about Jesus' closeness to them. Their faith in Jesus instilled in them a sense of freedom, in spite of material evidence to the contrary. Because, then, Jesus had existential rather than doctrinal meaning for the slaves, Cone asserts that "Jesus in the black religious experience is not reduced to a theological concept" (ibid., 36). Thus, for blacks, Jesus is no abstract trinitarian Person, but a fellow sufferer. For Cone, moreover, Jesus " . . . is a living reality in the lives of black people, able to lift them out of the slave-condition and grant them freedom" (ibid.). However, in spite of Cone's view that Jesus for the slaves was not reduced to a theological concept, it seems that the slaves felt free when reflecting on the *theological* meaning Jesus had for them. That meaning, in addition, appears traceable to the penultimate and ultimate ramifications of the crucifixion-resurrection event. And those ramifications translate into theological *concepts*. Cone writes that Jesus, for the slaves " . . . [was] clearly more powerful than any earthly reality" (ibid., 38). It seems—conceptually, abstractly, and existentially—that one cannot think more theologically.

That slaves, the ancestors of black religion, were strongly in possession of theological concepts is further revealed—although perhaps unwittingly—in Cecil Cone's analysis of eschatology within black religion. Cone's analysis is disclosed in his discussion of the black church that the slave population joined in the postbellum period.

With Major Jones and J. D. Roberts, and unlike James Cone, Cecil Cone claims that the black church in the postbellum period was more continuous than discontinuous with the black church of the antebellum period (ibid., 61). For Cecil Cone deradicalization of the black church occurred only in proportion to the severity of white terrorism, disfranchisement, and Jim Crow. Under the weight of such oppression, ex-slaves and other persons of African descent were forced in their churches to lean on their notion of the righteousness of God:

It was in the midst of this situation that blacks after the Civil War encountered the Almighty Sovereign God. This encounter with its resulting conversion experience gave rise to a variety of responses. In the first place, this experience created a worshipping community where a "foretaste" of God's eschatological freedom is partially realized in the people's present existence [*Crisis*, 63].

Blacks in worship, then, celebrated the freedom they experienced in the encounter with God, especially in the ecstatic event of conversion. Essentially, they sublated their material condition in spiritual experience.

"While it is true," explains Cecil Cone, " that conversion always involves the ethical responsibility of shaping the world according to divine justice, . . . political justice in this world can never exhaust the fullest meaning of God's coming freedom" (ibid.). Thus, for Cone, the eschatology of the black church of the postbellum period was otherworldly in its assertion that earthly struggles pale in significance when compared to the "bliss" of heaven. Here, Cone is reminiscent of Major Jones. The "already" is not as crucial as the "not yet," which, in faith, makes the "already" bearable. In worship, oppressed blacks experienced a foretaste of "glory divine." That experience sustained and strengthened them in the face of awesome trouble: "Divine freedom is God's presence in the context of the people's existence wherein they are given a new life in Jesus Christ" (ibid.). It seems, then, that the eschatology of the black church, in its intrinsic relation to Jesus Christ, evinces again the depth of theological conceptualization in black religion. Divine freedom is not of this world—God is mightier than the Klan—and is experienced through a faith that lifts one's soul above suffering.

Cecil Cone, however, appreciates that the eschatology within black religion has a worldly dimension: "In the black religious experience, talk about heaven . . . has a double meaning." Thus, divine freedom *also* enables blacks "to endure oppression and gives them the . . . strength . . . to participate with the divine in the *final* destruction of oppression here on earth" (ibid., 71). Although a certain notion of resistance is implied here, "final" suggests an apocalyptic eschatology. In effect, therefore, resistance to oppression is still secondary to an initiative that only God may take at the event of the "second coming." As with Major Jones, Cone's notion of eschatology is tied to a notion of black awareness that emerges foremost from a sensitivity to the "otherworldly" ramifications of black religion. Thus, opposition to white supremacy is seen as being essentially "left up to" God. More specifically, it is believed that justice can never be established by way of revolution.

Major Jones

Jones attempts to come to terms with the radical tenor of black power rhetoric that pervaded the late 1960s and early 1970s. He, therefore, asks " . . . whether . . . liberation and freedom can be established by mere means of revolution" (*Ethics*, 159–60). For Jones, the answer is no; a government established by way of revolution is but a modified form of the old, oppressive regime. According to Jones, only God can truly liberate humankind. Thus Jones's doctrinal ideas of God seem to focus on God's righteousness.

Fundamentally, then, the righteousness of God, for Jones, negates all human efforts to secure forms of righteousness in this world. Humans, therefore, in their quest for liberation, justice, and equality—the goals of revolutions— are unequipped to achieve righteousness. Jones's focus on the righteousness of God, moreover, is intrinsic to his christology.

Jones asserts that the "good revolutionary" is Jesus. Jesus "is more than a zealot, he was and is more than a mere black messiah . . . he was and is the one [who] is always coming, and it is he who . . . calls for a *complete break with the present order*" (ibid., 161–62; emphasis added). Jones's christology is inherently eschatological. He rejects Cleage's Jesus, who was allegedly a black zealot, and James Cone's Jesus, in whom "blackness" functions metaphorically, signifying Jesus' historical identity as an oppressed Jew (ibid., 166). According to Jones, the christologies of James Cone and Cleage are too thisworldly. For Jones, Jesus transcends race and class and is revolutionary in that he requires the pious to thoroughly capitulate to the ultimacy of God's love. Such capitulation results in a radical love for humanity, which makes talk of race and class meaningless.

As with Cecil Cone, then, Jones emphasizes a radical dissimilarity between penultimate revolution and the ultimate revolution, which the pious await while enduring suffering. Thus, according to Jones, "current events have meaning only if they can be seen as they are and can also be interpreted in the light of the future" (ibid., 162). True revolutionaries, therefore, see beyond political ideology—as in black power—and focus instead upon the "eschatological dimensions" (ibid., 166). In more doctrinal terms, Jones writes:

> A Christian eschatology, relevant to black theology and to the politics of liberation, can be neither a tentative guess at how fragmented gains may be achieved nor a specific program of immediate utopia; it is rather the lighting up of a new dimension of life now [*Ethics*, 196].

Thus, for Jones, the life of black Christians is one " . . . of courage in suffering and hope, of suffering in courage and hope, and hope in courage and suffering" (ibid., 197). Hope is born from the faith that "trouble don't last always." That Jones's eschatological and christological reflections are intrinsic to his ideas of God should be apparent by now.

Clearly, then, Jones views notions of a black God with suspicion: they may result in a kind of idolatry. A critical question for Jones, therefore, is "whether it is possible for God to acquire color without becoming identified with that which is too narrow to [represent] the . . . human family, much less that which is Divine?" (*Awareness*, 116). Thus, as with the notion of a black Christ, Jones takes issue with James Cone's notion of the blackness of God. Such a notion for Jones is too reductionistic in its partiality to blacks, and ignores that God is the God of oppressors as well (ibid., 120).

Consistent, in addition, with the tenor of his theology, Jones asserts that God is synonymous with hope. Indeed, as we have seen, God, for Jones, has been the ground for black hope. Jones claims, moreover, that blacks' struggle to liberate themselves from oppression has found support in the biblical idea of "*God's* chosen people" (ibid., 107). If, therefore, suffering is redemptive, then redemption is being effected by blacks as they suffer in hope with the faith that they are God's people. Taking issue again with James Cone, Jones writes: "There would be a great weakness in . . . black theology if it did not inform [blacks] of the meaning of God's will for all people . . . . Blessings cannot be only for God's chosen people; they must be for the whole human family" (ibid., 119). "Chosenness," therefore, means an "apartness" in sanctification rather than a separateness on the basis of ethnicity (*Ethics*, 45). Blacks are set apart (chosen) by God in order to fulfill the ethical demands of Christianity. "To be different," writes Jones, "means to stand apart in an ethical sense" (ibid., 47).

Jones's notion of Christian ethics, in addition, is related to the idea that "the first and highest characteristic of Old Testament ethics is its comprehensiveness" (ibid., 48). According to Jones, the Jewish society of the Old Testament was a theocracy governed by an ethic in which love of humanity, justice, and care for the oppressed were all supremely central (ibid., 44–48). That biblical view serves as the hermeneutical basis for Jones's ethical imperative that blacks and whites love each other without surrendering their ethnic identity (ibid., 20). His ethical views, as I will show shortly, are highly reminiscent of J. D. Roberts's view that black liberation implies the ethical demand for reconciliation between blacks and whites. With reference to the New Testament, therefore, Jones asserts that ethics is "about relationships involving love, loyalty, forgiveness, and service" (ibid., 52). But, the greatest of these, for Jones, is love.

Drawing on the writings of Paul, Jones argues that liberation has, essentially, a spiritual meaning. Paul's command that slaves are to love their masters, says Jones, although inappropriate overall for the context of chattel slavery, has a hidden significance—namely, that the ex-slave, "if he is Christian, will act as a Christian in his struggle to liberate himself from the master" (ibid., 64–65). Liberation, then, will be "under the mandate of love" (ibid., 65).

Love is, for Jones, a spiritual power, on which Martin King based his ministry. Jones's view involves a commitment to nonviolence. Bearing an affinity to King's use of Gandhi's concept of satyagraha/ahimsa, Jones argues that blacks must first liberate themselves spiritually, in such a way that, in confrontation with whites in social struggle, blacks would never respond violently, even if they suffer violence themselves (ibid., 140–50).[22] Anything less, he asserts, is neither Christian nor ethical (ibid., 176). Jones's view here is undergirded by the fantastic notion that blacks "tend to be more explosively violent than . . . [their] white counterpart" (ibid., 133). Serious study of black history in the United States does not reveal they have been more "explosively violent" than whites. Although black rioting, especially in the 1960s, was explosive, that violence neither sublates whites' merciless persecution of blacks nor minimizes systemic violence done to blacks by whites. A case could be made for the view that black rioting was proportionate to the violence whites have perpetrated against blacks. But I think a stronger case could be made for the view that the cumulative effect of white violence far exceeds black violence. If the lamentable fact of black-on-black crime is the issue, then Jones may statistically have a point. Blacks do appear more explosively violent than whites in the way that they treat one another in their ghettos. If, however, the black ghetto itself is a product of white systemic violence against blacks, then it must be more critically stressed that black-on-black crime is but the outcome of that systemic violence.

J. Deotis Roberts

As already indicated, Roberts's notion of Christian ethics rests upon the premise that black liberation is essentially tied to reconciliation. With Jones, moreover, Roberts finds that James Cone has made a "religion of black power" (*Liberation*, 21). Although white supremacy still poses a problem for Roberts, and warrants for him the black power response, he asserts that liberation without reconciliation is meaningless (ibid., 21–25).

Roberts, like Jones, in addition, uses the biblical theme "chosen people" to communicate the ethical responsibility of black theologians. "Chosenness" again implies sanctification for a task consistent with the work of redemption, and is again entirely unrelated to Cleage's notion of blacks as "the chosen people" (ibid., 49–60). As chosen people, asserts Roberts, blacks must become "instruments of God's salvific purpose for all" (ibid., 59). Reconciliation with whites, then, is indispensable.

According to Roberts, moreover, Christian leaders advocate nonviolence. Violence, asserts Roberts, does psychological damage to blacks, and is pragmatically unable to effect true liberation (ibid., 186). Moreover, "violence . . . is inconsistent with the Christian ethic" (ibid., 190). Roberts's commitment to nonviolence is, in addition, partly supported by an African worldview (*Political Theology*, 74–75).

He asserts that that worldview discloses a notion of an interdependent universe (ibid.). Violence here is seen as a disruption of a certain equilibrium, and of an African sense of community. According to Roberts, Africans have traditionally believed that communal life is dependent upon a mutual sense of responsibility (ibid., 74–75). But he fails to wrestle with the problem of the wars and civil wars that set traditional Africa against itself. Indeed, Africa has been a continent in which ethnic groups, even though related by ancestry and language, have clashed violently with one another.[23] Africa was—and is—no haven.

Had Roberts focused upon *a* traditional society, and noted its similarities with others, his stand on an African notion of "wholeness" might have greater credibility. All the same, the notion serves as a point of departure for Roberts's rejection of violence:

The incidence of blacks killing blacks and taking their own lives is too great for [blacks] to tolerate an eschatological position that sanctifies despair and encourages the use of a type of teleological suspension of the "ethical" in the name of theology [*Political Theology*, 182].

Roberts's comment here is directed at James Cone. Implicit seems to be the view that black self-directed homicide is part of the same phenomenon that burned black ghettos during the middle and late 1960s. Roberts, then, views James Cone's acceptance of violence as a capitulation to despair, which ignores the theme of hope strongly evident within the black church (ibid., 182–83). Roberts's views here invite discussion of his notion of eschatology.

J. Deotis Roberts believes, as do James and Cecil Cone, that the struggle for liberation emerges, theologically, from an eschatological perspective based on the resurrection. For these three, particularly, eschatology in black theology is both thisworldly and otherworldly. Roberts and Cecil Cone, however, reject James Cone's *radical* thisworldly focus. According to Roberts, "an eschatology without a future dimension is only partially complete. It may include the cross, as [James] Cone has done, but it does not include the resurrection" (*Liberation*, 162). Although (as I will show shortly) James Cone does not ignore the resurrection, he has expressed little interest in life after death.

Roberts, however, is interested in an afterlife, and refers to the work of African theologians on that issue (*Political Theology*, 185–88). Occupied with the African roots of Afro-American religion, he is interested in African theologians' work on the relationship of ancestors to Christian eschatology. African theologians find a certain continuity between the traditional belief in ancestors and the Christian belief in a communion of saints (to be discussed in more detail in chap. 3, below). According to Roberts, however, the African view that the dead "live" as long as they are remembered is unsatisfactory for a Christian understanding of eschatology (ibid., 186). Life after death in the Christian mode, for Roberts, is dependent on grace, not on human recollection of the deceased. In rejecting the latter, though, Roberts fails to discuss an important question that African theologians have raised in this context. Might not the resurrection and the notion of prevenient and elevating grace include even forgotten ancestors? (to be taken up in chap. 3, below). Perhaps, then, Roberts has sacrificed African traditional beliefs too quickly on the altar of Western orthodoxy. Still, study of the significance that ancestors may have for black theology is important to Roberts, who seems in quest of a truly African-American doctrine of eschatology.

He thus criticizes James Cone for an alleged Teutonic method that fails to take seriously enough "the African roots of black religion" (*Political Theology*, 186). That may well be. But Roberts's example of Cone's failure in this is no indication of Cone's captivation by a Teutonic method. According to Roberts, Cone believes that the " . . . offering . . . of one's life for black liberation [is] a means toward partaking of a type of social immortality" (ibid., 187–88). (As well as attributing that view to a Teutonic method, it appears that

Roberts wishes to further discredit Cone's acceptance of violence.) It seems to me, however, that a notion of social immortality is intrinsic to African traditional life, and is seen in the crucial role attributed to ancestors. It was believed that without them, society would crumble. Failure to care for them properly, we are to understand, would bring great misfortune. A concept of social immortality is found also in African traditional notions of reincarnation (to be examined in chap. 3, below). In addition, human sacrifice, in Dahomey, for example, was seen in part as necessary for the safe passage of the king into death and, therefore, for protection of society.[24] James Cone's view, then, that life is expendable for the sake of a social immortality is not *necessarily* Teutonic, but bears an affinity to traditional African thought. That Cone did not intend for it to, however, is more than plausible and more than likely the case!

Roberts also has problems with the christocentric focus of James Cone's theology. Roberts says that Cone has "a narrow christocentric view of revelation that distinguishes between religion and the Christian faith" (*Political Theology*, 19–20). Such a "Barthian" distinction, Roberts argues, is "inadequate for a theological program that traces its heritage to the third world" (ibid., 20). Although James Cone has pointed out affinities between his thought and Karl Barth's, his christocentrism is hardly so narrow as to preclude his endorsement of Third World theologies that seek continuities between their traditional religions and Christianity. In fact, Cone strongly supports Third World theologies.

Roberts believes, in addition, that christology in black theology must explore the continuities between "God's revelation to peoples of Africa and his revelation in Jesus Christ," with the understanding that Christ "unlocks the meaning of all revelation" (*Political Theology*, 20). And Cone's notion of revelation in Christ, charges Roberts, impedes the emergence of a Pan-African understanding of the black religious experience (ibid., 20–21). Yet, Cone does not dismiss in his later writings the significance that African heritage may have for black theology. I find, moreover, no condemnation of black religions of the diaspora in Cone's writings.

In spite of Roberts's criticism of Cone's christology, he has in common with Cone a notion of a black messiah: "The black messiah encounters the black Christian on the level of personal experience . . . enabling black Christians to overcome their identity crisis" (*Liberation*, 130). Similarity between the two theologians here lies in their view that the blackness of Christ symbolically refers to Jesus' identification with the oppressed (ibid., 130–40). Although blackness, then, has universal implications, an appreciation of its universality emerges from an existential understanding of black suffering (ibid.). Sharp dissimilarity between them, however, is found in Roberts's insistence that the black messiah is as equally a reconciler as a liberator (ibid., 154–55). As we shall see, James Cone emphasizes more radically that Christ is liberator.

As with his christology and his notion of Christian ethics, Roberts relates his notion of God to African traditional religion. His exposition of the transcendence and otherness of God is derived in part from the African notion of the Creator's relationship to other gods and to humankind (ibid., 137). Roberts's notion of God's immanence, however, is more biblical than African: "The God of Moses, the God of the Exodus, has been real to black people . . . the God of the Exodus is the black man's God" (ibid., 99). For Roberts, God has been present to blacks in their suffering.

William Jones has asked a difficult question: Why does a just God of liberation, who identifies with the oppressed, permit their perennial suffering? He argues cogently that no empirical evidence can support the view that God has liberated, is liberating, or will liberate oppressed blacks (*Is God a White Racist?*). Roberts, however, answers Jones with the response of faith: "Here . . . it is better to trust God . . . than man" (*Political Theology*, 98). Referring to the Old Testament depiction of the pathos of God, Roberts stresses God's oneness with the oppressed in painful suffering: "Human pain is a symbol through which man is united to God" (ibid., 102). Thus, his argument that God identifies with the oppressed is buttressed by his notion that God empathizes with them. Attendant to his notion is the view that God's empathy with the suffering of the oppressed does not annul God's power to liberate blacks from white supremacy. "God's love," writes Roberts, revealing an affinity with the thought of Major Jones, "will prevail because God's power is unchallenged ultimately by all opposing power" (ibid., 113).

James Cone

If the Old Testament has influenced Roberts's doctrinal understanding of God, it is decisive for Cone's notion of God. As with Major Jones and J. D. Roberts, the exodus and the notion of a "chosen people" are featured in Cone's theology. On the basis of the exodus, and the idea of salvation history, James Cone claims that God has elected the oppressed to be the chosen people. He thus passes over the Platonic view that God's righteousness exists abstractly, and favors that which he claims is a more historical view (Cone, *Liberation*, 17–21). According to Cone, the Old and New Testaments attest to God as the enforcer of justice who raises up prophets to remind an apostate Israel of its charge to protect the widow and the orphan (ibid., 19). Theology, then, for Cone, must stress God's involvement in history in behalf of the oppressed, or it signifies nothing: "If God is not involved in human history, then all theology is useless, and Christianity . . . is . . . a hollow, meaningless diversion (ibid., 26).

Because of this view, Cone has also been forced to respond to William Jones. Cone's response to Jones is particularly warranted: "God is at work in the black community, vindicating black people against white oppression" (ibid., 27). As empirical verification of that claim is difficult, Cone asserts: "William Jones is right! . . . No historical evidence . . . can prove conclusively that . . . God . . . is actually liberating black people from oppression" (*God*, 191). But scientific, historical evidence is not at issue for Cone. With Roberts,

Cone distinguishes the faith of secularism from faith in Christ. Faith in Christ affirms that God-in-Christ is the liberator, is liberating, and will liberate the oppressed (ibid., 191–92).

Because he believes that God is the liberator of oppressed blacks, Cone says that God is black. It bears repeating—because Cone has been so frequently misunderstood—that this is an existential and symbolic rather than racial and literal description of God. Cone writes: "The blackness of God *means* that God has made the oppressed condition his own condition" (*Liberation*, 121; emphasis added). In other words " . . . a black [person] is anyone who says he is black, despite . . . skin color" (ibid., 124). Only by way of such an identification with the oppressed may one truly bear, for Cone, the image of God (ibid.).

I have noted similarities between James Cone's and J. D. Roberts's notions of the black Christ. Roberts accuses Cone of a "Barthian hangup." For Roberts, such a "hangup" renders Cone's Christ more kerygmatic than historical. According to Roberts, James Cone does not relate "the teaching and example of Christ to his so-called black Christ" of liberation (*Political Theology*, 123). Cone's Christ is allegedly "accessible only by a leap of faith" (ibid.). James Cone, however, clearly and substantially emphasizes the Jesus of history. Who Jesus was, what he did and taught, is intrinsic to who Jesus is as Christ. "Jesusology" is the foundation of Cone's christology. The historical example of Jesus reveals his blackness as the Oppressed One who "really enters . . . our world where the [oppressed] are . . . disclosing that he is with them, enduring their humiliation and pain, transforming oppressed slaves into liberated servants" (Cone, *God*, 136).

Indeed, the eschatological significance of Jesus Christ "lies in the totality of his existence in complete freedom as the Oppressed One, who reveals . . . that God . . . is present in . . . human liberation" (Cone, *Liberation*, 210). For Cone, then, God-in-Christ *chose* historically to be one of the oppressed. His resurrection, therefore, reveals his divinity, without erasing the condition of his humanity. James Cone's understanding of eschatology, then, is related, as I have noted, to the metaphysical ramifications of the resurrection. Noted as well, however, was that Cone's eschatology is radically thisworldly. This needs more explanation.

"The idea of heaven is irrelevant for black theology" (*Black Power*, 125). No doubt James Cone raised many eyebrows—of blacks and whites—when he penned those words in 1969. No long white robes? No ultimate consummation of the resurrection promise that would end this "time between the times"? Apparently not. Unlike Major Jones, James Cone's eschatology subjects the "not yet" to the "already." He appears so theologically committed to the notion of "freedom now" that any eschatology implying patience in lieu of suffering, and thus passivity in suffering, is flatly rejected. His "neo-orthodoxy," then, is discontinuous with Luther's notion of "the two kingdoms" and Calvin's notion of a theocracy. Indeed, Cone's theology invalidates

the claim that Protestants are "to obey constituted authority no matter how wicked it might be."[25] The " . . . key to Black Theology," writes Cone, is its refusal "to embrace any concept of God which makes black suffering the will of God." Black Christians "cannot waste time contemplating the next world (*if there is a next*)" (*Black Power*, 125; emphasis added). Justification solely by faith means for Cone not acceptance in heaven, but freedom to do "all for the neighbor," now! (ibid., 125). Thus Cone alludes to a futuristic eschatology only to illuminate the "ungodliness of the present" (ibid., 125–27). Eschatology here means transformation today (ibid., 126). And even though Cone writes later with more certainty on an afterlife, his eschatology will be no less urgently focused upon this present life.[26]

James Cone also focuses urgently upon the inappropriateness of black/white reconciliation prior to the complete liberation of blacks: "There can be no reconciliation . . . unless the hungry are fed, the sick are healed, and justice is given to the poor" (*God*, 234). Cone's notion of Christian ethics, then, is revealed in his passionate appeals for an end to starvation and disease, and the exploitation of humans. In his quest for the end of these forms of human suffering, Cone is neither committed to nonviolent struggle nor is violence abhorrent to him (ibid., 217–25). He sees the issue of violence in the light of the violence that whites have done to blacks (*Black Power*, 141). For James Cone, then, at issue is whether an evil system warrants—justifiably and necessarily—violent overthrow (ibid., 143).

In more theological terms the issue is not Jesus' nonviolence or the alleged incompatibility of violence "with love and reconciliation" (*God*, 222). The issue is what God-in-Christ is doing today, which, for Cone, hardly precludes violence as a Christian option (ibid., 223–24).

USE OF BLACK CULTURAL CATEGORIES IN RELATION TO AFRICA

The growing methodological dependence of Afro-American theologians upon cultural categories such as Afro-American music, black religion, and the institution of the black family is promising—in that these theologians, under each category, have related their thought to Africa. They refer to the African roots of black culture in the United States, or examine the ramifications of African traditional religion for black theology. In some cases, both factors are at issue. In each case, moreover, a close collegial relationship with African theologians would seem to strengthen the work of black theologians as they seek to "indigenize" black theology.

As I have posited, Afro-American theologians' more substantial engagement in studies of black culture is a consequence of their more substantive engagement in the study of black history. Focus here is upon the three cultural categories already noted: music, family, and religion. More specifically I shall examine the thoughts of James Cone in relation to black music; J. D. Roberts in relation to the black family; and Cecil Cone in relation to black religion.[27]

James Cone and Black Music

In spite of Cone's claim that he was deeply influenced by black culture even in his early writings, I have argued that they inadequately reflect this.[28] For this reason, black religionists, such as Charles Long, Gayraud Wilmore, and Cecil Cone, subjected Cone's first two texts to harsh critique (J. Cone, *Soul*, 59–60). As I noted, their focus was upon his captivation by Barth, Tillich, and Bultmann, and upon his paucity of references to Africa and black religion (ibid.). Long, writes James Cone, "even questioned whether a black theology was possible since theology itself is European and . . . imperialistic by . . . nature" (ibid., 60). Taking seriously his colleagues' critiques, James Cone wrote two texts that attempted to relate black theology to black sources: *God of the Oppressed* and *The Spirituals and the Blues*. The former reveals the definitive influence that "growing up black" in Bearden, Arkansas, had on his life and thought. Reference is made in that text, moreover, to the African heritage of black North Americans. Essentially, *God of the Oppressed* examines the black religious experience, from slavery to 1975, and concludes:

> The form of black religious thought is expressed in the style of story and its content is liberation. Black theology, then, is the story of black people's struggle for liberation in an extreme situation of oppression [p. 54].

Inasmuch as I, however, am interested in James Cone's reflections on the theological meaning of certain forms of black music, I shall focus upon his *The Spirituals and the Blues*. Revealing again his theological perspective, Cone asserts: "The message of liberation in the spirituals is based on the biblical contention that God's righteousness is revealed in his deliverance of the oppressed from [slavery] (*Blues*, 35).

In their earliest forms, spirituals were influenced by an African timbre, African rhythms, African patterns of call and response, and an oral tradition.[29] Cone writes that the spirituals reflect "mainly [an] African background . . . rather than white American Christianity" (*Blues*, 15). In asserting this, Cone rightly challenges the views of scholars who posit that spirituals are "the least African and most European of all Afro-American religious music."[30]

"The Africanism in the spirituals," Cone explains, "is directly related to the *functional* character of African music . . . [in that] it was directly related to daily life" (*Blues*, 32). Indeed, African worksongs, as with those created by enslaved Africans in North America, may be said to be functional in that they established a rhythm by which a task was accomplished.[31]

But, it seems to me, *African* music that related to initiation, burial, and other religious rites does not appear to be *merely* functional. It has meaning as well as function (Jahn, 164–69). The rhythms by which the gods possess their devotees, for instance, have no *function* in and of themselves. In Vodun and

Santeria, other American africanisms that Cone ignores, the polyrhythms themselves do nothing. It is their religious *meaning*, their association with a specific *Loa* or *Orisha* (divinities), that incarnates the divinity in the dance of the devotee (Jahn, 29-61).[32] Indeed, rhythm *functions* as the precondition of "possession trance" (Whitten and Szwed, 88). "If, [however], the rhythm, the division of accents fails to correspond to the meaning" of the ritual, then the music is insignificant (Jahn, 174). Although this suggests that possession depends upon and varies with drumming, and that this is a function of the *drummer*, it is believed that the rhythms produced are "voices" of the postulated gods, whose call to their devotees is not contrived by the musicians or by the priests who serve the gods.

Possession here, then, depends upon supplication and revelation rather than just musicianship, and the music produced is functional only in relation to a worldview (meaning). An outsider to this worldview, therefore, only hears the rhythm, but does not understand it. Thus, the function of African music, especially in its relation to religious rites, is sublated by its meaning. Music, then, functions in tandem with certain notions of the suprasensible or with certain community activities.

Had James Cone, therefore, given more attention to the intrinsic relationship between function and meaning, I think his view that the spirituals have African origins would have greater credibility.

Cone writes, in addition, of "the power and energy released in black devotion to the God of emotion" (*Blues*, 4). Apparently, he is referring to the specialness found in *the religious feeling* of black worship. Coming to a stronger conclusion, it seems that Cone is saying that the special spirituality of certain black churches is proportionate to the depth with which those churches experience the reality of God. Certain scholars, moreover, believe that that spirituality bears the marks of African traditional sensibilities.[33]

The gods did not survive the slave climate of the United States, but black worship there reveals a dynamism similar to that of Vodun and Santeria. The origins of these phenomena are believed to be traceable to West African spirit possession.[34] As Ben Sidran writes: " 'Spirit possession' became the manifestation of the Holy Ghost [in the black church] and was *always* generated through music. It was *felt* that 'the spirit will not descend without song' " (*Talk*, 20; emphasis added). Cone's notion of "the God of emotion," then, is related to a certain *feeling* generated in a certain rhythm and timbre, both of which move the community to ecstatic praise! Thus, Cone writes: "The interpreter [of the spirituals] must feel the Spirit . . . *feel* . . . the power of black music, responding both to its rhythm and the *faith* in experience it affirms" (*Blues*, 5; emphasis added). Faith, then, is that which puts feeling into music, impregnating it with religious meaning.

Cone, moreover, attributes the power of black music to the "Black Spirit," who attests to a different God from the one of white sacred music (ibid.). If, for James Cone, therefore, the "Black Spirit" is continuous with the spirituality of

West Africa, then his view here needs more support from a study of the relationship of the spirituals to African traditional religion and neo-African religion in the Americas.

An analysis of African music would have also strengthened Cone's significant theological interpretation of the blues, in which a falsetto timbre and blue tonality are strongly evident.[35] The blues are related to the spirituals. As one black preacher put it: "Ain't much difference in the blues and a sacred song, a church song . . . . The blues come out of the Church anyhow" (Wilmer, *Face*). The blues, however, as Cone rightly shows, have a different meaning from that of spirituals. The blues are, according to Cone, secular spirituals (*Blues*, 108–12). They are expressions of suffering and sorrow, which, therapeutically, overcome sorrow in the very act of lament. The blues, then, are balms for the lacerations of suffering. Depicting the daily vicissitudes endemic to human life, the blues tell of unrequited love, sexual pleasure and lust, and hard luck. Essentially, the blues are a survival music. Tapping the pulse of black life, born in the manger of black suffering, cynical but not utterly despondent, the blues are at once an artistic and practical expression (ibid., 128–40).

James Cone sums up their theological significance: "The important contribution of the blues is their affirmation of black humanity in the face of immediate absurdity" (ibid., 127). Blues, then, like jazz, are, according to Archie Shepp, "a symbol of the triumph of the human spirit, not of its degradation. It is a lily in spite of the swamp" (Wilmer, *Face*, Introduction).

J. Deotis Roberts and the Black Family

In his *Roots of a Black Future: Family and Church*, Roberts relates the two institutions—family and church—intrinsically. Survival of the one depends on survival of the other. I focus, however, on his reflections on the black family.

Roberts asserts that the black family is in crisis due to the tragic ramifications of slavery (*Roots*, 24–38). In spite of those hardships, however, the black family, according to Roberts, has survived by creatively adapting African patterns of the extended family to the North American context (ibid., 25–26). Roberts asserts, however, that the oppressive character of the United States threatens to undermine even that improvisation. As an example of the ramifications of that oppression, Roberts points to dangers in households headed by women (ibid., 120–25). The "black child" he asserts, "needs the love of mother and father" (ibid., 124). His alarm over the decision of black women to procreate without husbands is deepened by his analysis of the irresponsible way black men forsake the roles of husband and father (ibid., 126–29). (Here, Roberts displays a new perspective. In an earlier text, he asserted too generally that black women and children are without husbands and fathers because black men are captivated by white women [see *Political Theology*, 158].)

According to Roberts, then, black theologians must convey to the black church that strong nuclear and extended families are central for the preservation of that church and for black liberation. Useful for that task, asserts

Roberts, is an African notion of family. In Africa, "the family was an economic and religious unit, and through its ties with the wider kinship circles, was also a political unit. The family of Africa [then] . . . was central . . . and [exerted] great influence upon personal life" (*Roots*, 30).

Roberts finds an additional African model for the Afro-American family in Julius Nyerere's notion of "Ujamaa" (ibid., 85; *Political Theology*, 163). According to Nyerere, a form of socialism existed in Africa before any liberal and Marxist notions were introduced there. He claims, moreover, that "the idea of 'class' or 'caste' was non-existent in African society" (*Ujamaa*, 11). Today, however, this view is easily discredited by a critical examination of African history.[36] Even Nkrumah, who once strongly advocated African communalism, later wrote: "In pre-colonial Africa, under conditions of communalism, slavery and feudalism, there were embryonic class cleavages" (*Struggle*, 22). Indeed, traditional societies such as Dahomey revealed not only a caste system but a proto-mercantilism in which trade in slaves with the West was strictly regulated to insure, militaristically and economically, the interests of the king.[37] One journalist has even speculated that traditional Africa has been more capitalist than socialist (Lamb, 189). Roberts, then, as with all black theologians, must beware of romanticization of Africa. Although African patterns of kinship (extended families) reveal an emphasis on communal equity, any theological appropriation of them must be critically undertaken in light of the problematics uncovered (see Radcliffe-Brown and Forde).

Cecil Cone and Black Religion

Cone analyzes Afro-American religion with attention to its African roots. He asserts that Afro-American religion is the soul of black North American theology, and that African traditional religion is the soul of Afro-American religion. Cone does not wrestle with the problematical nature of the latter assertion.

Problems lie in Cone's position that the monotheism of Afro-American religion is but a continuum of the monotheism of African traditional religion. He asserts Afro-American religion "is African in root and branch" (*Crisis*, 39). For him, moreover, "The black religious experience [of the Almighty, Sovereign God] has in common with its African roots the concept of the divine as all-encompassing" (ibid., 143). According to Cone, it is in that holistic understanding of God "that the African religious tradition makes its greatest impact upon black religion" (ibid.). Cone, however, gives too little attention to the plurality of traditional African worldviews; although similar, they have different nuances, which differently accent the notion of God's transcendence and immanence. Nonetheless, in arguing that African traditional religion is monotheistic, Cone relies upon the research of John Mbiti.

Mbiti claims that God for Africans is omniscient, omnipresent, omnipotent, and thus utterly transcendent (*Concepts*, 3–18). Yet, asserts Mbiti, God is imminently near to Africans (ibid., 16–18). Here Mbiti counters a contradictory claim that the Africans' God is remote, removed from daily life, invoked—with few exceptions—only in times of catastrophe (ibid., 12). Cecil Cone, then, has rightly based his assertion that African traditional religion is monotheistic on the conclusions of an African theologian (*Crisis*, 30–31).

In spite, however, of Mbiti's position that the notion of a remote God is false and foreign, he makes reference to that with which Cone has not sufficiently wrestled:

> Since people are more immediately concerned with the daily affairs of human life, their awareness of God's presence is not uppermost in their consciousness [*Concepts*, 8].

Thus, Mbiti says that Africans believe in God paradoxically: "they know him and yet they do not know him. He is not a stranger . . . and yet they are estranged from him. He knows *them*, but they do not know him" (ibid., 27). Mbiti claims, therefore, that God for the Africans is "the very *Mysterium Tremendum par excellence*" (ibid.). In light of Mbiti's analysis here, two critical questions seem to challenge Cecil Cone's notion of an *Afro*-American God: Do adherents of black, Christian religion claim they do not know God-in-Christ? And is not God uppermost in the consciousness of black Christians who embody the spirit of black religion?

Avoiding the view that the Africans' supreme God is estranged from them, I must note that Mbiti's review of Africans' traditional notions of God show that they differ starkly from Christian notions of God. Although God, for Christians, in addition, is also "the very *Mysterium Tremendum par excellence*," the relationship of revelation to christology provides Christians with a transcendent God who in divine immanency is also a man, a personal savior—in some sense, a brother. Studies of African traditional religion present little that resembles an incarnation of the Supreme God as a human being. Cecil Cone, then, it seems to me, has not wrestled satisfactorily enough with the problem of radical discontinuity between the notions of God in African traditional religion and Afro-American Christian religion.

In general, moreover, African traditional religion reflects at points a monotheism that differs radically from the Christian notion of God. Christian monotheism is essentially triune. Posited is a Creator who became incarnate as Jesus and who becomes manifest through a third person, the Spirit. Africans, however, although having a notion of a transcendent Supreme Being, traditionally focused upon ancestors and the lesser gods (some of whom may have been ancestors). In addition, more emphasis in that religion is given to human agency than is the case with Christianity. As an African scholar explains:

> The religion of the African is not founded upon man but for man. . . .
> He does not [however] . . . equate God to man . . . . No man . . . is
> . . . good [enough to] be . . . considered God, or even worshipped as a
> special son . . . of God.[38]

Traditional African religious life is more related to human beings than to God. African theologian Kwesi Dickson writes:

> Man . . . is of considerable importance not only because he is created by God, but also because he is a moral being with a sense of right and wrong. Man is so important in the African conception that it might be wondered whether in African thought man is . . . at the centre of reality [*Theology*, 60].

Dickson's view of the centrality of humans to African traditional religion is supported by his colleague Harry Sawyerr,[39] and by French africanist Dominique Zahan. Zahan writes:

> Before beginning the study of African religion and spirituality . . . the position occupied by man in African thought and culture [must be established]. From one end of the continent to the other the African affirms his conviction that the human being is superior to all else in existence. Man is the supreme and irreducible reality; the divinity itself enters his affairs in the same way as do other beings which [man] is close to and uses [*Religion*, 6].

For certain scholars, then, African traditional religion is anthropocentric, whereas Christianity—including Afro-American Christianity—is theocentric.

Concepts of eternal life in the two religions are also radically dissimilar. Christians believe their deceased are, or will be, in heaven. Most Africans believe their deceased "live" with them. Found as well in many traditional societies is the notion that the deceased may reincarnate as infants. Thus a point of continuity exists between the dead and the unborn; one phenomenon feeds into the other. Immortality is therefore a concept to be understood in the "here and now"; notions of a heaven are absent in most traditional African cosmologies.

All this simply stresses again that the focus of traditional African religion is more upon the human than the divine. (To minimize, however, that Africans have traditionally traced their being to a Supreme Being, is wrong.) Cecil Cone's God of black religion, then, appears more Christian than traditional African, especially since the African belief in reincarnation, the practice of certain African funerary rites, and African acts of libation were scarcely evident in the United States.[40]

All the same, Cone asserts: "If it is kept in mind that religion was the whole system of being [in Africa], then it is only natural that religion would be the primary means by which [the slaves] could attempt to cope with their condition" (*Crisis*, 31). Yes. But the gods died in the United States: Da Ayido Hwedo, Legba, Shango, and Ogun, for example (Raboteau, *Religion*, "Death of the Gods"). And the names of their African ancestors are lost to most black North Americans.[41] The phenomenon of "working roots" reveals something

African, as do "Hoodoo," the "sanctified church," the blues, jazz, and certain aphorisms and folktales. But the God in whose presence the slaves experienced conversion was, essentially, the God of Moses and the father of "King Jesus."[42] Their God is not, strictly speaking, the African God.

Needed, I think, is an explanation of how the biblical God replaced the African God and why.[43] It seems that chattelization destroyed much of the human-centered character of African traditional religion; Jesus and the almighty, sovereign God replaced the ancestors and lesser gods.[44] But inasmuch as Cecil Cone fails to give an adequate account of this transposition, the claim that the almighty, sovereign God is African appears to be too hastily made.[45] Discontinuities between black religion and African traditional religion must be better taken into consideration. Though an essential monotheism undergirds each, the two do not seem to me to be at all synonymous.

In sum, Cecil Cone, J. Deotis Roberts, and James Cone have contributed immensely to the quest to ground black theology in black culture and the African heritage. More investigation, however, into that heritage—and its problematical relationship to black North American culture—might have greatly enriched their work.

Charles Long

A critic who suggests that black theologians more critically study Africa's cultural relationship to black religion is Charles Long. I have noted Long's view that the literary and dogmatic character of Western theology renders it poorly suited for an assimilation of black religion. More appropriate for Long, according to James Cone, is a method that emerges from the "value-free" discipline of the philosophy of religion.[46] Long's appraisal of the Frazier-Herskovits debate, however, concerns me more than the issue of method. I am interested in the conclusions he draws in light of that debate, and its ramifications for the relationship of black theology to African theology (an issue more fully explored in chap. 5, below).

Long finds middle ground between the positions of Frazier and Herskovits. The African heritage, he asserts, has neither greatly nor insignificantly influenced black culture in the United States. Afro-American religion in the United States reveals African influences, but not nearly as much as with blacks in other parts of the Americas.[47] According to Long, the most significant impact of Africa upon black consciousness in the United States has been its *image* rather than the vestiges of African culture.[48] Indeed, many black North Americans believed that Africa was the place where they could live freely as human beings. Long asserts, moreover, that Africa, as a place (image), has historically had profound religious meaning for blacks in the United States.[49]

The importance of that image, moreover, for black religious awareness is due, according to Long, to the "involuntary structure of the black religious conscious."[50] "Involuntary" here means that the dearness of Africa as a place—as "Zion"—was born from the pain of blacks' experience of rejection by the white society of the United States. Blacks did not choose separation from the United States, but were *forced* into separatism.[51]

American society for blacks of the United States has not been a theonomous, transparent milieu in the Tillichian sense.[52] For blacks, God did not come *through* the society in which they were pariahs, but *in spite of* it. In the United States, society was opaque rather than transparent to the revelation that God is no respecter of persons.[53] Opacity, on the one hand, represents white rejection of blacks: blacks from this perspective are "dirty," "evil," "sinful," "inferior." But, as Long explains, blacks transformed opacity into a positive symbol. Left only with their pariah status, a "hardness" of reality in suffering, blacks transformed opacity into a symbol that absorbed their experience.[54] Christology for blacks, as a result, has been darkened by black suffering. Long writes:

> Paul Tillich in his systematic theology made explicit the meaning of transparency in his Christological formulation. In the crucifixion, Tillich affirms that Jesus became transparent so that through Him the believer could see God. The theologians of opacity [however] with their emphasis on suffering . . . force one to deal with the actuality of the suffering itself, and to that human act whereby one human being or community forces another person or community to undergo an ordeal for the salvation of one or both.[55]

Long concludes that theologies of liberation, which celebrate the nonwhite, are theologies of the opaque. Naturally, black theology is included here, especially as it is defined by James Cone.[56] In order, moreover, for black theologians to fathom the symbolic ramifications of "opacity," Long suggests they must probe the depths of black culture, " 'way down yonder' [where God is met, and] some other strange brothers."[57] (Long implies that such probing will uncover more substantially the traditional African spirituality, which has a certain continuity with Afro-American religion.)[58]

RELATIONSHIP TO BLACK FEMINISM, MARXISM, AND THE THIRD WORLD

Black theologians reveal an insensitivity to feminist issues generally and to black feminist issues in particular. Their writings have been sexist, with minimal attention given to issues raised by black scholars such as Bell Hooks, Angela Davis, Michele Wallace, and Gloria Wade-Gayles.[59] "Black man" has served generically for black humanity; the affirmation of black manhood has tended to exhaust the meaning of black awareness; and God is too often defined in masculine terms. Little, if any, reference has been made to the formative and substantive role black women have played in the black church; and certain black clergymen have not, in general, been criticized for their views that border on misogyny.[60] Though most black theologians applaud the heroism of Harriet Tubman and Sojourner Truth, few have noted the courage of Ida Wells Barnett and Maria Stewart (Loewenberg and Bogin, *Women*). Stewart and Barnett were devout Christian heroines of black liberation. Stewart fought gallantly against slavery and Barnett courageously fought against lynchings (Loewenberg and Bogin, 183-200; Wells, *Crusade*). Paucity of reference to black feminism has caused black female theologians to ask the question: How can a black theology of the oppressed ignore the oppression of black women, who, bearing the burden of racism and sexism, are the most sorely oppressed? Their question inspired their quest for a black feminist theology. Black women are looking critically at black males' theological works, celebrating the contributions of black women to the black church and black history, and attempting to write black theologies with inclusive language. In the vanguard of this movement are Pauli Murray, Jacquelyn Grant, Theresa Hoover, and Kelly D. Brown.[61]

Today, James Cone, more than any other black male theologian, has substantially taken the black feminist critique to heart. He insists that the problems of sexism must receive critical attention by black male theologians:

> Black women (and also black men) [must] . . . discover their sisters of the past and . . . find community with those of the present so they can share experiences with each other and thereby be encouraged to keep fighting for recognition and justice in the church. . . . I firmly believe that the black church cannot regain its Christian integrity unless it is willing to face head-on the evil of patriarchy and seek to eliminate it [*People*, 138-39].

Cone asserts that capitalist exploitation must also be eliminated.[62] When workers are the means of production and yet are alienated from the benefits of their labor, they, like women and blacks, are oppressed. Alienated laborers suffer from the control that monopoly capitalists have over their lives and over the products of their labor. Karl Marx put it succinctly: "Political economy starts from labour as the real soul of production; yet to labour it gives nothing, and to private property everything."[63] Kwame Nkrumah has highlighted the intrinsic relationship of monopoly capitalism to the colonization of the Third World.[64] Capitalism, moreover, undergirds and maintains white supremacy. Capitalism was a principal cause of chattel slavery, and is the foundation of both the apartheid policies of South Africa and neocolonialism within the rest of the continent.[65] Small wonder, then, that James Cone is engaged in the study of Marxist thought in order to engage the problems of capitalist exploitation. And J. Deotis Roberts has also expressed interest in Marxist thought.[66]

Examining Marxist and black church differences in worldview and historical development, James Cone shows that black churches and white Marxists have encountered one another only minimally. According to Cone, the atheism of Marxists has been an affront to the theocentrism of the black church; and dogmatic, self-righteous white Marxists have tended to look down upon the intellectual capacity of black religionists (*People*, chap. 9). Still, Cone has the hope that " . . . black religion and Marxist philosophy may show us the way to build a completely new society" (*Soul*, 138).

Cone's vision is shared by philosopher Cornel West, who has criticized black theologians for their failure to criticize monopoly capitalism. West implies that black theologians' silence on capitalist issues is proportionate to the benefits black theologians receive from capitalist structures (*Prophesy*, 113). West advocates an Afro-American revolutionary Christianity that will succumb neither to a bourgeois liberalism nor to a right-wing Marxism. According to West, middle ground between those two extremes is a "revolutionary Christian . . . praxis . . . rooted in . . . Afro-American culture and . . . the . . . black church [and informed by] progressive Marxism" (ibid., 145). His analysis of Afro-American revolutionary Christianity, however, has little use for African norms and notions:

> While it might be possible to articulate a competing Afro-American philosophy based principally on African norms and notions, it is likely that the result would be theoretically thin [*Prophesy*, 24].

Although J. Deotis Roberts expresses interest in Third World theologies (*Political Theology*, 20), it is James Cone's writings that reveal a substantial engagement in the theologies of liberation and indigenization that have emerged in Africa, Asia, and Latin America. Cone has stressed the need for dialogue among the oppressed of the Third World, with the hope that the virtue of listening will overcome dogmatic, partisan exposition.[67] Referring to the well-known imperialistic strategy of "divide and conquer," Cone has advocated solidarity among members of the Ecumenical Association of Third World Theologians (EATWOT) (Fabella and Torres, 235–44). According to Cone, Third World theologians share in the experience of domination by the European West, and were thus inspired to write by "political movements of liberation in the countries of their origin" (*Soul*, 100). Cone asserts, moreover, that: " . . . if third world people build a coalition in their struggle, then it would be more difficult for Europeans and [white] North Americans to control [them]"—politically, ecclesiastically, and theologically (ibid., 102).

Such a coalition might well be achieved in an alliance between black theologians of Africa and the United States. Both groups have members in EATWOT, and represent a tension that divides Third World theologians: indigenization versus liberation. Should they successfully construct a method inclusive of issues of liberation and indigenization, it might serve as a model for EATWOT. According to James Cone, Asian and black North Americans have had "few conflicts in [their] dialogues," which bodes well for a joint construction of a theology of liberation and indigenization.[68] Afro-American and African theologians, on the other hand, cannot agree on their relationship. I am brought again to my principal concern.

CHAPTER III

African Theologies of Indigenization

We believe that the God and Father of our Lord Jesus Christ, Creator of heaven and earth, Lord of history, has been dealing with mankind at all times and in all parts of the world. It is with this conviction that we study the rich heritage of our African peoples, and we have evidence that they know of Him and worship Him.

The Consultation of African Theologians,
Ibadan, 1965

I investigate African theology of indigenization with the hope that textual differences between it and black North American theology will be more clearly in evidence, and that black North American theologians may see more clearly the particularity of African theological discourse.

African theologians rely upon at least three principal sources for their work: (1) the Bible, (2) the African independent churches, and (3) African traditional religion.[1]

The Bible is an essential source for all Christian theologians. Little, then, need be said of African theologians' use of the Bible but that their engagement in the study of African traditional religion is subject to its authority. The Old Testament, moreover, is particularly attractive to many Africans, who find an affinity between the ritual life of ancient Israel and traditional Africa.[2]

The historical relationship of independency to African theology has been examined in chapter 1, above. To briefly reiterate, independency reveals an africanization of Christianity that emerges from an African traditional spirituality. Greatest emphasis within these churches appears to be placed upon healing and prayer. With the exception of churches such as the West African Church of the Lord (Aladura), independent churches make little effort to express themselves in an academic African theology.[3] Inasmuch as the African theologians with whom I am concerned do not engage in the topic of independency with the intensity with which they engage in the study of African traditional religion, I shall not focus on independency in the course of this chapter.

African traditional religion is the most important source of African theology. African theologians concentrate largely on the creative interaction between elements of that religion and Christianity. Indeed, discussion of African traditional religion is undertaken here because it is indispensable for an analysis of African theology. In this chapter, then, I first discuss, broadly and generally, African traditional religion. Secondly, I examine the ways in which African theologians are engaged in the study of the problematical relationship of Christianity to African traditional religion in order to clear the way for a theology more indigenous to black Africa. Thirdly, I look at critical views of African theology.

AFRICAN TRADITIONAL RELIGION

Caution must be observed by Westerners attempting to analyze the traditional religion of black Africans. Temptations to interpret this orally transmitted heritage *solely* by way of Western concepts should be resisted: African traditional religion is decidedly not a Western phenomenon.

Westerners initiated into African traditional religion by way of literature (secondary sources) rather than experience (primary sources) should be particularly cautious. Primary sources are gleaned from firsthand observations of traditional rites, with an introduction to their meaning by traditional priests, oracles, diviners, and other religious specialists. An understanding of African languages is indispensable here.

My discussion is conducted from secondary sources: the writings of those who have lived within traditional milieus and witnessed the traditional African approach to religion with an understanding of African idioms. Such an examination is complicated by the different ways that writers interpret this phenomenon. Because my discussion is confined to the relationship of this religion to African theology, I focus primarily upon African theologians' interpretations, with some reference to the work of European and Euro-American africanists, such as Geoffrey Parrinder, Dominique Zahan, Basil Davidson, Melville Herskovits, and E. E. Evans-Pritchard. (In general, these interpreters have rejected terms such as "animism," "ju-ju," "fetish," and "primitive" as inaccurate descriptions of the phenomenon now under examination.)[4]

An examination of African traditional religion is further complicated by thematic variations. Scholars have analyzed African traditional religion thematically: God, gods, disembodied spirits, ancestors, humankind. Scrutiny of diverse ethnic groups reveals radical variation in certain of these themes. Harshness of environment and other historical factors led to migrations hundreds of years ago with the result that traditional peoples, though often related, speak different languages and practice different customs.[5] Zambian President Kenneth Kaunda, for example, claims that the elderly are revered in Africa— waited on hand and foot as age progressively weakens them (in Shorter,

Spirituality, 138). Among the nomadic Bushmen of the Kalahari, however, infirmed elderly are surrendered to hyenas (Zahan, 46). Among the Sudanic Nuer, twins have traditionally been revered, whereas among the West African Igbo, tradition dictated that twins be destroyed at birth.[6] Other examples of variance abound, revealing that African traditional religion varies considerably from place to place. Rain doctors, for example, are more prominent in areas susceptible to drought than in those in which the climate is more temperate (Mbiti, *Religions*, 236). In the flatlands, God may be associated with the sky; in mountainous regions, with the highest summit; in the rain forest of the pygmies, with impregnableness (Mbiti, *Concepts*, 3–7).

Thus, because of differences among African traditional cosmologies, it seems best to talk of African traditional religions. Use of the singular here is based upon African theologians' view that, in spite of differences, a certain unanimity of belief is evident (Mbiti, *Religions*; Idowu, *Religion*). My discussion of African traditional religion, then, attempts merely to reflect the views of theologians such as John Mbiti, Vincent Mulago, and Bolaji Idowu.

Structurally, my discussion is adopted from Mbiti's categorization of African traditional religion:

1. God as the ultimate explanation of the genesis and sustenance of both man and things.
2. Spirits . . . made up of superhuman beings and the spirits of men who died . . . long . . . ago.
3. Man . . . human beings who are alive and those [unborn].
4. Animals and plants, or the remainder of biological life.
5. Phenomena and objects without biological life [*Religions*, 20].

Mbiti asserts that these categories form the ontological structure of African traditional religion.

Placide Tempels makes a similar point in his *Bantu Philosophy*: in traditional Africa a hierarchy of being interacts and overlaps. Tempels describes this matrix as "vital force." All entities participate in it and all possess it with more or less potency according to their position within it (Tempels, *Bantu*). At the center of this matrix are human beings, who manipulate their milieu in order to promote equilibrium or disequilibrium.

Mbiti and Idowu find Tempels's notion of vital force problematic because it reduces African traditional religion to magic.[7] Magic is the human attempt to control the natural environment, and other religious phenomena, through harnessing what Mbiti calls "power" or "force" (Mbiti, *Religions*, 257). On the other hand, the influence of Tempel's notion of vital force is evident in the work of African theologian Vincent Mulago of Francophone Africa. Mulago has modified Tempels's notion of vital force with the term *union vitale* or *participation vitale*.[8]

If Mulago conceives African traditional religion as a unified system in which all participate interdependently in a hierarchy of being, the key to Mbiti's ontology is time. If for Mulago the link between human beings and the divine stretches in some sense upward from humankind to God,[9] it stretches backward into Zamani (an African philosophy of time that includes the ancestors, spirits, divinities, and God), for Mbiti.[10] Zamani has no teleology; the past eternally swallows the present. Yet the past is unable to swallow the present fully due to procreation and (partial) reincarnation.[11]

As I now briefly examine categories within African traditional religion, no attempt is made to adjudicate between Mbiti's ontological terminology and Mulago's. Under the heading of "humankind," I shall discuss humans, animals, plants, and other visible elements within the natural milieu. God, divinities, spirits, and ancestors will be discussed under the heading of "the invisible and the divine." Under both headings, focus is upon the traditional societies to which African theologians refer when writing about African traditional religion. These are the Akan, Igbo, and Yoruba of West Africa; the Akamba of East Africa; certain Bantu groups of southern/central Africa; and certain Nilotic groups of East Africa. Attention is given as well to the Bambara and Dogon of Mali, and the Senufu of the Ivory Coast and Burkina Faso (Upper Volta).

Humankind

As noted in chapter 2, above, scholars are agreed that humans are the focus of African traditional religion. Believing themselves regents over nature, Africans attempted to manipulate their natural milieu by knowledge of its properties and by appeals to the invisible: to divinities, spirits, and ancestors. Africans, then, have lived in dynamic, symbiotic relationship with their natural environment.[12] Primordial avatars, as in the case of the Senufu, are often believed to be animals: snakes, hornbill birds, crocodiles, chameleons, and tortoises. Animals such as these have totemic significance and are sacred.[13]

Religious meaning is found as well in the significance Africans attach to hemispheres. The Bantu of Kavirondo, for instance, attribute goodness to the east and badness to the west (Zahan, 67). The homesteads of the Dogon chief are "so built as to present a model of the universe," with left and right, east and west, north and south, embued with religious significance (Forde, 100–101). The relationship of the hemispheres to cosmological ideas indicates that natural environments are the "temples" of African traditional religion.

With the exception of sites such as Great Zimbabwe, physical temples perish quickly.[14] Tropical and desert conditions, moreover, make internal gatherings highly impractical (Parrinder, 19). Harshness of climate may also help explain the absence of literate traditional religions (except among the Ejagham of Cameroon) (see Thompson, chap. 5). Intense heat and humidity render writing surfaces, such as papyri, too susceptible to decay (Jahn, 187). Thus, once again, humans are central to religion, for they must transmit it orally. Without them, there would be no record of religion.

The Akan, Yoruba, and Igbo believe that God has given humans a part of the divine essence. For the Akan that divine spark is called *Kra*; the Yoruba call it *Ori*; and the Igbo call it *Chi*.[15] Intriguing as well is the Dogon belief that they possess "two souls of opposite sexes, one of which inhabits [their] body while the other dwells in the sky or in water" (Forde, 88). The Dogon believe, then, that one has a spiritual double. As a result, one may be in two places at the same time (Zahan, 8). Humans are quite malleable. Other notions of spiritual duality are found throughout sub-Saharan Africa (ibid.).[16]

In the social milieu, "blood" figures intimately into patterns of kinship and establishes societal identity.[17] The Ashanti (Akan), for instance, trace their blood to the paramount chief (king) and through him to God. Indeed, the supreme chief is the people's link with God.[18]

One's status in society, moreover, is determined by one's relationship to certain *rites de passage*. Discussion of these rites will show that notions of human composition are intrinsic to social patterns, which rest fundamentally in religious worldviews.

Among the Akan, one is at birth the embodiment of one's mother's blood; the father imparts the personality-soul; and God imparts *Kra*.[19] Among the Bambara an infant may be a reincarnated ancestor (Zahan, 136–37). Most traditional societies attach taboos to surviving babies, which insure their ritual adoption into society. Upon adoption, infants are accorded a fully human status (Mbiti, *Religions*, chap. 2; Zahan, 9).

If birth comes first in a series of initiations—the Bambara have at least six initiations (Zahan, 134–45)—closely behind it is initiation into adulthood. In many societies, circumcision and clitoridectomy mark that initiation—one's death to childhood and rebirth into adulthood (Mbiti, *Religions*, chap. 12).[20] According to Harry Sawyerr, blood shed in these operations is seen as libation to ancestors (*Evangelism*, 24). Blood, in this case, must flow liberally onto the ground to seal the union between the human and ancestral communities (ibid.).[21] Bambara circumcision, in addition, is seen as the removal of vestiges of "femaleness" (Zahan, 135). In societies in which male and female circumcision is practiced, initiates are accorded the status of adult upon thorough recuperation from the operation. Imperative soon after is marriage (Mbiti, *Religions*, chap. 12; Sawyerr, *Evangelism*, 24).

Marriage is essential to procreation and thus ensures the bond between humans and their ancestors. According to John Mbiti, childless marriages are unconsummated (*Religions*, chap. 13). Children ensure that "life" will continue to be shared by the living, the dead, and the unborn. They preserve society.

In death, as in birth, taboos are observed. The deceased must be given safe passage into the invisible, which includes the domain of the ancestors (ibid., chap. 14). Improper burial would cause the deceased to bring misfortune upon the family responsible for interment (ibid., 204). And, because the cosmological milieu of traditional religion—its warp and woof—is delicate, a rupture at one "point" may send out "negative vibes" elsewhere (Davidson, *Genius*, chap. 6–7, 10–16). Thus Africans are careful to honor their ancestors. They must daily provide them with food and drink to avoid trouble: sickness, death, barrenness, impotency, accidents, and the like (ibid.).[22] Misfortunes such as these concern specialists, who identify the cause of trouble.[23]

Religious specialists, such as diviners, when consulting the ancestors, may determine that the cause of trouble rests in an angry ancestor who must be appeased by sacrifice (ibid.). Other specialists include medicine men, priests, mediums, and herbalists (ibid.). Herbalists have impressive knowledge of the medicinal value of plants found among abundant toxic vegetation. (The Dogon, for instance, "classify the plants they know in twenty-two chief families of which some are divided into as many as eleven sub-families.") (Davidson, *Genius*, 112). Mediums are often possessed by ancestors or divinities and reveal their messages to diviners or to the priests who serve a god (Parrinder, chap. 9). Medicine men combine the roles of diviner, herbalist, and magician (Mbiti, *Religions*, 217–24). Identification of witches and sorcerers are a principal activity of medicine men (ibid.).

Belief in witches pervades traditional Africa (ibid., chap. 16).[24] Unlike sorcerers who *learn* harmful magic, witches are *born* evil.[25] Most misfortune is attributed to the activities of these despised and feared beings. Witches, moreover, are believed to "eat" persons, especially their relatives, at night. It is believed that witches consume even their own infants. (Consumption here is of the spiritual double—a notion intrinsic to the traditional notion of the self. The spiritual doubles of witches consume the spirits of persons who are asleep.) (Idowu, *Religion*, 175–76; Parrinder, chap. 9).

The Invisible and the Divine

Spiritual energy permeates the invisible and the visible. By way of that energy, humans interact with the invisible, manipulating the cosmos in order to promote fortune or misfortune.[26] It bears repeating that witches and sorcerers promote chaos, whereas medicine men preserve order and fecundity with the help of the supreme God, lesser gods, and the ancestors (Mbiti, *Religions*, 258).[27]

That the ancestors are a prominent part of most traditional societies also bears repeating. Seen as a part of families, they reveal how intensely Africans believe themselves a part of the invisible. When ancestors, however, are no longer remembered by name, they become dangerous, unpredictable spirits inhabiting the bush or forest.[28] In general, according to Idowu, only the ethically upright and physically sound become ancestors.[29] Outstanding ancestors have been apotheosized (Idowu, *Religion*, 186). Among the Yoruba, for instance, the god Shango is thought to have been the fourth king of the Oyo dynasty (Parrinder, 47). Vincent Mulago reports that the entire cosmology of certain Bantu peoples of central Africa may be understood as a *culte des ancêstres*—an invisible dimension joined to the visible realm, inhabited by ancestors, disembodied souls, apotheosized heroes, and God.[30]

Large pantheons are found in West Africa (Murray, 33; Parrinder, chap. 4).

The Yoruba count at least seventeen hundred gods. Olodumare (Olorun) is their supreme God (Mbiti, *Concepts*, 120–21; Idowu, *Olodumare*). The Bantu of southern and central Africa have fewer divinities than certain of their West African cousins who are also Kongo-Kordofanian (Parrinder, 43). Fewer gods are also found among Nilotics such as the Nuer and Masai, who show little interest in ancestors (Murray, 28; Evans-Pritchard, *Religion*).

Olodumare, the supreme God of the Yoruba, does not seem to be a creator—one who *solely* brought forth the world *ex nihilo*, or after subduing primordial chaos. What, then, is the relationship of Olodumare to the lesser divinities? Perhaps a clue lies in Idowu's assertion that divinities were not created but "brought into being, or . . . came into being with the nature of things with regard to the divine ordering of the Universe" (*Religion*, 169). Harry Sawyerr explains that Orisha-Nla created, whereas Olodumare instilled in the inanimate creatures the principle of life (*God*, 42).

If the Yoruba pantheon is in some sense gradated, then second in status to the supreme God, Olodumare, is Orisha-Nla.[31] Well-known lesser divinities are Ogun and Shango, who are revered in parts of the African diaspora as well.[32] A well-populated pantheon is also found in Dahomey (Benin) and several of these gods are prominent in Haiti.[33] (The Igbo of Nigeria, however, have fewer gods than the Yoruba. Their most important divinity appears to be Ala—the earth mother) (Ilogu, 35–37).

Mbiti claims God was traditionally known in Africa as Creator. And in spite of the myriad gods found in West Africa, African theologians assert that African traditional religion is essentially monotheistic.[34]

Their assertion is an abstraction distilled from the majority of African societies that possess a notion of a supreme or creator God. Mbiti has greatly contributed to the credibility of this view in his *Concepts of God in Africa*. His Pan-African study of three hundred ethnic groups concludes that God for the Africans is utterly transcendent but nonetheless immanent. Traditional African belief holds that God is omniscient, omnipotent, ubiquitous, and unequivocably holy. The African thus carefully avoids profanation. If God is too closely approached, cosmic equilibrium is lost and catastrophe ensues. "The concept of intermediaries," explains Mbiti, is widespread in African societies. "[Humans feel] that [they] cannot or should not approach God alone or directly and must do so through special persons or beings" (*Concepts*, 220). Priests who serve the gods, mediums, oracles, ancestors, and the gods, then, are the intermediaries in and through whom most Africans have had intercourse with the divine.

Mbiti claims, moreover, that Africans traditionally sought God practically rather than spiritually. Alien, then, to traditional sensibilities is an "Augustinian" piety dominated by an insatiable love of God in quest of the beatific vision. Mbiti writes: "Africans do not thirst after God for [God's] sake alone. They seek to obtain what [God] gives . . . [with little concern for] the final reward or satisfaction of the human soul or spirit" (*Concepts*, 219).

That the African God, then, is as remote as certain scholars suggest appears true at first glance. A God who is for most societies approachable only through intermediaries, and beseeched only during crisis, appears indeed uninvolved in human affairs. Yet, I have shown that Mbiti and Idowu reject that judgment as foreign and assert, rather, that divine transcendence must be kept strictly in tension with divine immanence, and that this dialectic must be understood in traditional terms. Although few traditional societies worship God directly, God "is a reality and . . . not an abstract concept" (Idowu, *Religion*, 150).

An example of God's nearness to humans is observed in further examination of the Akan notion of *Kra*. I noted *Kra* as the divine spark within humans that simultaneously imparts the essence of life and governs human destiny. Harry Sawyerr's analysis of J. B. Danquah's *The Akan Doctrine of God* reveals, in addition, the way in which a triadic God (or a God with three praise names: Nyame-Nyankopon-Odonomankoma) is believed to be of the same blood as the Akan and, therefore, their supreme ancestor (*God*, 25–33, 95).

In many societies God is associated with the sun and moon, and it may be that belief in a supreme god was preceded by sun and moon cults from which notions of a supreme God developed (Mbiti, *Concepts*, 131–36; Sawyerr, *God*, 19–21).

In sum, God in African traditional religion is related to but not synonymous with humans. Humans, however, are intrinsically related to their ancestors. Relationships between humans, their unborn, their ancestors, and their gods, represent the essential union between the visible and invisible world, which is bound by an energy that pervades the entire cosmos. Manipulation of this energy, for good or evil, and communion with the invisible are the traditional vehicles in and by which Africans have lived with their God. Their religion is dynamically pregnant with *archetypal symbols* that are *ritually* manifested in dance, colors, sacred objects, masks, sculptures, and rhythm.[35] These reveal, on the surface, the intensity with which Africans—always in transition between being and becoming—feel themselves within a vibrant milieu imparted to them by God and controlled by customs handed down by primordial ancestors.[36]

These traditions remain somewhat enigmatic to the Westerners and the westernized, for even the most reverent observer must await initiation into that which may have been withheld.[37] And, *perhaps*, due to the negative ramifications of colonialism, much has been lost due to the passing of a master priest-diviner who had no apprentices to whom to entrust traditional secrets. Indeed, the black continent is no longer under the sway of its traditional worldviews. As shown in chapter 1, traditional societies have been, since the Berlin Conference, subjected to Western mores, Western Christianity, and an epistemology that render certain African views archaic. Divine (or ritual) kingship has given way to the office of president; political catastrophe, drought, disease, and famine are no longer problems to be solved by religious specialists, but are instead tackled from Western paradigms of the political, social, medical, and natural sciences.

CHRISTIANITY INCARNATED IN AFRICAN FORMS

That discussion and assessment of African theology is confined to and representative of a small, select group of African theologians must be sharply stressed here. My intention is to examine, for the most part, the work of African theologians who have been involved in the consultations between Afro-American and African theologians.

African theologians want to produce *Christian* theologies that incorporate certain *traditional* religious concepts. In order to achieve that goal, African theologians have been engaged in the study of African traditional religion and its problematical relationship to Christian doctrine.

Problems for them arise from an appreciation of the tension between the continuities and discontinuities between African traditional religion and Christianity. Only by giving attention to this problem do African theologians feel they can precisely identify the traditional idioms through which a Christian doctrine may be expressed. In no case, then, is africanization essentially repristinization: only elements truly complementary to a Western, Christian orthodoxy appear desirable in African theology.

Obviously discontinuous with Christianity are the sacrificial practices of homicide and infanticide and the murder of twins and deformed babies. The notion of reincarnation is also outside the pale of Christian belief, as are metempsychotic notions associated with animals. What, however, is to be thought about the divinities and the ancestors? What relationship has the notion of sin to belief in sorcery and witchcraft? How far may polygyny be tolerated within an African church? Some of these questions will be examined later, but I look now at another problem with which African theologians are concerned.

That problem hinges upon distinctions often made between theologies of adaptation (contact theology) and more incarnational theologies. According to Mbiti, contact theology is "built upon areas of apparent similarities and contact between Christianity and traditional African concepts and practices" (*Eschatology*, 187). The danger here is that apparent continuities may be too superficially adapted to fit a Christian framework. Indigenization here occurs only minimally. In adaptation, the African clergy barely assumes ecclesial leadership, and although liturgies may be linguistically and musically African, the theological content of African churches remains essentially European.[38]

Incarnational theology, on the other hand, emerges from a sustained and critical enterprise in which the relationship of Christianity to a people's traditional religion is examined in depth.[39] How can a Christian theology reflect the traditional ethos of a people and be, nonetheless, an orthodox theology? To be examined, then, are African theologians' conscious attempts to go beyond the superficialness of adaptation to a theology as indigenous as the Bible and the strictures of Western orthodoxy will allow.

Discussed first, and briefly, will be the continuities among elements of

African traditional religion and Christianity. Secondly, African theologians' attempts to communicate certain Christian doctrines by way of certain of these continuities will be examined.

Examples of Continuities

E. W. Fashole-Luke and John Mbiti assert that African theology should be pluriform and plural. Because Africa, they reason, is a continent of great diversity, African theological reflection should be equally diverse (Anderson and Stransky, 135–48; Mbiti, *Eschatology*, 185). I have concluded, however, that African theologians work under the same theological agenda: the critical interpretation of Christianity through elements within African traditional religion that appear to be continuous with Christianity. Exposition of one such element is found in J. Omosade Awolalu's essay "Sin and Its Removal in African Traditional Religion."[40]

Awolalu demonstrates that a notion of sin is evident within traditional life. According to Awolalu, Africans live traditionally in an ethical covenant relationship with one another and with their ancestors, their divinities, and the Creator. Humans' "rights and obligations are prescribed, [their] duties are enjoined, and [their] relation to [one another is] regulated" ("Sin," 279). Thus, Awolalu asserts that African traditional society is a moral theocracy in which " . . . sanctions [are] recognized as the approved standard of social and religious conduct" (ibid.). Failure to respect these sanctions constitutes sin and invites the wrath of the beings who inhabit the invisible realm. More specifically, sin is incurred in the violation of taboos, the neglect of ancestors, and asocial behavior. What disturbs equilibrium in society disrupts the union between the human and the divine (ibid., 279–83).

According to Awolalu, rites of purification, practices of confession and reparation, and the act of sacrifice have been the traditional means by which Africans sought to remove the consequences of sin (ibid., 283–87). Awolalu stresses, moreover, that although sinners are "punished by either the divinities or the ancestors, . . . sins are . . . regarded as offenses against God . . . the Creator and Sustainer of the universe" (ibid., 287).[41] His view, then, that sin is primarily an affront to the righteousness of God implies that the traditional notion of sin is compatible with the Christian notion of sin.

Vincent Mulago has researched a Bantu cosmology that he calls *participation vitale*, a notion of the relationship between the living and the dead sustained by God. The notion that God created and sustains *participation vitale* has led Mulago to assert that continuity exists between it and the Christian image of the body of Christ, and the notion of the Trinity:

The life-relationship on which, among Bantu, the unity of communities and individuals is founded, this communication which is a sharing in life and in the means of life, this effort towards ontic growth, self-transcendence, and enrichment, find a sublime and transcendent realization in the Church of Christ, which is also a community of life, whose vital principle is a sharing in the life of the Trinity, humanized in the Word of God made Man [Dickson and Ellingworth, *Revelations*, 157].

For Mulago, then, Jesus is the "founder of the Church, the 'clan' which came down from heaven" (ibid.).

In revealing continuities between Igbo culture and Christianity, Edmund Ilogu explains that Igbo culture prior to colonization was a well integrated matrix with patterns of decentralized authority embodied in the Ozo title (a symbol of authority) and the priests (Ilogu, 24). Missionaries' disregard for that culture caused disruption and societal crises (ibid., chap. 4). Ilogu asserts, therefore, that if Christianity is to be relevant to the Igbo today, it must "be based on sound relevant theology [aware] of Igbo life" (ibid., 170). Such a theology would include "traditional morality, Christian teachings, and modern technological influences" (ibid.). Igbo traditions that Christianity might absorb and transform are polygyny and the Ozo title of authority (ibid., chap. 8). According to Ilogu:

> The Igbo belief in continuity with the ancestors . . . with the symbolic honour to them through libation, can provide for Christians, together with All Saints Day, moments for . . . thought and prayer for our ancestors in the faith [and those] in flesh and blood [ibid., 219].

"If we are true to the spirit of the Bible," writes Bolaji Idowu, "we must admit . . . God's self-disclosure is . . . to the whole world and that each race has grasped something of [this] primary revelation according to its native capability" (ibid., 12). On this premise Idowu asserts that African notions of a supreme God are continuous with the biblical God (ibid., 17–29). Both notions are based on a belief in a reality of which nothing greater can be conceived. Denial, then, that Africans had a general conception of revelation is for Idowu a lapse into bigotry (ibid., 18–19).[42]

Idowu asserts, moreover, that all concepts of God are provisional in that they fail to capture the essence of God, who exists in reality before existing in thought (ibid., 22). He states, however, that the concept of God is probably "clearer to those who grasp the fact of God intuitively and know Him to be the . . . basis of their existence and the ultimate motive of their lives than it is to those who are able to read about Him" (ibid.). In short, Idowu discredits the view that knowledge of God was imparted to Africans by missionaries. "Africans," he asserts, have their own distinctive concepts of God and that God . . . is not 'a loan-God from the missionaries'" (ibid., 29).

African Traditional Concepts in Dialogue with Christian Doctrines

Continuities between Christianity and African traditions have encouraged African theologians to more substantially investigate the relationships of their traditional religions to Christian doctrines. Their efforts provide examples of the problems incurred as Christianity encounters African traditional religion in greater depth. I focus upon their attempts to africanize ecclesiology, christology, and eschatology. Theologians on whom I concentrate are Harry Sawyerr on ecclesiology; John Mbiti and John Pobee on christology; and Mbiti on eschatology.

Harry Sawyerr asserts that the African church needs, first, sound doctrine: "the teaching by which Christians are led to possess and so to impart to others . . . knowledge . . . that God . . . is motivated by love" (*Evangelism*, 67). Africans need, secondly, worship, " . . . humble and grateful response in a manner appropriate to the voice of God" (ibid.). Thirdly, the African church must reveal a character suited to the spirit of ecumenism (ibid., 68). And, fourthly, African Christians must know Christ as "the goal of all revelation. He must not be worshiped as one of several deities. Pluralism has no place in Christianity" (ibid., 70–71). Sound ecclesial doctrine for Sawyerr, then, includes emphasis on *agape*; implies a certain decorum in worship; requires a catholic ecclesiology; and makes christology the axis on which all ecclesiology revolves.

Magic, propitiation of ancestors, devotion to gods, and fear of spirits have no place in Christianity, according to Sawyerr. Indeed, Christianity must replace the traditional approach to personal crisis:

> Anxiety turns the pagan to improvise his own solution of his problems, sometimes invoking the aid of God. The Christian, on the other hand, turns his attention towards God in total surrender to the will of God [ibid., 77].

Thus, African Christians need not " . . . scout around through diviners to discover what spirit or deities [have been] offended" (ibid., 78). Sufficient for them is a view that God understands their suffering (ibid.). Sawyerr, then, conservatively makes a case for an African theology based solidly on scripture and the Christian tradition from Paul to Barth. At issue for Sawyerr is not so much the africanization of christianity as the christianization of aspects of African traditional religion:

> Christianization of Africa should mean not merely a transplantation of cultures from cultures foreign to Africa but the integration of African culture into the fabric of Christianity. . . . In this way, the Church in Africa will . . . develop an originality of its own [ibid., 80].

From that perspective, he asserts, the traditional notion of ancestors can be absorbed and transformed by Christianity.

Disagreeing with Bolaji Idowu and Jomo Kenyatta, Sawyerr argues that ancestors were not *revered* but *worshiped* (ibid., 122–28).[43] Coming to a stronger conclusion, it seems that Sawyerr is saying that ancestor worship is a form of idolatry, and must be eliminated with the rationale that

Christian doctrinal teaching should be directed towards first presenting
the Church as a corporate body with a unique solidarity transcending
. . . anything akin to it in pagan society [in Shorter, *Spirituality*, 131].

Still, doctrinal teaching should discover a means to preserve "the tribe, the
solidarity of living and dead, as Africans understand that relationship, but
within the idiom . . . of . . . the community of the Church" (ibid.).

An African ecclesiology, therefore, would include ancestors "within the
framework of the Universal Church and be included in the notion of the
communion of saints" (ibid.). Thus, for Sawyerr, African Christians should
pray that their ancestors receive salvation in God's providence, though they
were pagan. Conversion is thus posthumously accomplished (ibid., 131–32).
Libation to the ancestors, however, is strictly forbidden by Sawyerr, because it
is a "pagan," idolatrous practice (ibid., 133).

If African theologians have been encouraged by continuities between notions of ancestors and the *sanctorum communio*, christology appears more
problematical for them. As one source suggests, the humanity of Christ could
be a stumbling block for an African appreciation of Jesus' divinity. Traditional
notions of God have been so awesome that worship of a *man as God* seems to
stretch traditional imagination too far. According to John Mbiti, African
theologians must uncover ways in which "the Person of Jesus Christ fits into
African conceptualization[s] of the world, [and must uncover the continuities]
between the New Testament portrait of Jesus [and] African traditional concepts" (Mbiti, "Concepts," 52).[44] Mbiti's quest for an African christology,
then, proceeds first from an identification of the "christological points" that
interest Africans. In this way, he seeks to determine their understanding of
Christ and the proximity of that understanding to an orthodox christology.

Based on his study of the Aladura churches, Mbiti claims that the birth and
temptation of Jesus, Palm Sunday, and the crucifixion and resurrection of
Jesus Christ are the New Testament themes that attract Africans (ibid., 53).

"Regarding the practical works of Jesus, great emphasis is laid on the
miracles of healing, miracles of deliverance, blessing, and judgment" (ibid.).
Essentially, asserts Mbiti, Jesus is worshiped in Africa as *Christus Victor* (ibid.,
54).

Mbiti explains that the title *Christus Victor* appeals to Africans because it
implies Jesus' triumph over phenomena that Africans traditionally fear (ibid.).
Mbiti is encouraged by this syncretism because the notion of Christ as cosmo-
crator may provide traditional eschatology with the teleological perspective it
lacked, and may introduce into traditional piety concepts of resurrection and
"rejuvenation" (ibid., 60).

"For generations," writes Mbiti, "Africans [have orally recounted myths of]
paradise lost, how death came about, how God and men are separated" (ibid.).
Absent in traditional life, however, was a notion of paradise regained. "But in
Jesus," states Mbiti, "all this falls into place; it makes sense, . . . becomes a
revelation, a hope, and a destiny to which the Church and [salvation history]

are moving" (ibid.). Because, then, Jesus, in some sense, saves humankind from death and reconciles it to the Creator, the notion of Jesus as savior is attractive to Africans. Study of the independent churches reveals, moreover, "that the chief preoccupation of African Christians is redemption from physical dilemmas" (Mbiti, "Savior," 408).[45] And "Savior," like the title *Christus Victor*, suggest Jesus' power to solve these problems (ibid., 410).

Titles, however, such as "Messiah, Christ, the Son of David, and the Son of Man have no special relevance to traditional African concepts" (Mbiti, "Concepts," 58). According to Mbiti, this is because nothing analogous to them exists in traditional societies. But "Son of God," "Lord," "the servant of God," are titles that are continuous with traditional thought (ibid., 58–59). Certain African mythologies, for instance, reveal a notion of a son of God. The notion that Jesus is God's obedient servant, in addition, "fits . . . into . . . traditional concepts of father-son relationship in the home" (ibid., 59). Africans, furthermore, have traditionally referred to God as Lord or Master. Thus, writes Mbiti, "the Lordship of Jesus can be fitted into [an] African concept of his person and position. He would indeed shine through as the Lord of Lords, since Africa knows also other Lords besides God" (ibid.).

If "Messiah" and "Son of David" prove to be stumbling blocks for an appreciation of the humanity of Christ, traditional notions of intermediaries adequately interpret Jesus' divinity, according to Mbiti. Divinities have been traditionally conceptualized as parts of the deity (Idowu, *Religion*, 169). Yet, they are closer to humans and may work in their behalf. Certain folktales, for example, reveal that humans are referred by God to divinities who may best serve human needs. Similarly, Jesus, as part of the deity, as in Trinity, is that Person to whom Christians feel closest, and for whose blessings they frequently ask.

Traditional concepts of divinities as intermediaries, then, might serve an African christology (Mbiti, "Concepts," 61). Mbiti posits, in addition, that notions of the humanity of Christ may find continuity with certain *rites de passage*. For Mbiti the birth, baptism, and death of Jesus portray him as a "perfect man in the African sense":

> In the eyes of African peoples, for [whom] those *rites de passage* are so meaningful, Jesus fulfills everything which constitutes a complete, corporate member of society [ibid., 56].

By interpreting, then, the Christ event as a series of initiations, Africans appear to interpret the humanity of Christ on their own terms.

John Pobee also asserts that African notions of human nature help incarnate an African christology. He focuses upon the Akan notion of human composition. To reiterate, Akan believe humans are composed of their mother's blood (*mogya*); a personality-soul derived from the father (*sunsum/ntoro*); and a spark of divinity (*Kra*) imparted to the person by God.[46] I have shown, moreover, that this notion of human composition is intrinsic to patterns of kinship. Akan believe they share the *same* blood, tracing their descent patri-lineally. "Since kinship," writes Pobee, " . . . is a mark of a [person] . . . an [Akan] Christology would emphasize the kinship of Jesus, [whose] identity . . . was . . . demonstrated by his relationship to Mary, which gave him status and membership in a lineage and clan" (*Theology*, 88). Pobee's reference to Jesus' relationship to Mary, then, is an attempt to reveal continuities between notions of community in traditional Jewish and African societies. Pobee, however, does not fully explore the implications of his analogy.

Although Jesus' blood relationship to Mary links him to the community, Jesus' descent was recounted through Joseph. Inasmuch as Joseph did not sire Jesus, problems arise in accounting for Jesus' personality-soul (*sunsum*). The notion of *Kra*, however, is promising for an Akan christology. Indeed, Pobee mentions that Jesus' *Kra* may be viewed as *homoousious* with God in a sense unparalleled in Akan traditional thought (ibid., 93–94).

Pobee additionally finds accounts of Jesus' circumcision relevant for an Akan appreciation of the humanity of Christ. According to Pobee, circumcision incorporated "a child into a kinship group. . . . Thus in the Akan context, the circumcision of Jesus would underline Jesus' belonging to a kinship group [in order to] demonstrate his humanity" (ibid., 89). As with Mbiti, moreover, Pobee argues that Jesus' baptism may be seen as an additional initiation. Baptism, then, is viewed as "a rite of solidarity which went into the making of this man Jesus in the African sense." Pobee also relates Jesus' death to the Akan notion of "person." In death, therefore, Jesus' *Kra* returns to God, for it has fulfilled its human destiny (ibid.).

Pobee expresses the divinity of Jesus in terms of Jesus' sinlessness, and in relation to the Akan notion of morality. Reminiscent of J. Omosade Awolalu, Pobee writes:

> In Akan society, the essence of sin is an antisocial act. It is not an abstract transgression of a law; rather it is a factual contradiction of established order [*Theology*, 90].

Because Jesus perfectly loved his people, was an inimitable healer, and was unprecedentedly in communion with God, he thus perfectly models the Akan notion of the ethical person, according to Pobee (ibid., 92).

Christology is intimately related to eschatology, and Mbiti has explored problems that arise when New Testament eschatology encounters a traditional African eschatology. Mbiti focuses upon the Akamba of Kenya—his people.

According to Mbiti, the Akamba had no concept of a distant future and thus lacked a teleological perspective. As a result, Akamba Christians expected the parousia to come soon; their traditional notion of a future event implied its imminency (*Eschatology*, chap. 2). Mbiti asserts that missionaries' ignorance of this fact exacerbated the conflict that would naturally emerge as New Testament teleology encountered the linguistic and conceptual world of the Akamba (ibid., 54). Mbiti believes that had missionaries taught a "realized" eschatology rather than a more apocalyptic notion of eschatology, Akamba Christians would not have had such great expectations (ibid., 56–57). Emphasis would have been placed, therefore, on the resurrection rather than the parousia (ibid., 42–44, 163).[47] As it is, however, Akamba Christians, as of 1971, expected "an immediate realization of this futurist eschatology, [and] many [were] deeply disappointed . . . when they . . . [realized] that early generations of Christians [were] passing away and the . . . end of the world [had] not come" (ibid., 57).

According to Mbiti, then, the Akamba must learn that "time is subject to eschatology and not vice-versa" (ibid., 61). Time is, therefore, subject to Christ who may become incarnate in the African background. Thus, for Mbiti, africanization of eschatology first requires the Akamba to gain more theological insight into the uniqueness of Christ, and into the sacraments of baptism and the Eucharist (ibid., 90).

Because the Akamba had no sacramental life in the Christian sense, they associated the Eucharist with magical ideas (ibid., 112–13). Mbiti writes that the Akamba may "unconsciously . . . transpose associations of magic and witchcraft with food and drink on to the elements at the Eucharist. The service [then] becomes an occasion of fear and dread" (ibid.). For Mbiti, the Akamba must view the Eucharist as "a blessing rather than a curse" (ibid., 123). Therefore, as the Akamba are a sensitive people, "every possible appeal through the senses should be made to excite [Akamba] emotion, capture their imagination, *direct their attention and focus their attention . . . upon [Christ]* at the Eucharist" (ibid.; emphasis added).

Baptism, on the other hand, suggests Mbiti, might be associated with birth in order to convey to the Akamba the theological significance of that sacrament:

> Akamba . . . put great value on family and kinship ties. Infant baptism presents an occasion to convey the transposition of [a] traditional sense of kinship to the Christological kinship created through baptism. It is this community of kinsmen which then must be nourished and sustained through the Eucharist [*Eschatology*, 118].

In short, because the Akamba think more concretely than abstractly, Mbiti claims that sacraments must be related to aspects of traditional life (ibid., 120). The Akamba traditional notion of eschatology, moreover, must become a vehicle for their initiation into Christian eschatology.

Traditional eschatology, for instance, takes the Akamba "back to the remotest possible point in Time, beyond [the] point of beginning to, in reality, a point of non-being, [which goes beyond creation]" (ibid., 134). "Existence" in that eschatological realm comes by way of death, for death may mark one's entrance into the realm of one's ancestors and the spirits. As with Christians, then, the dead are "geographically nearer to God than [are humans]" (ibid., 138). Still, writes, Mbiti, "God's mode of existence is outside that of the departed, and in this respect [God] is transcendent to them" (ibid.). The

Akamba notion of God's transcendence then, also finds an affinity with Christian thought. According to Mbiti, however, the Akamba neither believe that God punishes the departed "nor rewards them for whatever they did in this life. . . . [Ancestors, moreover, neither] thirst for [God's] righteousness; nor do they have spiritual communion with [God]" (ibid.). Thus, although the Akamba believe their departed are close to God, they, unlike Christians, have no notion of heaven, with attendant themes of retribution, new creation, and the mass resurrection of new creatures. "To the Akamba," asserts Mbiti, in addition, "the spirit world becomes dangerous if it gets too near, and sacrifice as offering must be given to restore the right equilibrium." Christianity presents nothing comparable to such a worldview (ibid., 155).

In order to preserve elements of Akamba traditional eschatology, Mbiti suggests Akamba Christians adopt the view that the human and spirit world "overlap in Jesus Christ" (ibid.). And, according to Mbiti, the sacraments would excellently symbolize this symbiosis in teaching the Akamba that baptism and the Eucharist maintain in themselves equilibrium between humans and the spirit world. Inasmuch as Christ made the one, perfect, ultimate sacrifice of himself, no additional (penultimate) sacrifices are needed. Indeed, equilibrium between the human and the divine was flawlessly and permanently regulated upon Jesus' resurrection. Mbiti claims, moreover, as does Sawyerr, that traditional eschatology would be further christianized if the notion of ancestors would be absorbed in that of the communion of saints (ibid., 147).

I have noted, that the resurrection, for Mbiti, has rendered time subject to the authority of Christ. Past, present, and future, then, converge into the "nowness" of the resurrection. Mbiti asserts, therefore, that "if . . . the temporal implications of the Resurrection [are followed], Jesus [on Easter] was placed in the dimensionless present, the presence of God" (ibid., 174). The "dimensionless present," moreover, is manifest within one's daily, faithful relationship with Christ. Mbiti's interpretation of the resurrection, then, leads him to conclude that eschatology need not be exclusively teleological. A linear understanding of time—past, present, future—is thus dispensable. It follows that, for Mbiti, the Akamba lack of teleological perspective is no great barrier to their christianization. Their "two-dimensional concept of time is equally valid" (ibid., 182). Indeed, Mbiti claims that a two-dimensional concept of time is found in the New Testament as well: the duality of New Testament time "has been realized in the historical present of the Church, and what is to be consummated at the parousia."

Mbiti points out, however, that the Akamba notion of time and the New Testament notion are not in any sense synonymous (ibid., 182–83). But the notion of the historical present of the church is still applicable to Akamba Christians and their traditional milieu. In other words, standing irrepressibly in the middle of the resurrection and the parousia is the nowness of Christ in the church. Ecclesial experience of Christ, then, transcends time, though it is, nonetheless, a present reality. And, although an appreciation of Christian apocalypticism must come to pervade Akamba eschatology, the problem of indigenization hinges less on a notion of the future and more on an understanding of the present lordship of Christ. As Mbiti explains, "Christian Eschatology [is] a Christological phenomenon [which is] . . . impervious to temporal limitations, whatever understanding of eschatology we derive from linear and other concepts of Time" (ibid., 182).

In sum, Mbiti believes that Akamba Christians can retain a notion of their spirit world if they focus on the resurrection. From that perspective, their ancestors are seen as within the communion of saints. Focus on the resurrection, moreover, might help the Akamba develop a sense of teleology. "The End," writes Mbiti, "is a teleological End . . . which means a corporate and conscious participation in the presence and nature of God" (ibid., 185). Christian knowledge of the nearness of God, then, ensures the pious of an abundant spiritual life and frees them from the finality of death. "For that," concludes Mbiti, "is the mode . . . which [we will have received in Christ] and attained [in Him] all . . . promised us: the mode in Christ in which there is . . . no beyond for us to become" (ibid.). The resurrection, for Mbiti, has taken the Akamba worldview into Christ. It is in this sense that one may speak of an African, Christian eschatology.

CRITICISMS OF AFRICAN THEOLOGY

My examination of African theologians has disclosed their quest for a discourse that renders central Christian doctrines intelligible to the traditional sensibilities of specific ethnic groups, in order to better christianize them. Their consensus is that African theologies are indispensable to the africanization of the mission church and in keeping with the spirit of independence that seeks to overcome the negative ramifications of colonialism.[48]

Their views appear to have been reflected, to a certain degree, at the fifth international conference of the Ecumenical Association of Third World Theologians, in 1981. There, in New Delhi, a group of African theologians stated:

We Africans are . . . committed to take historical destiny, and the future of Christianity on our continent, in hand. This is our sacred task, and no intimidation can deter us from it. This is why African-type liturgies are developing, slowly but surely. This is why an African Christian literature is being born. This is why a properly African spirituality is beginning to nourish the devotion of searching souls. This is why an African ecclesiology is drawing more and more . . . theological attention. This is why African religious orders are springing up, to enrich the tradition of a consecrated life at the heart of the universal church. This is why a catechesis, and a pastoral ministry addressed to . . . the social classes of God's people are beginning to bear fruit. We are beginning to see a new African theology . . . relentlessly on the march—shoulder to shoulder with the great movement for the total liberation of Africa [Fabella and Torres, 60].

These are inspired words, succinctly outlining the breadth of African theology.

Certain scholars, however, have criticized the work of African theologians. Their critiques touch on possible impediments to the attainment of the goals of African theologians, as stated in New Delhi. I begin with the critique of African theology by African women. (In chapter 4 the black North American critique of African theology will be examined.)

Today many educated, Westernized, and urbanized African women feel that African traditions may be oppressive to women.[49] The passion with which many African women feel their oppression was made forcibly clear in the context of South Africa.

To paraphrase a bold, sharp statement made by a Xhosa woman in 1982 at the Federal Theological Seminary of South Africa during a forum on black theology in the United States:

> When you men are praying, I must go outside. I cannot pray with you because you do not consider me an equal before *God*! You talk about the white men, but it is *you black men* who oppress me! Really! What has your black theology of liberation to say about that!!![50]

Her indignation, though expressed in reference to black North American theology, seems no less relevant to African theology.

In many African societies, the traditional role of women seems to be largely passive. African theologian Mercy Oduyoye exposes this problem as she writes: "I did a study of Akan proverbs, . . . [attempting] to demonstrate that women fall victim to linguistic imagery that socializes them to accept *their place* in society and to view with caution any call for more space" (Fabella and Torres, 253). Oduyoye's study has led her to conclude that male chauvinism is a problem in Africa, "and not one . . . created . . . by the arrival of Islam and Christianity, but [one that] is an integral part of our African worldviews" (ibid.). If Oduyoye's views represent the impact of a developing African feminism upon African theology, many issues related to africanization may need to be examined in a new light.

Male African theologians, for instance, have been involved in the debate over polygyny: Should it be banned from the church? May it be provisionally accepted? Are polygynists to be denied the sacraments? (Ilogu, 220–24, Sawyer, *Evangelism,* 81–83). Little discussion, however, is given to the effects of polygyny on women. Perhaps, traditionally, polygyny helped ensure survival (infant mortality was high) and it was crucial to patterns of descent (Radcliffe-Brown and Forde, *Systems*; Mbiti, *Religions,* 186–89). Still, as Lamin Sanneh writes with insight, the issue of polygyny "has lost sight of the important contribution Christianity has made to the emancipation of women" (*Christianity,* 248). Polygyny was often abusive of women, and to quote Sanneh, "its benefits [did] not always . . . embody all the ideas of the African past" (ibid.).

Male African theologians, in addition, have examined the relationship of traditional initiations to Christianity. Too little attention, though, has been focused upon the problems certain African women have with initiations involving female circumcision. Controversy surrounding that tradition suggests that female African theologians may identify it as glaringly discontinuous with Christianity.

If Mercy Oduyoye has implied that African theologians are insensitive to women's issues, Adrian Hastings asserts that African theologians have too uncritically accepted Western values as normative for their theology:

> The theology of Mbiti . . . Idowu and Fashole-Luke . . . remains, despite its African concern, remarkably controlled in language and methodology by its European medium and by the European academic centres and traditions where its proponents studied and shone [*Christianity*, 58].

If, as Hastings suggests, African theologians have been only minimally indigenizing Christian doctrines, if their theology is more continuous with the theologies of Europe than with the traditions of Africa, how African is African theology?

Ambrose M. Moyo ponders this question from a different perspective. He asserts boldly that "very little [African] theology of real significance has come forth" ("Quest," 95).[51] African theologians, he claims, "mostly talk about doing such a theology. [But] the actual working out of such a theology is still a thing of the future" (ibid.). Could the conservatism of African theologians, which Hastings perceives, and the slow progress of African theology, which Moyo perceives, emerge from the conservatism of the "africanized" mission church in Africa? Seemingly so.

Indeed, the African theologians at New Delhi (EATWOT, 1981) stated:

> African churches are often faithful copies of their missionary mother churches, and so they refuse to admit any theological thought, any ecclesiology, or any church law but that developed in and sent here from the West. Hence the development within the churches of a reactionary movement opposed to any and all efforts at inculturation [Fabella and Torres, 59–60].

Moyo asserts, in addition, that "some Christians and theologians in Africa are very reluctant to accept or are even opposed to the whole idea of an African theology" ("Quest," 95). Is that opposition to African theology a result of a colonization that, according to Moyo, has "produced minds and hearts that . . . only think, feel, and express themselves the white missionary's way?" (ibid.). Obviously Moyo believes that is the case: "Our problem today is . . . not one of the white missionary discriminating against . . . African counterparts and looking at African culture with disdain, but that of the African successors of the white missionaries" (ibid., 99). Moyo concludes that if African *theology* is to be *African* theology, it must incorporate African traditions far more substantially than has so far been done (ibid., 107).

Moyo's critique of African theology is buttressed by that of F. Eboussi Boulaga. In his *Christianity without Fetishes*, Boulaga describes an African middle-class Christianity of which, by implication, African theology now is a part:

> A simple substitution of black . . . missionaries for white ones has been the primordial act. There is something of the carnival about the Africanization of the colonies. It is the inauguration of a playful, imaginary, cruel, tragic praxis. The inability to face up to the real turns to resentment against those whom one can caricature but can neither equal nor do without [p.74].

Those to whom Boulaga refers here are the African masses who, gathering themselves into independent churches, are resisting the spiritual poverty of African middle-class Christianity (ibid., chap. 3).

For Boulaga, then, the current state of African theology, as a theology of africanization, is pathetically weak. He writes further:

> For want of radicalism, Christianity's reappropriations in Africa make up a collection of heteroclitic characteristics, gathered from the Bible and various Western Christianities, with a few elements of the "African genius" thrown in by way of anecdote, curiosity, and folklore [ibid., 72].

Thus, Boulaga asserts that African theology, despite protestations to the contrary, is no more than adaptation—a very superficial syncretism.

According to Boulaga, that which the church in Africa must lose, in order to save its soul, is its captivation to the West:

> What the church [in Africa] has accomplished to the time of this writing, it has accomplished with the resources, personnel, and protection of the Christian West. The contribution of African Christians is yet to come. Their current power is but borrowed, subordinated, auxiliary [ibid., 223].

Boulaga feels deeply that the African church and African theologians must struggle for power and self-determination, must substantially relate to the African masses, and must communicate with one another in a way that is as yet without precedent (ibid., 218–27).

Theologian Allan Boesak, a South African of mixed racial descent, has also critiqued indigenization. His critique is based on the view that black South African theology is an African theology:

> A black liberation theology shares a common basis with African theology. . . . The search for true and authentic human identity and libera-

tion is also to acknowledge that one's Africanness is a God-given blessing to delight in rather than a fate to be lamented [*Innocence*, 40].

The similarity that Boesak discerns between black South African and African theologies derives from his realization that the majority of South Africans are descendants of Africans who migrated southward from West-Central Africa over a thousand years ago. Thus, Boesak writes correctly that "black theology [in South Africa] is, after all, profoundly African." He argues, moreover, that black South African theology " . . . takes seriously the processes of the struggle for humanity and justice, of secularity and technology" (ibid., 14). For Boesak, the South African context—in which blacks are more severely oppressed than are "colored" and Asians—does not commend focus upon the theme of indigenization to the exclusion of the theme of liberation.

What is more, radical distinctions made between the two themes are unacceptable to Boesak, because indigenization is encouraged by white oppressors:

Some white theologians are trying to separate black theology from African theology as if the two have nothing in common. In South Africa white South African theologians have declared themselves prepared to accept black theology if it means "indigenization" . . . something they contrast with the "revolutionary," "anti-white," and "unchristian" elements in black theology [*Innocence*, 14].

As I will show in chapter 4, however, certain widely read African theologians also separate black theologies from African theology. Thus it is not the case that only white theologians are trying to separate black and African theologies. In any case, Boesak's critique of indigenization relates to a problem peculiar to the South African situation:

Because indigenization has always meant isolation and fragmentation of groups, we fear that within the *Apartheid* context such a theology would become nothing more than a "homeland theology" [ibid.].

Let me digress a bit and briefly discuss the South African homelands in order to explain what Boesak means by "homeland theology."

Forcibly and callously removing blacks to 13 percent of the most unarable land, the South African government has instituted a homeland policy that intends to perpetuate denial of citizenship to blacks in the land of their birth.[52] Disfranchised, forced by economic necessity to work for low wages in mining, farming, manufacturing, and domestic enterprises, relegated to urban townships and hard, barren hostels if "employed," the majority of South Africans are already controlled with ruthless police-state efficiency. Confined to use of second-class transportation and inadequate public facilities, forced to carry an identification pass, and forbidden to be outside black areas after midnight, the majority suffer in a racist and fascist state. With the exception of a small middle class, blacks of the townships, squatter camps, hostels, and homelands live in squalor, suffering from deprivation and disease.[53]

The homeland policy is but the logical outcome of a repressive, white supremacist system strikingly similar to that of the southland of the United States prior to 1965. Placing blacks in ethnic homelands, the Pretoria regime has effectively undermined attempts to establish a democratic South Africa as envisioned in the Freedom Charter.[54] Homelands, in addition, were established in an attempt to ensure that only blacks of service to the economy would be allowed in "white" South Africa. Entrenching the hegemony of whites, homelands polarize blacks in order to control them. The supremacists' goal, moreover, is to grant independence to the homelands in order to make blacks citizens of "independent states" pathetically dependent upon the Pretoria government. Among homelands already "independent" are Transkei, Baphuthatswana, and Venda. Nurturing traditional cultures, the homelands fortify Xhosa identity in distinction from Zulu identity, and Sotho identity in distinction from Nguni. By dividing blacks in this way, Pretoria effectively maintains the praxis of a peculiar neo-colonialism. As Allan Boesak writes:

> Indigenization has too much of a colonial aura clinging to it and has been used too one-sidedly in the sense of response to the gospel in terms of traditional culture [*Innocence*, 14].

For Boesak, myopic focus upon indigenization in South Africa helps maintain black political suffering. Indigenization, he asserts, yields " . . . to uncritical accommodation, becoming a 'cultural theology' or a 'religion of culture'" (ibid.).

By no means, however, does Boesak reject the theme of indigenization. If, Boesak reasons, black South African theology is to be truly contextual, it must be indigenized. But for Boesak: "An authentic contextual theology is . . . prophetic; it is not merely an exhumation of the corpses of tradition as African theology was sometimes understood to be" (ibid.).

According to certain African philosophers, African theology has been proceeding from mistaken premises. Three African philosophers, for instance, assert that Tempels, Mbiti, and Mulago have been masquerading "folktales," "religious rites," and superstition as African philosophy. According to these philosophers, Tempels's philosophy of *force vitale*, Mulago's philosophy of *participation vitale*, and Mbiti's philosophy of Zamani are not philosophies but mere interpretations of traditional worldviews.[55]

Theophilus Okere, Kwasi Wiredu, and Paulin Hountondji believe that philosophy is a Western, literate tradition that is a continuum of Greek philosophy. Although these philosophers maintain that Western philosophy must be africanized to some degree, they assert that African traditions are aphilosophical. They find the notion of a Pan-African philosophy, gleaned from a study of diverse ethnic groups, absurd.

Hountondji claims, furthermore, that talk of an African philosophy has been for the benefit of a non-African public. But, he asserts:

> ["True" African philosophy must be] for an African public. . . . That will stop . . . purring . . . about Luba ontology [and] Dogon metaphysics . . . simply because such themes do not interest fellow countrymen but were aimed formerly at satisfying the western craving for exoticism [*Philosophy*, 54].

Hountondji, then, believes that attempts to force Europeans to reevaluate their assessment of the African "savage" wastes time:

> In a completely sterile withdrawal, [Africans] go on vindicating our cultures, or rather, apologizing for them to the white man, instead of living fully their actual splendor and poverty, instead of *transforming* them [ibid., 50].

With these criticisms in mind, I must move toward solving the problem with which this study is concerned: a determination of the nature of the relationship of black theology to African theology. Historical comparisons have been made, and I have examined black and African theologies back to back as discourses of liberation and indigenization. Chapters 2 and 3 have shown that the two theologies are, indeed, radically different from one another.

What concerns me now is what Afro-American and African theologians are saying about one another. A study of the relationship of black theology to African theology must deal substantially with the dissent among the two groups of theologians regarding the extent to which they are similar. The next chapter, then, examines what black and African theologians have written in regard to their interrelationship.

CHAPTER IV

Dissent among African and
Afro-American Theologians

*Long ago, the pig and the baboon used to live together on the hillsides.
One day, it was very cold and a cutting wind was blowing. As the pig and
the baboon sat in the sun trying to get warm, the baboon turned to the
pig, and said, "This wind is enough to wear the end of one's nose to a
blunt point." "Yes," answered the pig, "it's really enough to blow the
hairs off one's buttocks and leave a bare, dry patch." "Look here," said
the baboon, getting cross, "you are not to make personal remarks!" "I
did nothing of the kind," retorted the pig, "but you were rude to me first."
This started a quarrel, and they came to the conclusion that neither cared
for the other's company. So they parted, and the baboon went up on the
rocky top of the hill, while the pig went down to the plains, and there they
remain to this day.*

Wayao

Have theologians correctly assessed differences and similarities between
black and African theologies, and have they adequately assessed the nature of
their relationship? In order to answer these questions, I must critically examine
their writings on this topic. Thus I now focus upon the essays emerging from
meetings between black theologians of Africa and the United States that best
disclose dissent among them.[1]

DIFFERENCES

"An African Views American Black Theology"

John Mbiti's article with this title best represents the African position that
the two streams of theology are radically dissimilar.[2]

His views surprised Afro-American theologians who had met with a delegation of African theologians at Union Theological Seminary, New York City, in 1973 (see Wilmore and Cone, 448). The meeting at UTS was a sequel to an encounter between the two groups held in Tanzania in 1971. The UTS meeting, moreover, had encouraged Afro-American theologians. They had taken the initiative in organizing the consultations, urgently feeling the need to confer with African theologians. It seemed that the two groups were indeed in the process of forming a strong alliance.[3] James Cone, moreover, believed that the UTS consultation had been in preparation for another meeting scheduled for 1974, in Legon, Ghana. It was believed that in Ghana the two groups would wrestle in depth with issues arising from their similarities and differences (ibid.).

However, before the Legon meeting, John Mbiti published his article. James Cone says that Mbiti's essay disturbed North American black theologians because it misrepresented their theology (ibid.). Did Mbiti misrepresent them? And did his own views represent a significant group of African theologians?

I shall examine those questions by abstracting central arguments from Mbiti's essay and from essays written by E. W. Fashole-Luke, and Harry Sawyerr. The last two essays more specifically describe the nature and scope of African theology, but Fashole-Luke and Sawyerr do so at points in relation to black North American theology. The essay by Fashole-Luke, moreover, was prepared for the consultation in Legon, Ghana, 1974.[4] And although it is alleged that Mbiti had "jumped the gun," I can, nonetheless, examine his essay within the context of that meeting in Legon.[5] I now critically analyze the views of Fashole-Luke and Sawyerr, saving Mbiti for last because his critique is considered to be the most significant.

In delineating the contemporaneous trends within African theology in his "The Quest for African Christian Theologies,"[6] Fashole-Luke quoted from the essay "What is African Christian Theology?" by Harry Sawyerr.[7] Sawyerr wrote that "African . . . is primarily a mythological term, expressive of love for a continent or commitment to an ideal" (p. 23). Thus, for Sawyer, whites and Asians, for instance, who may be third-generation nonblacks born in Africa, qualify as "Africans."

Fashole-Luke finds Sawyerr's concept valuable. According to Fashole-Luke, it is:

First, . . . an inclusive definition which excludes no one, precisely because the Gospel is for everyone, oppressed and oppressor alike. Second, it is a clarion call to African theologians in the Republic of South Africa to rise above the racial tensions and cleavages of that unhappy land and to proclaim the message of reconciliation of men to men and the brotherhood of all men in Jesus Christ ["Quest," 75].

Fashole-Luke focuses on black theology in South Africa:

> Who should participate in the quest for African Christian theologies? These questions are of primary importance, *particularly* in the Republic of South Africa where whites oppress blacks, racial discrimination is enshrined in legislation, and African theology is *identified* with *Black Theology*. Non-blacks . . . are excluded from participating in the creation of Black Theology; perhaps because Black Theology is defined as "a theology of the oppressed, by the oppressed, for the liberation of the oppressed" [ibid.].

Harry Sawyerr also emphasizes that African theologies, unlike black theologies, must transcend racial emphases. Sawyerr asserts, for instance, that Africans should:

> Deplore any attempt to define a *Theologia Africana* as specifically devised and produced for Africans *per se*, in spite of the stir caused by . . . James H. Cone's *Black Theology and Black Power* ["African Theology," 22].

Let me now examine Sawyerr's and Fashole-Luke's rejection of black North American theology more substantially.

If their rejection of the black theology of the United States emerges from the view that it has no universalist ramifications, they are mistaken. Although dissent exists among the Afro-American theologians I have studied, their work reveals that, indeed, their theology has global significance.

James Cone, for instance, the most radical voice, has made blackness a symbol both of oppression and of God's identification with the oppressed. Although his theology is strongly contextual, it is no less universal. Its universalness expands as the logos of black theology is abstracted from the particularity of black suffering and translated into other contexts of oppression. Indeed, Sawyerr and Fashole-Luke fail to explore the dialectic that forms the structure of Cone's theology: God's yes to liberation and no to oppression; God's yes to the oppressed and no to the oppressor. Abstracted from the context of the oppression of blacks in the United States, divorced from the influence of black power rhetoric, Cone's assimilation of a Barthian dialectic may well be relevant to Africa.[8]

Consider, for example, the case of the Hutu of Burundi. For nearly a century, they have been oppressed by their Tutsi overlords (Lamb, 12). Reportedly, some two hundred thousand Hutus were butchered by the Tutsi in 1972 for opposing Tutsi domination. And consider the Hutu Christian priest, Michel Kayoya, who criticized the oppression and corruption within independent Burundi. "In the wake of the Hutu rebellion he was arrested and shot without trial on 17 May [1972]. . . . He was buried in a common grave with some seven thousand other victims" (Hastings, *African Christianity*, 15). Shortly before his murder, the martyred Kayoya wrote:

> I was a Christian
> I wanted my people
> to shape a real
> eternity by fighting against hunger
> Famine
> Injustice
> Dishonour.[9]

Without ignoring the need for africanization, Kayoya recognized the relationship of Christianity to the liberation of the oppressed, and issues of societal reform.[10] Coming to a stronger conclusion, there is, heuristically, it seems to me, an affinity between the thought of Kayoya and Cone.[11] Discovery of that affinity teaches—or at least suggests—that a black North American theology of liberation may contribute to an African theology. Sawyerr, then, is mistaken when he says that black North American theology has little relevance for African Christians.

Fashole-Luke and Sawyerr also assert that the theme of reconciliation should be intrinsic to theologies concerned with race relations. They believe Christians should overcome racism and that theologians should speed that process by proclaiming "the brotherhood of all men" ("Quest," 75). For Sawyerr and Fashole-Luke, then, reconciliation is intrinsic to liberation. For Cone, the former without the latter is—to make an allusion to Bonhoeffer's thought—cheap grace.[12] There are thus significant differences between Cone's notion of reconciliation and that held by Sawyerr and Fashole-Luke. My analysis of the thinking of J. Deotis Roberts and Major Jones, however, discloses their affinity with the views of Fashole-Luke and Sawyerr. The four make reconciliation essential to theological reflection on racial conflict and appear unanimous in the view that James Cone overemphasizes the relationship of blackness to theology.

Compare, for instance, Fashole-Luke's statement that "the Gospel is for everyone, oppressed and oppressor alike" ("Quest," 75), with Roberts's statement that "the only Christian way in race relations is a liberating experience of reconciliation for the white oppressor as well as for the black oppressed" (*Political Theology*, 222). They are obviously similar. There is, then, a certain similarity among black theologians in Africa and the United States, a similarity revealed in their disagreement with James Cone. Thus, not only have Sawyerr and Fashole-Luke failed to see the way in which black theology has relevance to Africa, they have also ignored that which they have in common with certain Afro-American theologians. I noted that Fashole-Luke's essay distinguishes African theology from black theology in South Africa. Moreover:

> Black South Africans can only produce genuine and relevant Christian theologies if they take account of the theological insights of their white

oppressors and include them too in the quest for a South African Christian Theology ["Quest," 74].

Implied here is that blacks in South Africa depend too heavily upon the theology of James Cone.[13] The question is, however, in what way should blacks in South Africa include the theology of their oppressors?

The Afrikaners' peculiar brand of Calvinism, as embodied in the Broederbond, unequivocally supports white supremacy and undergirds Boer intransigence to majority rule.[14] Indeed, Charles Villa-Vicencio, in his *The Theology of Apartheid* asks:

Whether . . . Afrikaner neo-Calvinism is [merely the projection] of white nationalists [who] would like to believe [that] apartheid is God's "calling" and "mission" for them?[15]

Afrikaner neo-Calvinism is indeed the servant of apartheid. Boers believe they are God's chosen people—*elected* to usurp the land from the "black Canaanites" (Villa-Vicencio, 19). It appears, then, that the policies of "separate development" and the fascist purging of all opposed to that system converge with a theology that supports white rule. Thus, it seems that if black South Africans accept the theological "insights" of their white *oppressors*, they will slowly perish in the homelands (or continue to be shot in the back)![16] Perhaps the theology of James Cone attracts black South African theologians of liberation because Cone emphasizes that reconciliation without liberation is nonsense. Indeed, even the most pacific black protest in South Africa has caused the Pretoria regime to murder, torture, and exile hundreds of black South Africans.[17] Fashole-Luke's statement, then, that "black South Africans can only produce genuine and relevant Christian theologies if they take account of the theological insights of their white *oppressors*" is quixotic. The theology of apartheid is neither Christian nor insightful but racist and fascist. Had Fashole-Luke made reference to the theology of Beyers Naudé, a former member of the Broederbond, he would have been on safer ground.[18] But the theology of the *oppressor*, I believe, must be as anathematized as the "theology" of Adolf Hitler! Indeed, study of the theology of the oppressor within the context of South Africa would seem to drive black theologians of *liberation* irresistibly to the theology of James Cone.

If Sawyerr and Fashole-Luke have examined black North American theology too superficially, John Mbiti has discussed it more substantially. He rightly asserts that it must be understood historically, within the context of the oppression of blacks in the United States (Wilmore and Cone, 477–78). Mbiti correctly concludes that the history of Afro-Americans is a significant factor accounting for the differences between black North American and African theologies: "Black [North American] theology cannot and will not become African theology" (ibid., 481). Indeed, I have shown that the two theologies are not synonymous: their histories and their discourses are significantly dissimilar. Still, the histories from which they emerged overlap in the lives and thoughts of blacks who were forerunners of black and African theologies. My textual interpretations, moreover, uncovered evidence that Afro-American theologians have studied African traditional religion in relation to the African roots of slave religion. Significantly, then, black and African theologians are engaged in the study of African traditional religion in relation to Christian theology. Therefore, although Mbiti rightly emphasizes that black North American theology cannot be contextually African theology, he has not focused enough on what they have in common.

As a result, Mbiti makes these curious statements: (1) African theology "grows out of . . . joy in the experience of the Christian faith, whereas black [North American] theology emerges from the pains of oppression" and (2) "black [North American] theology hardly knows the situation of Christian living in Africa, and therefore its direct relevance for Africa is either non-existent or only accidental" (ibid.). These two statements invite closer scrutiny.

That Africans were largely christianized in a milder socio-political climate than blacks of the United States should be clear. Furthermore, the experience of colonialism appeared to be, overall, less harsh than the history of black suffering after the Civil War. Certainly, then, as I have shown, the oppression from which black theology emerged was more severe than that from which African theology emerged. Nonetheless, that African theology emerged in the postcolonial period links it to African revolution and thus to colonial oppression. Moreover, African theologians' professed intent to overcome the negative ramifications of colonialism, as seen in relation to mission, further highlights the emergence of African theology from a certain kind of oppression.

It seems to me, then, that Mbiti's statement that African theology emerges out of joy in the experience of the Christian faith is reductionistic. The undeniable joy with which certain African theologians approach the task of theological reflection tends to obscure the fact that resistance to colonial oppression influenced quests for African theologies. Thus, cautiously and provisionally, it is fair to assert that both theologies *emerged* from contexts in which white structures were found to be oppressive; and there is little joy in oppression.

Mbiti's implication, moreover, that joy is absent in the work of Afro-American theologians caricatures their theology. Although James Cone, for instance, has written with anger against white complicity in the maintenance of black suffering, joy is, nonetheless, revealed in his work as well. Joy, for instance, is found in his celebration of courageous black Christians such as Henry H. Garnet and Sojourner Truth.[19] Intense satisfaction is derived from the achievements of these persons. Intense satisfaction is derived as well from finally being able to say "black is beautiful" in a nation where beautiful "Negroes" were believed to be "octoroons." Thus joy is found in black theologians' celebration of an ancestry more Kongo-Kordofanian than Anglo-

Saxon. And, as African ancestry has become less regrettable among blacks, the joy that black theologians take in the doing of their theology has increased.[20]

Mbiti says that "one would hope that theology arises out of spontaneous joy in being a Christian, responding to life and ideas as one redeemed" (Wilmore and Cone, 478). I find this curious. The gospel is good news when Easter bursts with joy, but there is also a dark side to the gospel. It seems that the joy of Easter only blossoms in the darkness of the cross. Cross and resurrection form a dyad in Jesus Christ. And it seems that joy without suffering leaves one with a somewhat monophysite christology. The suffering of *Christ* helps one appreciate the divinity of Jesus. And the joyous resurrection of *Jesus* sublates his crucifixion, but does not annul his suffering. It is, therefore, the pain, the terror, and the horror of the torture of the man-God that points to the emergence of theology from suffering. Joy, then, is as intrinsic to suffering as resurrection is to crucifixion; and resurrection is as intrinsic to crucifixion as divinity and humanity are to Jesus Christ.

If one is still repulsed by the emergence of black theology from suffering, one may consult tradition: the Christian martyrs of the patristic period; Augustine's struggle in conversion; Luther's anguished quest for a gracious God; and Bonhoeffer's prayers before his execution. Indeed, one would prefer that theology emerge from joy. But bearing the weight of the cross—suffering for the sake of redemption—is the awesome cost of discipleship. Joy comes in the morning.

Mbiti's second statement, that "black [North American] theology hardly knows the situation of Christian living in Africa, and [that] therefore its direct relevance for Africa is either non-existent or only accidental," seems untrue. That Afro-American theologians cannot know existentially what it means *to be* an African Christian is unquestionably true. They are aware, however, that many African Christians suffer from disease, famine, and drought, and that many have been victims of an African holocaust and corrupt African governments. J. Deotis Roberts puts it this way:

> Many Africans need to decolonize their minds. . . . In many cases they have accepted without question the values of the colonies. . . . In some sense oppression in South Africa [and] in Uganda . . . is quite similar [*Political Theology*, 79].

Reportedly at least three hundred thousand Ugandans perished under Idi Amin's rule from 1971 to 1979 (Lamb, 78). Under Marcias Biyogo's rule, 1968 to 1979, it is said that at least fifty thousand persons were murdered as a result of ethnic tensions in Equitorial Guinea (ibid., 105). I have noted that in 1972 the Tutui exterminated at least two hundred thousand Hutu. Bokassa, former "emperor" of the Central African Republic, allegedly had eighty school children clubbed to death for refusing to wear uniforms stamped with his picture (ibid., 53). Sharpville and Soweto are not the only African tragedies. Holocaust has also come to Africans due to civil wars that erupted because elites manipulated ethnic animosities (ibid., 9–14).[21] The classic example is the war between Biafra and Nigeria. Reportedly, at least one million persons—mostly Igbo—died in that war, which, with the help of the West and the Soviets, raged from 1969 to 1970 (ibid.; see also Dudley, 67–73).

Perhaps reference to the thousands who perished in African holocausts appears to cater to sensationalism. But the point is simply that there is crisis in postcolonial Africa that affects African Christians. Thus Mbiti's statement that Afro-American theologians are ignorant of the *situation* of Christian living in Africa must be questioned. Mbiti could well be contradicted by African Christians who reveal situations of Christian living in Africa to black Americans. Here, the prophetic words of Michel Kayoya seem hauntingly profound. He asks:

After one colonization, were we going to be subjected to another? Another, more terrible colonization? A colonization by the meanness which every heart conceals laziness and pride. Burdens that weight on the heart of man and prevent him from growing. *The struggle for liberation becomes a struggle between brothers tearing each other apart* [*Footprints*, 126; emphasis added].

A fair question at this point seems to be: "After all, these events took place some twelve years ago. So how relevant is this critique today?" Unfortunately, very relevant.

As recently as July 20, 1984, a headline on the front page of the *New York Times* read in bold type: "Spokesman Says 15,000 Have Died Since Obote's Return." Apparently, President Obote cannot control his army; civil war threatens to erupt again in the Sudan; civil war in Chad may yet erupt again; and the situation in Zimbabwe evinces again that political conflicts are still exacerbated by age-old ethnic tensions.[22] I could go on: coups in Nigeria and Cameroon; war between Ethiopia and Eritrea; problems of growth versus development; disease, famine, drought. Indeed remarks that Canon Burgess Carr made in 1974 seem no less relevant today:

What explains the deep antagonisms that have erupted in Nigeria, Burundi, Uganda, and which are a menace in every African nation today? I put it to you that there are only two tribes in Africa: the elites and the masses! As such what is usually described as tribalism in Africa is essentially a class struggle.[23]

Canon Carr's perspective here is echoed by that of Bishop Henry Okullu. Mourning the inhumane execution of Father Kayoya, Okullu writes:

In Africa the Society for the Prevention of Cruelty to Animals should be changed and instead be called the Society for the Prevention of Cruelty to Human Beings. In the history of independent Africa, there has never been such a large-scale killing of animals in the way human life is repeatedly wasted in various parts of the continent. Not even in Kenya's Tsavo National Park, where nearly 5,000 elephants died in 1972 through drought, can the situation be compared to a large-scale massacre of . . . men, women, and children in a tribal war. . . . Let the evil of tribal governments be uprooted from the soil of Africa and the civil wars be minimized [Shorter, *Spirituality*, 92–93].

From a Christian perspective, Canon Carr and Bishop Okullu attribute civil war and "tribalism" to the unwillingness of humans to struggle for a humane society. Carr writes, therefore, that civil war is really war "among the elites competing for the limited opportunities, privileges, and power available in our dependent societies. The masses get caught in the cross-fire and become victims" (*Struggle Continues*, 77; see n. 23). It has been African Christians like Canon Carr and Bishops Tutu and Okullu who have informed North American theologians of "the situation of Christian living in Africa"; and, in the case of Carr and Tutu, precisely because they believe black theology is relevant for Africa. To quote Burgess Carr:

The forthrightness of black theology . . . presents a dual challenge to our Christian style of life [in Africa]. In a profound way, it challenges . . . African theology to advance beyond academic phenomenological analysis to a deeper appropriation of the ethical sanctions inherent in our traditional religious experience [ibid., 78].

As long as African theologians believe black North American theology is relevant for Africa, how can one maintain that it has no relevance for Africa? Mbiti's mistreatment of black North American theology is evident.

As with Sawyerr and Fashole-Luke, Mbiti believes that black North American theologians are too preoccupied with blackness. According to Mbiti, black theology sees "blackness in everything. It speaks of a Black God, Black Church, Black Liberation, Black this and Black that" (Wilmore and Cone, 478).

That the blackness of God is a symbolic notion in the thought of James Cone bears repeating. Indeed, Mbiti states that "James Cone [tries] to give a wider ontological meaning to 'blackness'" (ibid.). J. Deotis Roberts and Major Jones use the theme of blackness more conservatively than does James Cone. As with Miles Jones, a black theologian whom Mbiti approvingly quotes, Major Jones has warned that notions of a black God may be incipiently idolatrous (ibid.; see also M. Jones, *Awareness*, 117). And although Roberts asserts that black theology is contextual and related to blackness, he nonetheless relates blackness to whiteness in a way that commends universalism more than ethnocentrism: "The only Christian way in race relations is a liberating experience of reconciliation for the white oppressor as well as for the black oppressed" (*Political Theology*, 222). Black theologians do not see blackness *in everything*, but, very specifically, in certain things.

Talk of a black God refers to God's identification with the black oppressed. Talk of a black church refers to the history of black ecclesiastical institutions that developed in distinction from white institutions. And black liberation is that for which the black church has struggled with the faith that liberation was within God's providence.

The theme of blackness, then, emerges from a historical context that has been at once oppressive to and redemptive for blacks. As Mbiti puts it, the emphasis on blackness is, in part, a "cry of protest against conditions that have persisted for nearly four hundred years" (Wilmore and Cone, 478). But by narrowly focusing upon black theologians' dependence on "a color terminology arising out of the color consciousness of American society," Mbiti loses sight of the wider ramifications of black theology.

Mbiti, in addition, even attempts to undermine Afro-American theologians' appeal to scripture by stating that racial color is not a theological concept in the scriptures (ibid.). Scriptural support for black theology, however, rests in Jesus' ministry to the oppressed rather than in explicit references to race. Mbiti's rejection of black theology on the basis of scripture misrepresents black theology. Mbiti would deprive Afro-American theologians of the option to deduce meanings from the biblical text, to make use of a hermeneutic that contemporizes what is perceived as the "truth" of the gospel. (Could not one say that African theology is abiblical inasmuch as the New Testament makes no explicit reference to African traditional religion?)

Mbiti, however, does find scriptural support for the black theology focus on liberation. But he writes that: " . . . an excessive preoccupation with liberation may well be [its] chief limitation. . . . [And] when the immediate concerns of liberation are realized, it is not at all clear where black theology is supposed to go" (ibid., 479). According to Mbiti, in addition, black theology is eschatological, but "its eschatological hopes are not clearly defined. There is no clue as to when one arrives at the paradise of liberation. One gets the feeling that Black Theology has created a semi-mythological urgency . . . that it must at all costs keep alive" (ibid.). Mbiti has posited, then, that: (1) black theologians overemphasize liberation; (2) their notion of eschatology is muddled; and (3) they believe that liberation is synonymous with paradise.

Critical examination of these thematic areas reveals, first, that blacks— especially the poor—urgently need liberation from a system in which there is little room for black advancement. Neither the depth of the oppression of blacks in the United States nor the insidious way their oppression is perpetuated is mythological.

Secondly, whose eschatology is *clearly* defined? Eschatology has reference to a suprasensible reality that in its ultimacy escapes human comprehension. Thus it cannot be clearly defined within the limits of human discourse. Still, within these limits, black theologians have articulated their views of the way in which liberation relates to eschatology. For Major Jones, the relationship is expressed in a theology of hope that stresses God's love for the oppressed and assures the oppressed of final victory. Roberts asserts that black/white reconciliation would be a penultimate sign of a more ultimate grace. Thus his eschatology has thisworldly and otherworldly implications. And James Cone's radically critical eschatology places less emphasis on a futuristic realm in favor of one in which the oppressed will live less miserably, due to the humanization of structures that exploit and ignore them *now*. Indeed, black theologians *have* defined their eschatological visions.

Thirdly, black theologians distinguish liberation from paradise. Liberation is equated with justice rather than paradise. For Jones and Roberts, moreover, paradise is inherent in a consummated eschatology.

And as for Mbiti's remark that black theology avoids issues unrelated to liberation, could it not be said that African theologians ignore theological issues unrelated to indigenization?

My assessment of Mbiti's views, however, should not obscure that the two theologies differ radically from each other. Mbiti rightly emphasizes that the two groups of theologians "must recognize simultaneously . . . the dangers of encroaching upon one another's theological territories" (Wilmore and Cone, 482). To be sure, North American theologians should not attempt to dictate the terms under which African theologians must do their work. Fundamentally, though, all Christians claiming service to Christ are accountable to one another for his sake and in the Spirit of his love. Mbiti says as much:

> Black [North American] theology and African theology have each a variety of theological concerns, talents, and opportunities. Insofar as each contributes something new and old to Christian theology, as such, it will serve its immediate communities and also the Universal Church [ibid.].

That Sawyerr and Fashole-Luke would agree with Mbiti is a fair guess. And if the three, moreover, would first explore the universal ramifications of black theology in relation to the problem of human suffering in black Africa, and recognize that a sensitivity to such suffering is theologically imperative, black theology might be viewed as something more than "water buffalo theology" in relation to African theology.[24] If African theologians will see, in addition, that the African descent of black North American theologians figures in the content of their work, statements like "black North American theologians hardly refer to Africa" may be avoided.

SIMILARITIES

Desmond Tutu, James Cone, and Gayraud Wilmore actively participated in consultations between black theologians of Africa and the United States. I shall examine their views on the nature of the relationship between the two streams of theology, beginning with Tutu.

"Black Theology/African Theology—Soul Mates or Antagonists?"

This essay[25] was delivered *in absentia* at the 1974 conference in Legon, Ghana, in response to Mbiti's "An African Views American Black Theology." The South African bishop refers to the meeting in New York in 1973 and to the 1971 meeting in Kampala:

> These . . . consultations [reflect] a noteworthy phenomenon—a new and deep desire for [blacks] to find each other, to know one another as [siblings] because we belong to one another. We are bound together by close bonds on three levels at least [Wilmore and Cone, 483].

The first level, according to Tutu, is blackness. But cultural and historical differences weaken this similarity. Even within black Africa, ethnic, cultural, linguistic, and historical disparities impede a Pan-Africanism based solely upon racial similarity. Tutu, however, places the theme of blackness within a context that tends to undermine cultural and historical disparity. Addressing the assembly at Legon, Tutu wrote: "If anyone assembled here today goes into a situation where racial discrimination is practiced, would he ever escape the humiliation and indignity heaped on us?" (ibid.). Tutu's point is well taken: blacks are still subject to white contempt for blackness.

Although white supremacy in the United States has been weakened by the impact of the civil rights movement, black Africans visiting the United States can experience subtle indications of discrimination; and there are cities and suburbs they would be advised to avoid. And most blacks visiting South Africa must tour that country through the strictures of apartheid. White supremacy is shamelessly enforced there.

Are the contexts of South Africa and the United States critically important to blacks who live outside them? Blackness understandably bonds black North Americans and black South Africans: apartheid is highly reminiscent of Jim Crow. But for Africans whose identity is more related to ethnicity than to skin color, blackness is less binding. Indeed, many Africans are not Pan-Africanists; they feel no kinship with other Africans. Ideological pluralism subjects the bond of blackness to different interpretations, some of which may emerge from a position that does not value blackness. Blackness, then, does not in any a priori sense bind Africans and Afro-Americans.

According to Tutu, the second level of bonding between black theologians of Africa and the United States is that of "mother Africa." Discernable again is the Pan-African perspective that characterizes Tutu's essay:

> All of us are bound to mother Africa by invisible but tenacious bonds. She has nurtured the deepest things in us as blacks. . . . No matter how long and traumatic our separation from our ancestral home has been, there are things we are often unable to articulate, but which we feel in our

bones, things which make us . . . different from others who have not suckled the breasts of our mother, Africa [ibid., 484].

These poetic words have emotional appeal and some basis in fact. Blacks of the United States have been inspired by their relationship to Africa. Martin Delany and Henry McNeal Turner attest to the way that black Americans have embraced Africa in the past. J. Deotis Roberts and Cecil Cone evince black theologians' current fascination with Africa.

Problems arise, however, upon closer scrutiny of Bishop Tutu's prose. Although Afro-Americans have retained African elements in their music, religion, speech, folktales, and dance, not all feel bound to Africa. On the other hand, not all Africans feel bound to Afro-Americans. And what does it mean that Africa "has nurtured the deepest things in . . . blacks?" If culture nurtures the deepest things in a people, and if black culture is in many ways a continuum of African culture, then Africa has nurtured the deepest things in North American blacks. But sharp differences exist between Afro-American and African cultures, and the degree to which the latter has nurtured the former is open to diverse interpretations.

At points, in addition, Bishop Tutu's words are reminiscent of such concepts as "negritude" and "African personality." He says that there is something ineffable that blacks "feel in [their] bones, things which make [them] . . . different from others who have not suckled the breasts of our mother, Africa." In "negritude" and in the notion of "African personality" reference is made as well to this intangible *something* that distinguishes blacks from whites. For Senghor it was an emotionalism that would form the basis of a new humanism; for Nkrumah it was something abstracted from a traditional ethos.[26] Both views have been criticized as being over-romantic and insensitive to differences among African peoples. Not all blacks, moreover, feel—or want to feel— different from whites. Some may feel they are Anglo-Saxon in their bones, even if their Anglo-Saxon ancestry is minor. Still, Desmond Tutu recognizes that the image of Africa has functioned to bind black members of the North American and African clergy. Analysts of the relationship between black and African theologies should discuss the importance of Africa to the American black clergy, in the past and in the present.

"The third level of unity," writes Tutu, "comes through . . . baptism and . . . membership in the Body of Christ which makes us all His ambassadors and partakers in the ministry of reconciliation" (Wilmore and Cone, 485). Unquestionably, Christianity in some sense binds the two groups of theologians, but not necessarily by the very nature of what is involved.

Christianity encompasses penultimate and ultimate notions; distinctions can be made between thisworldly and otherworldly realities; a certain disparity is revealed in empirical facts about the churches and in the suprasensible notion of the church. Prescinding from metaphysical notions of Christianity, I note that Christianity is a complex phenomenon. Its diversity is especially glaring when viewed critically from the social science disciplines. The theology of the Nazis differed radically from that of the confessing church.[27] There is radical difference between the Calvinism of the Broederbond and the Calvinism of the Broederkring.[28] And James Cone's theology differs from John Mbiti's. Christianity is not axiomatically synonymous with ecumenism, even though there is an ecumenical movement. Thus, Tutu's appeal to an eschatological oneness in Christ is weakened by vivid examples of disparity, hostility, and disunity. Such examples, then, make his appeal to Christian unity applaudable but problematic.

Another similarity between Afro-American and African Christianity, Tutu finds, is the emphasis both place on the ramifications of the incarnation. Seemingly, for Tutu, God's incarnation for the purposes of redemption and reconciliation implies a certain universalism. The humanity of Christ is understood as God's descent into the human milieu, which is culturally and racially diverse. Appreciation, therefore, of the universalist ramifications of the incarnation is contingent upon the insight that the humanity of God encompasses human diversity. According to Tutu, black North American and African theologies, in radically different ways, reveal this same insight. Desmond Tutu puts it this way: "Both [theologies] have [firmly repudiated] the tacit claim that white is right, white is best" (Wilmore and Cone, 489). In other words, the hegemony of white theologians over the making of theology has tended to obscure universalism in diversity, and it has tended to condone, often explicitly, the destruction of black culture and black human rights. Correctly, then, Tutu stresses that black and African theologies have liberated theology from the poverty of the view that "white is best."

In exposing that similarity, however, Tutu exposes as well a difference to which I have paid close attention. He asserts that, although black theologians uncompromisingly condemn institutions upholding white supremacy, African theologians have "tended to be more placid; to be interested . . . [in] anthropological concerns" (Wilmore and Cone, 490).

Tutu refers to the problems of postcolonial Africa, which I have discussed. Reminiscent of the criticisms leveled against African theologians by Boulaga and Moyo, Tutu asserts that African theologians have "failed to produce a sufficiently sharp cutting edge" (ibid.). According to Tutu, African theologians must not shun the task of prophetic denunciation of the forces that plague the poor of Africa. And for Tutu, such denunciation "can only happen when a radical spirit of decolonization occurs within each exponent of African theology" (ibid.).

Tutu's views here, however, must be examined with an appreciation of the way in which experience influences perspective. As a black at the front of ecclesiastical opposition to "separate development," as a priest ministering to those tortured in detention and pushed into "homelands," as the one who presided over the funeral of Steven Biko and who confronted Prime Minister Vorster over the holocaust in Soweto, Desmond Tutu is radically politicized.[29] Although no excuse is intended here for the silence of other African theologians vis-à-vis black Africa's "plethora of problems," that black South Africans and black North Americans have known the demonic character of white supremacy longer than most other blacks provides insight into the affinity of

Tutu's views with those of James Cone. Tutu writes: " . . . I am an exponent of Black [North American] Theology coming as I do from South Africa" (Wilmore and Cone, 490). Yet, he also writes: "I also believe I am an exponent of African theology coming as I do from Africa" (ibid.). But it seems that Tutu is more strongly an advocate of black theology of liberation.

"Black Theology and African Theology"

Co-authored by Gayraud Wilmore and James Cone,[30] this essay takes us back to 1971 in Tanzania where it was delivered to a "consultation between American black churchmen and African religious and government leaders."[31]

Themes of similarity examined in Tutu's essay appeared as well in Cone and Wilmore's essay: rejection of the notion that theology is synonymous with white theology; the current and historical importance of the image of Africa to black North America; the celebration of blackness. Wilmore and Cone's discussion of these themes is very similar to Tutu's; thus further discussion of them here is unnecessary.

Cone and Wilmore identified areas of dissimilarity between the two theologies as well. They first noted the historical differences I have identified. Then the authors focused upon the difference between African theology as a theology of indigenization and black North American theology as a theology of liberation, explaining the relationship of black liberation to the liberation themes of the Old Testament (Wilmore and Cone, 463–65). "In the New Testament," assert the authors "the same theme is carried forward by the appearance of Jesus Christ the Incarnation of God" (ibid., 467). As noted in chapter 2, above, Jesus' identity as an oppressed Jew reveals for black theologians "not only who God is and what he is doing, but also who [they] are and what [they] are called to do about human degradation and oppression" (ibid.).

From that perspective and with reference to the universal significance of black theology, the authors critique African theologians' neglect of the theme of liberation. And like Tutu, Cone and Wilmore suggest that certain African theologians may be reluctant to embrace the liberation focus of black theologies because of African theologians' ties to a neo-colonial matrix:

> Africanization must involve liberation from centuries of poverty, humiliation, and exploitation. A truly African Theology cannot escape the requirement of helping the indigenous churches to become relevant to the social and political ills of Africa, which are not unrelated to Euro-American imperialism and racism [ibid., 475].

Indeed, the specter of neo-colonialism casts a shadow over Africa. But black theologians must carefully insert the problem of racism into the contexts of West, East, and Central Africa. Although neo-colonialism and white supremacy are intrinsic to prevailing problems of underdevelopment, those problems are exacerbated in Africa because of traditional divisions among blacks. Thus, for Tutu and Carr, an *African* theology must emphasize liberation from corruption and the ethnic and caste conflicts that fed the slave trade and, in certain cases, facilitated colonization. The better question, then, which Wilmore and Cone should pose, is not so much "What can African Theology learn from Black [North American] Theology about the demonic power of White racism?" (ibid.), but how can Afro-American theology teach African theology that oppression of any sort is anathema to the Spirit of love? I think, moreover, that Cone and Wilmore put the shoe on the wrong foot when they asked: "What can the black churches of America learn from the African churches about reconciliation between tribal groups?" (ibid.). Indeed, according to Carr, the African church has identified with the "elites in [African] societies" who have fanned the fires of ethnic conflicts for personal gain.[32]

The authors' questions, however, were posed in an attempt to clear the ground for an alliance between black North American and African theologies. As with Tutu, Cone and Wilmore write out of a desire to see Afro-American and African theologians work together. Indeed, as I have noted, certain Afro-American theologians intensely desired to draw closer to African theologians. But unfortunately, as Cone and Wilmore wrote in 1971, "one of the peculiar features of our present situation is that Black Theology is reaching out to African Theology but the reverse is not necessarily true" (ibid., 473). Indeed, Carr, Tutu, and Boesak appear to be the only well-known African theologians interested in a joint enterprise between the two groups of theologians. But in spite of the cool reception of Afro-American theologians, Cone and Wilmore assert: "there exists . . . a mysterious bond of blood brotherhood between black theologians and African theologians" (ibid., 475–76).

What, however, is the big mystery? Blacks of the United States are of African descent. The only mysteries are often the exact identity of the African peoples from whom Afro-Americans are descended. Mystification of historical reality can lead Afro-Americans to romanticize their relationship to Africans. Very possibly, and most probably, the Afro-American and African theologians whom I have been discussing are not at all genealogically related. They more than likely have no common ancestor, but *australopithecus afarensis*.[33] With such romantic notions about their "mysterious" blood relationship to African theologians, Afro-American theologians are bound to suffer a certain frustration. The value of the image of Africa to their life and thought is confused if they are shown ambivalence by Africans.

De facto emergence of this problem is mentioned in Gayraud Wilmore's report of a consultation that took place in Accra in 1977:

It was apparent that the courtship between African and Afro-American theologians would no longer preclude an open confrontation on the issues of blackness as a symbol of radical alienation, and struggle and liberation as the defining concept of biblical faith. . . . It broke out most decisively between African and Afro-American perspectives on the significance and meaning of black theology [Appiah-Kubi and Torres, 204].

As Wilmore reports, Mbiti and Cone angrily locked horns on those issues. As would be expected, Allan Boesak sided with the Afro-American theologians. But Gabriel Setiloane of Botswana accused blacks from the United States of "trying to tell Africans how to do theology in Africa" (ibid.).

Understandably, though, most Africans do not see "blackness as a symbol of radical alienation," because they live in the *blackest* continent in the world. And although black North American theologians, because of their radical alienation in a predominantly white population, feel that liberation and struggle are of the essence of biblical faith, such themes are hardly pertinent to those who—however mistakenly—believe themselves to be liberated.

Yet, in spite of the fact that Afro-American and African theologians became openly antagonistic toward one another in Accra, James Cone's address there, "A Black American Perspective on the Future of African Theology," was conciliatory.

Cone stated that, indeed, black theologians' focus on issues pertinent to black suffering in the United States could "blind them to the uniqueness of the African situation" (ibid., 176). He asserted, on the other hand, that Mbiti's misrepresentation of black theology, and his opinion that the two theologies have nothing valuable to contribute to one another, had helped kindle hostilities (ibid., 176–77). And if Setiloane accused American theologians of trying to tell Africans how to do theology, Cone stated just the opposite: "There is much truth to the widespread belief that the future of African theology belongs to Africans alone" (ibid., 177). Nonetheless, Cone attempted to explain to the Africans why Afro-American theologians tend to insist upon the importance of blackness in relation to liberation.

Cone refers to the identity crisis identified by W. E. B. DuBois. It is a conflict between blackness and "Americanness," the peculiar doubleness of an Afro-American awareness:

> It is a peculiar sensation, this double-consciousness, this sense of always looking at one's self through the eyes of others, of measuring one's soul by the hope of a world that looks on in amused contempt and pity. One ever feels his twoness—an American, a Negro; two souls, two thoughts, two unreconciled strivings; two warring ideals in one dark body, whose dogged strength alone keeps it from being torn asunder [ibid.; see also DuBois, *Souls*, 16–17].

Cone's assimilation of this conflict led him to write self-effacingly:

> How can I speak about the future of African theology when my black identity is so inextricably tied to North America? [Appiah-Kubi and Torres, 177].

Cone makes a strong point here. But why experience today a conflict in terms of a double identity? "Afro-American" means black American. The dual terms denote a single reality. Within the context of the United States, to be black means that one participates in particular cultural and historical experiences that are tempered by the fact of African descent. "Americanness," moreover, is not a uniform fact of life; it can be Amerindian, Italian-American, Irish-American, and so forth. Separation of blackness from Americanness emerges from a conflict resulting from an inability to accept that blackness in the United States is inseparable from Americanness.

Unfortunately, to be Afro-American is to be in some sense oppressed. Thus conflict emerges in the United States from Afro-Americans' second-class status in spite of a Constitution that promises equity. Conflict here, however, should produce a crisis more in historical and socio-political terms. That many Afro-Americans want to trace their roots back to Africa in a celebration of their African heritage is wonderful. The African heritage is part of Afro-Americans' birthright as black persons. But black theologians experiencing an identity conflict should overcome it and accept themselves as black Americans who are African only in a remote sense.

Indeed, James Cone, in spite of his admission of the experience of that conflict, said as much. "Aside from the technicality of my genetic origin," he writes, "what right do I have to participate in the future development of African theology?" (ibid.). Cone's sensitivity to this problem is attractive, inviting examination of what he believes joins the two theologies.

According to Cone, black North American and African theologies have in common a historical option. As in the Pan-Africanism of Desmond Tutu, Cone claims "there is some sense in which the black world is one, and this lays the foundation and establishes our need for serious dialogue" (ibid., 178). In what sense, however? Is it to be found in a certain unanimity among certain Pan-Africanists? Is it because Santeria, Vodun, and the sanctified church are continuums of an African spirituality? In other words, references to Pan-Africanism must be more clearly explained. Also necessary is an awareness that a religious continuum does not necessarily create solidarity. Moreover, Pan-Africanists often violently disagree with one another.

Cone more precisely identifies the oneness of the black world when he writes: "International economic and political arrangements require a certain kind of African and black nationalism if we are to liberate ourselves from European and white American domination" (ibid.). Kwame Nkrumah showed that white supremacy is all the more formidable because of its links to monopoly capitalism (*Neo-Colonialism*). Multinational corporations with enormous investments in African resources are headed by Euro-American billionaires who undergird the neo-colonial matrix. Cone's point, then, is well taken in that he has identified the relationship of white supremacy to neo-colonialism. Thus he writes: "The oneness that I refer to is made possible by a common historical option available to both Africans and black Americans in their different social contexts" (Appiah-Kubi and Torres, 179). That option, according to Cone, would also include standing with Asia, Latin America, and the Caribbean against neo-imperialism.

Have all African theologians, however, made that choice in the terms Cone suggests? If they have not, it seems to me that there is no unequivocal "oneness" between Afro-American and African theologians that is "grounded in a common historical option for the poor and against societal structures that oppress them" (ibid). If theologians such as Mbiti and Sawyerr fail to mention the African holocaust, and the problems of drought, disease, famine, civil war, and corruption, how likely is it that they will join Latin American theologians in struggles against imperialism?

Attendant to Cone's notion of a common historical option is his notion that the two groups of theologians share a common faith. According to Cone, if they have solidarity in Christ, it should be manifest in a joint, effective commitment to "create societal structures that bear witness to our vision of humanity" (ibid.). I have concluded, however, that an eschatological notion of oneness in Christ is contradicted by the empirical fact of ecclesiastical plurality. Pluralism, I said, is exacerbated by variations in experience and in the disparity of value judgments. Cone's statement, then, that "the unity of the church can be found *only* in a common historical commitment" adds just another view to ecclesiological ferment (ibid., 180; emphasis added). His view that imperialism is anti-Christian and that Christ is profoundly revealed in those who suffer from political oppression, starvation, disease, and awesome poverty seems correct. But it is unlikely that Africans captivated by a Western conservatism will find Cone's views attractive. Naturally, then, Mbiti bristled when Cone said:

The theme of liberation as interpreted by the particularity of the African economic and political situation provides the most creative direction for the future development of African theology [ibid., 183].

If, however, Cone believes that black theologians may contribute to the development of African theology by emphasizing the importance of the theme of liberation, he asserts that African theology may equally contribute to the development of black North American theology. He asks:

If liberation theology in any form is to represent the hopes and dreams of the poor, must not that representation be found in its creative appropriation of the language and culture of the people? [ibid.].

Cone concludes that the themes of liberation and indigenization are equally vital to the development of Third World theologies. He writes: "I contend . . . that indigenization and liberation belong together" (ibid., 184).

Examination of James Cone's essay concludes my analysis of the positions taken on the interrelationships between black theology and African theology.

Posed now is the question: Have the two groups adequately assessed each other's work?

Apparently, John Mbiti, E. Fashole-Luke, and Harry Sawyerr have failed to see that black theology transcends racial categories. They have also failed to acknowledge that J. Deotis Roberts and Major Jones agree with them that the theme of liberation is intrinsic to the theme of reconciliation. Mbiti, Fashole-Luke, and Sawyerr have also neglected to explore Afro-American theologians' study of African traditional religion—a significant point of similarity between the contents of certain black and African theologies.

James Cone, Gayraud Wilmore, and Desmond Tutu, on the other hand, have identified what the two streams of theology have in common, but too uncritically. In addition, their focus on the theme of liberation in relation to blackness has tended to obscure the uniqueness of the African political situation. They have allowed the problem of neo-colonialism to sublate the problem of African disunity.

In general, though, I find the arguments for similarities more commendable: they have been less prone to caricature African theology. Tendencies, however, of their protagonists to force issues of liberation upon a theological view that clearly rejects them, and their failure to adequately discuss the significant differences between Afro-Americans and Africans have muddied the waters.

Nonetheless, my task now is to clearly review the issues in order to offer a resolution on the nature of the relationship between the two streams of theology. I have come to the heart of this study.

CHAPTER V

Toward Pan-African Theology

The boy was called N'po, the girl, N'ko, and they were as one flesh. They grew up side by side, breathed one breath, spoke and sang with one voice, wore the same rings and coloured necklets. And the girl's golden tears . . . might have fallen from the boy's eyes, for he was both himself and her. Each was so much the other that it was quite bewildering, but no doubt this was how Teulete meant it to be. We all have our kindred spirit; no [one] walks alone.

> *It's you who are singing in my heart*
> *With the voice of the fountain,*
> *With the voice of my sister*
> *And with my voice.*
> *My sister is a gazelle*
> *And she is the wind on the plain,*
> *And the plain.*
> *I am the plain under her blue heels,*
> *I am the wind in her hair,*
> *She is the wind under my heels,*
> *She is the moving plain of my love.*

> *(from "Voices inside the Crocodile,"*
> *Guillot's African Folk Tales)*

It is time to offer an answer to the question: Are the two theologies siblings or distant cousins?

With the exception of a few, well-known African theologians such as Desmond Tutu and Burgess Carr, the most widely read African theologians clearly feel no close kinship with black North American theologians. John Mbiti, E. W. Fashole-Luke, and Harry Sawyerr have little use for the theme of liberation and appear to have rejected the call for an alliance between black and

106

African theologies. Therefore, inasmuch as the principal exponents of African theology stress their distance from black American theology, the two streams of theology are now only distant cousins.

That the two, however, today are distant cousins does not mean that certain Afro-American and African theologians are not closely related. On the basis of the preceding chapters, it is clear that certain theologians—Cone, Tutu, and Carr—have found similarities more crucial than differences. They have informally achieved a certain synthesis that appreciates the dissimilarities between the two theologies but transcends them in an accord that is weighted in what they have in common. Their affinity for one another, in addition, has been strengthened by arguments on the radical dissimilarity of black North American and African theologies. Theologians who stress dissimilarity, such as Mbiti, appear to have been inexact on the scope of black theology, often surrendering it to caricature. Because such African theologians have failed, on the basis of their arguments, to establish the credibility of their claims, they have helped remove suspicions that a future alliance between Afro-American and African theologies is implausible, due to radical dissimilarity between them. Thus, when similarities are critically valued—which makes appreciation of differences imperative—the door is opened to a future alliance between Afro-American and African theologies. A brief review will substantiate this conclusion. Focus will be on examples of the theme of *similarity in difference*.

That white supremacy has influenced the emergence of black and African theologies has been noted throughout the course of this study. Noted as well have been the different contexts in which that racism has been operative in relation to the content of both theologies. Ramifications of that difference can be seen in the theologies of John Mbiti and James Cone. Here an anglicized African influenced by American missiology encounters a black North American AME clergyman. On the surface, liberation conflicts openly with indigenization. Beneath the surface, coming to a stronger conclusion, the forces that have influenced the values of the two theologians are in conflict. Here, slavery confronts mission; a pariah minority confronts an "independent" majority; and the struggle for first-class citizenship pushes hard against the ideology of independence.

In sum, conflict between the theological perspectives of Cone and Mbiti derives from historical and textual dissimilarities between them. Yet, tension between Cone and Mbiti is not pervasive; their conflict neither precludes efforts toward alliance between Afro-American and African theologians nor obscures thematic similarities among their theologies.

Similar forces have shaped the lives of E. W. Fashole-Luke and Major Jones. Nonetheless, they both emphasize the theme of reconciliation and they deemphasize race as a theological symbol. J. Deotis Roberts also supports the theme of reconciliation, and supports the study of African traditional religion, as does Cecil Cone. Thus, in the climate of dissent a certain thematic similarity has been overlooked.

I found, in addition, that Desmond Tutu and Burgess Carr advocate the inclusion of the theme of liberation with that of indigenization in African theology. Indeed, the contexts in which they live, as seen in relation to their theological values, are seminal to an appreciation of the affinity they feel to Afro-American theologians. But they are no less African theologians and the close relationship they feel to North American theologians commends the feasibility of the prospect of a deeper synthesis. As a Xhosa, for instance, Desmond Tutu knows of the cultural problems with which many African theologians are occupied. And, as a *South* African, he would bring to the task of synthesis a perspective that has already in some sense incorporated the themes of liberation and indigenization. If, moreover, the differences between Cone and Mbiti may be seen, heuristically, as the continuation of the differences between Nat Turner and Samuel Crowther, then Cone and Carr and Cone and Tutu symbolize the continuum of an affinity between the Afro-American and African clergy that is traceable to the fraternity between Turner and Blyden, and Turner and Dwane. Critical analysis of this continuum has disclosed much resembling myth: mystical bond of blackness; African personality/negritude; the providential design, and so forth. Yet the stubborn recurrence of a certain Pan-Africanism in the thought of Afro-American theologians suggests that this notion has profound value for them.

Examples of thematic continuity, therefore, within the broader framework of thematic difference, and the examples of a certain continuum within historical discontinuity reinforce the position that *synthesis has been latent within the context of dissent*. More specifically, as the ideas of James Cone, J. Deotis Roberts, Desmond Tutu, and Burgess Carr are abstracted from their writings, they appear to be rudimentary sources for a joint theological enterprise. Their commitment to liberation, their engagement in the study of African traditional religion, and their sensitivity to the interrelationships between white supremacy, neo-colonialism, and micro-nationalism await correlation in the writing of an African/Afro-American theology. (African theologians such as Jesse Mugambi and Kofi Appiah-Kubi, in addition, have expressed views in which the themes of liberation and indigenization converge.)[1] In sum, kinship would rest in the construction of a Pan-African theology, which, in the tradition of Blyden and Turner, can overcome historical and cultural differences in Pan-Africanist sentiment.

Accord here would be found in a "new" theological enterprise that does not annul the distinctiveness of both theologies. Apart from synthesis, there will still be black and African theologies of liberation and indigenization. But by way of synthesis themes of both theologies would converge in such a way that the end result would be a theology deriving from both. Interplay between liberation and indigenization, slavery and colonialism, white supremacy and neo-imperialism would become complementary in a discourse addressing these formidable problems.

THEOLOGY OF PAN-AFRICANISM . . .

Theologies must be made of sterner stuff than imaginative sentiment. Pan-Africanism can be an amorphous notion, and attempts to achieve a symbiosis between it and Christianity should indeed raise eyebrows. These two problems will be examined shortly. Critical now is that certain Afro-American and African theologians *want* to form an alliance, and there is historical and thematic ground for it. Volition can speed the task of writing a text that represents a certain feeling of kinship. Indeed, the position that the two are siblings can be *taken* only when it produces the ground on which it can stand. Without such a production, the two theologies *are* now more distant cousins, as I have concluded. My historical analysis, and especially textual analysis, commend that without question.[2]

Thus, rather than assert that the two theologies are siblings, it is merely the potential for the establishment of that kind of relationship that I am positing. I am not attempting, moreover, to convince the reader that the two groups of theologians are siblings as if that conclusion were *common sense*.[3] Too much commends that opposite view. Still, "change can come from recognition of limits and concentration on realities.[4] In other words, *those who feel bonded to one another must step out of the waters of dissent onto the ground of accord.* Such action would strengthen them as siblings.

Criticism of my proposal is as inevitable as is ideological conflict in general. My appeal to synthesis, moreover, makes no pretense to "truth," as if the dissent emergent in past consultations would end. (And it is highly unlikely that African theologians such as John Mbiti will be interested in a theology of Pan-Africanism). Indeed, critique is desired for the sake of theoretical clarification which introduces another set of questions.

Upon what would a theology of Pan-Africanism rest? How would it stand philosophically, and around what doctrinal themes would it revolve?[5] What would be its practical implications? Here are traditional, yet intriguing questions, and thorough scrutiny of them does not fall within the scope of this study. But in order to defend the view that Afro-American and African theologians may collaborate in a Pan-African theology, I must explore these questions, at least provisionally.

What is needed is an account of the rationale for a theology of Pan-Africanism in a theological milieu rightfully suspicious of contrived symbioses between secular ideologies and Christianity. Indeed, juxtaposing Pan-Africanism and Christianity raises problems of the relationship between ideologies and revelation. Demonic consequences of such relationships have been revealed in the examples of Naziism and the theology of apartheid. Such aberrations show that alliances between certain ideologies and Christianity can lead to horrendous misanthropism.

God's revelation in Christ points to the bestowal of grace that contradicts genocide and fascism. If, then, it is God's revelation in Christ that "thou shalt love thy neighbor as thyself" and that "there is neither Jew nor Gentile," then theologies should fundamentally reveal an appreciation of the cosmic proportions of sanctifying, actual, elevating, and healing grace. Thus a Pan-African theology must foundationally avoid notions of black superiority. Within the broad context of black experience, one must convey an even broader vision for the world. A concern for the poor and the denunciation of the propensity toward nuclear annihilation, for instance, must be clearly expressed. It is evident that Christianity can do this. But can Pan-Africanism?

I have noted early notions of Pan-Africanism in the aspirations of the black clergy and laity in North America and Africa. Paul Cuffe, David Walker, Alexander Crummell, Samuel Crowther, James Pennington, Edward Blyden, James Holy Johnson, Majola Agbebi come easily to mind. Indeed, Africa for these members of the clergy was a new Zion that, in God's providence, would reclaim an ancient glory, but under the reign of a Christianity with the advantages of Western technology. What is now called Pan-Africanism has antecedents in a black Christianity of emigration, liberation, westernization, and indigenization.[6] It would be reductionistic, however, to see Pan-Africanism as an essentially Christian ideology. Its broader, more secular, context must be examined.

Earliest expressions of Pan-Africanism emerged from the mix of views of a group of westernized blacks of the Americas and Africa. Exigencies created by the slave trade and colonization, and the intrinsic relationship of British abolitionism to mission, gave rise in the eighteenth and nineteenth centuries to a tradition of resistance, emigration, and African nationalism. In studying those centuries I found seminal sources of a Pan-Africanism as dissimilar as that of Africanus Horton and Samuel Crowther; Marcus Garvey and W. E. B. DuBois; Harold Moody and George Padmore; and Felix Hophouet-Boigny and Kwame Nkrumah. In addition, scrutiny of early sources of Pan-Africanism reveals an interesting literature.

As a literary tradition, Pan-African discourse incorporates several major themes: the refutation of the myth of black inferiority; focus upon the black identity of ancient Egyptians, and the glorification of Egyptian achievements; the argument that Canaan, rather than Africa, was cursed; the argument that Egypt imparted civilization to the Hellenistic world; glorification of the western Sudanese states; the lack of African technological achievement due to isolation rather than inherent inferiority; Africa needed the West only until the technology needed for development was in place; Africa could humanize the world; Africa should combine an essential African background with the best of western liberalism; Africa must be independent and interdependent.[7]

Pan-African discourse, moreover, gave impetus to the founding of Pan-African organizations, which gave institutional shape to Pan-Africanist ideas. More specifically, Pan-African organizations were formed in response to colonization and white supremacy. Significant forerunners of the Pan-Africanist organizations of the twentieth century were the Fanti Federation and the African Church Movement. These emerged largely in response to the British, who already were controlling large areas of West Africa prior to 1884.[8]

By World War II, four Pan-African Congresses had been convened.[9] The Fifth Congress, however, is considered the most significant. As noted in chapter 1, it was convened by some of the future leaders of independent Africa. With African independence, the struggle for Pan-Africanism was led by an African vanguard that strove for continental unity. Two groups deserve mention: the radical Casablanca group and the more conservative Brazzaville/Monrovia group. In spite of internal differences, the Organization of African Unity was formed in 1963.[10]

My brief discussion of Pan-Africanism should have made clear its differentiation, as a political ideology, from Christianity. Yet, as I have shown, it has roots in the piety of the North American black clergy in the past. And there seems to be an important relationship between root and branch. Blyden and Nkrumah, Crummell and Casley Hayford, Turner and DuBois all believed in the equality of human beings.[11] Rarely have exponents of Pan-Africanism descended to diatribes on the inferiority of other races. Thus, even though some Pan-Africanists held notions of a certain black superiority, Pan-Africanism emerges historically from assumptions as to the equality of races.[12] Pan-Africanism reveals some compatibility with Christianity.

Pan-Africanism and Christianity also have in common a commitment to the poor. And today Afro-American and African theologians would be on solid ground if they made the uplift of the suffering black poor of Africa and the United States a plumbline for the profession of concern for the general category "the poor."

Disease, drought, pestilence, famine, and poverty make Africa one of the most uncomfortable places to live, especially for anyone who has meager resources. The political climate, plagued with corruption, micro-nationalism, and violence, only exacerbates the calamitous situation. Within the United States, poverty, illiteracy, and societal marginalization plague black communities from north to south. A vivid example of black deprivation can be seen in a segment of contemporary black youth. They are products of black suffering. The point here is that a certain concern for the poor and oppressed should be fundamental to theology. Afro-American and African theologians would be on solid ground in stipulating that a concern for the black poor of Africa and the United States be a springboard for joint enterprise. Unquestionably, concern for all poor and oppressed peoples should be a central theme. But in confronting the depth of the problem of human suffering, what better place to start than "in your own backyard"? A sense of charity that begins at home refers me once more to the examples of black clergymen in the past.

Though many, especially black Americans, were bigoted in their captivation by a Western notion of civilization, members of the black clergy championed the liberation of the African masses (Wilmore, chap. 5). Dissection of their notion of liberation, however, suggests the need for modifications. Needing revision, for instance, is a notion of God's providence that paternalistically sees Afro-Americans as indispensable to the redemption of Africa. Indeed, from a Pan-African perspective, Afro-Americans need Africans as much as Africans need Afro-Americans. Thus, black theologians of the United States should not feel they are "saviors," ordained to bring a modern epistemology and technology to Africa. But they might encourage black churches to be more involved with African churches in schemes for African development. Mission may indeed be a practical expression of a theology of the poor. There is room, moreover, for a more prophetic emphasis within that mission.

Bold talk of liberation in black Africa, moreover, is risky business. It takes a martyr's courage to prophetically denounce corruption in the face of notoriously autocratic governments. Going back a few years, imagine a theology of liberation in the context of the Uganda of Amin! Still, a Pan-African theology would take just such a prophetic stand because of a doctrine of God and a christology that explicitly denounce fascism, genocide, capitalistic greed, and a divisive elitism. My discussion of the views of Carr and Tutu, moreover, evinces that certain African theologians are prepared to take just such a stand. Thus it is again clear that Afro-American theologians may play a sibling role in the elaboration of a Pan-African theology of liberation. But what about indigenization? How would that theme serve the diaspora?

Although Kwesi Dickson resists use of the term "indigenization," he argues that indigenization is essential to the postcolonial context of Africa. Embracing the legitimacy of a black South African theology of liberation, Dickson writes, for instance:

> Such a theology should . . . be part of a larger theology . . . [which] will make a greater impact where it addresses . . . the situation in such a way as to underline the *fullness* of a people's humanity. . . . Africans' full humanity would come from not only the winning of socio-economic and political freedom, but also—and more importantly—the winning of the cultural battle, for it is the latter which defines more fundamentally the humanity of a people [*Theology,* 139].

Issue may be taken with the emphasis Dickson gives to culture, inasmuch as African socio-economic and political problems are so formidable. Yet, the issue he raises stresses the particularity of an African theology of indigenization. Indeed, engagement in the problem of indigenization must be a leading feature of a Pan-African theology.

Afro-Americans have tended to be insensitive to the African focus on africanization because of the lack of appreciation of African culture in North America. Indeed, the gap in the appreciation of African heritage among the black clergy may be seen historically in the difference between Turner and Agbebi. Turner found certain traditional practices shocking, whereas Agbebi sought to preserve many of them. Contemporary Afro-American theologians and religionists, however, seek greater insight into the significance of African traditional religion for black theology. Thus, they have already suggested the need for indigenization of black theology. As I have noted, their interest promises that African theologians might be instructive in the task of relating black theology to the image of Africa and the vestiges of africanisms within the United States, and those in relation to their prototypes in Africa and the Caribbean. Gayraud Wilmore describes these africanisms succinctly:

In the formation of a new common language, in the telling of animal tales and proverbs, in the leisure-time practice of remembered handicrafts, in the preparation of foods, homemade medicines, and magical potions and charms, in the standardization of rituals of birth, marriage, and death, in the creation of modes of play and parody, in the expression of certain styles of singing, instrumental music, and the dance . . . the slaves wove . . . the tapestry of a new African-American culture [*Religion,* 222].

Jazz and blues, gospel and spirituals, a certain timbre; tap dancing, certain social dances; a certain style of living; the presence of root doctors and the distinctive worship of the sanctified church all evince Wilmore's point. Blacks of the United States are an African people of a peculiar sort. On this basis, he claims that:

A third source of black theology is the traditional religions of Africa . . . and the concepts by which African theologians seek to make the Christian faith contextual and effective in Africa today. This is to insist that Afro-Americans are not only a spiritual people, but also an African people. [They] need to know what ancient and modern Africans have to contribute to our knowledge of God *and the survival and liberation of the human race* [ibid., 238; emphasis added].

Certain Afro-American religionists, then, are already, in *classic Pan-Africanist fashion,* seeking to collaborate with African theologians in quest of a theology that would relate African traditional religion to Christianity. Clear again, then, is the plausibleness of the view that Africans and blacks of the United States might develop a Pan-African theology that would interpret Christian doctrine by categories derived from traditional African idioms.

Further evidence of black theologians' willingness to embark on such an enterprise is marked by J. Deotis Roberts's comment that: "An adequate theological method must be sought which will create fruitful dialogue between all peoples of African descent" (*Roots,* 18). Roberts writes, in addition, that: "Pan-Africanism is a marvelous concept for those seeking a continuous heritage with their African ancestry" (*Political Theology*, 54).

Fundamental, here, to the notion of Pan-Africanism is that there appear to be affinities between African and black North American Christianities. They both display, though obviously in varying degrees, a certain "African" initiative in the transformation of Christianity from, for the most part, a Western Protestantism to one bearing the cultural impress of Africa. Black religionist George B. Thomas puts it this way:

African Christianity is both an evolutionary process in the African and black religious experiences and church movements and the main source

and resource of African and black theolog[ies]. *Pan-African theology*
[then] *evolves from Pan-African Christianity*, now . . . manifested in
black and African theolog[ies] [in Bruce and Jones, 80; emphasis added].

I reiterate, however, that the extent to which *black* church movements of the
United States are *African* is debatable. And Thomas appears to speak as
though a Pan-African theology is a fact rather than a possibility.

A more balanced assessment of the relationship of Africa to black theology
is made in Henry Mitchel's statement that "the faith of the black masses in the
USA is not by any means purely African, but is an adaptation of African roots
to American experience and Christian exposure" (ibid., 119). I quote Thomas,
however, merely to show that certain black theologians in the United States
would welcome a Pan-African theology.

Inasmuch as African theologians such as Burgess Carr and Desmond Tutu
also appear to be amenable to such a task, it is evident that African and Afro-
American theologians may be siblings not only in their separate contexts but
also in the quest for a Pan-African theology—a new theology within an old
tradition.

Study of Allan Boesak's thought indicates he too would be receptive to the
quest for a Pan-African theology. It was noted earlier in this chapter that
Desmond Tutu and James Cone represent a continuum of a historical relationship between James M. Dwane and Henry M. Turner. Boesak, it seems,
recognizes that historical continuum:

> As long as white Christians have been preaching the gospel to blacks,
> there have always been rather strong ties between black Christians in
> South Africa and the United States [*Innocence*, 36].

From my discussion of Tutu's views, I think it is clear why Boesak, also a
member of an oppressed people of color, wants to continue that historical
relationship. Also understandable, therefore, is why Boesak strongly feels
related to James Cone.

As with James Cone, white supremacy is a theological problem for Boesak
because that heinous bigotry oppresses *him!* Like Cone, Boesak is unable to
reconcile the gospel with human oppression, especially inasmuch as he believes
that the theme of liberation is the essence of that gospel. Unsurprisingly, then,
Boesak " . . . protest[s] very strongly against the total division . . . some
make between [the black theologies of South Africa and the United States]"
(ibid., 7). Because, therefore, the Pan-African theology I envision here would
focus intensely upon the theme of liberation, as that theme has been developed
in black theologies, it seems likely that Boesak would contribute much to the
development of a Pan-African theology.

Boesak, in addition, is sensitive to the problem of the africanization of
Christian theology. Indeed, we saw in chapter 3 that Boesak believes black
South African theology is profoundly African. I noted, moreover, that Boesak

believes black South African theology must be culturally indigenous to black Africans if it is to be truly contextual. Explaining in more depth the relationship he sees between contextualization and indigenization, Boesak writes:

> In calling for this actualization of the gospel for the black situation, Black theology in South Africa is also an essential correction of traditional western theological thinking. There is also a call for the church to go back to the roots of broken African community and tradition. It must examine why certain traditions were considered wholesome for the African community and whether these traditions can have a humanizing influence on contemporary society [*Innocence*, 14].

Boesak's statement here on the need for blacks to liberate themselves from "western theological thinking," his call for an exploration of the significance of African traditions for the church, and his question of whether those traditions can contribute to contemporary society may well help refine methodical inquiries into the nature, scope, and content of a Pan-African theology.

As with Tutu, then, Boesak would bring to the task of synthesis a perspective in which the central themes of black and African theologies are already inextricably related. Without question, the views of Allan Boesak on liberation and indigenization strengthen my argument that certain Afro American and African theologians are siblings who may produce texts that develop from the sense of kinship.

. . . WITH A FEMINIST PERSPECTIVE

That black theologians of Africa and the United States can function as siblings gains even greater credibility if a theology of Pan-Africanism includes a feminist perspective. Themes of liberation and indigenization would seem to easily complement one another in a Pan-African feminist theology. Women in their quest for liberation have exposed myths that support male chauvinism. Indeed, my reference to Mercy Odoyoye in chapter 3 showed that African female theologians are already reflecting on this problem. Challenging traditional assumptions about women's roles, and their bodies, Oduyoye asserts that tradition must accommodate women's new image of themselves (Appiah-Kubi and Torres, 112).

Black North American feminist theologians are similarly rejecting traditional *myths* about their place in society. They are part of a black women's studies movement that is asserting new positions on the meaning of the term "woman." Describing that movement, Barbara Smith writes:

> A viable, autonomous Black Feminist Movement in this country would open up the space needed for the exploration of Black women's lives and the creation of consciously Black woman-identified art. At the same time

a redefinition of the goals and strategies of the white feminist movement would lead to much needed change in the focus and content of what is now generally accepted as women's culture [Hull et al., *Brave*, 158].

Jacquelyn Grant, a black feminist theologian, is part of the black women's studies movement. Critiquing black theology, she writes: that because "Black women are the poorest of the poor, and the most oppressed of the oppressed, their experience provides a most fruitful context for doing Black theology" (ibid., 146).

Examination of the relationship of black female theologians of Africa and the United States to a wider feminist discourse reveals that the contexts in which they live have led them to focus on the themes of liberation and indigenization. In other words, they demand liberation from sexist institutions, and are in quest of indigenous idioms appropriate for a black feminist literature. Mercy Oduyoye, moreover, has already expressed interest in the problems of other Third World women (Fabella and Torres, 246–54). This suggests her openness to the problems of Afro-American women.

Suggestions, however, as to the content of a Pan-African feminist theology remain the prerogative of the women. Still, I must include the notion of such a Pan-African feminist theology in my vision of the ground on which Afro-American and African theologians may work as siblings.

Adoption of a critical method would be the watchword here. It bears repeating that sharp appraisal of the differences between the two streams of theology is critical in order to clarify the basis of a theology of Pan-Africanism. Thus if Afro-American and African theologians are to develop a theology premised on Pan-African assumptions, such assumptions must be more sharply defined.

Here, the broad contours have been merely suggested. Many difficulties must be overcome if such a theology is to take shape. And it also bears repeating that construction of a theology of Pan-Africanism is contingent upon the degree to which Afro-American and African theologians are committed to it. Only a fierce commitment to such a theology will produce it. Afro-American and African theologians who feel related as siblings must venture forth onto the ground cleared by the black clergy in the past—ground that is overgrown now from disuse.

In sum, creation of a Pan-African theology certainly offers a solution to the problem on which I have focused. It would no doubt stir up more controversy and add a new dimension to the dissent, but at least it would liberate a fresh perspective from that dissent. What is more, for those blacks of opposite sides of the Atlantic who feel a kinship with one another, the entire enterprise would seem to fulfill a desire. It is one born from a commitment to those who are different from, yet similar to, one another. And as certain blacks are not repulsed by that difference, the creation of a Pan-African theology would seem to be indeed a labor—for it would certainly be that—of love.

Notes

1. Although Afro-American theologians and African theologians have informally conferred with one another in the contexts of the WCC and EATWOT, I focus on their formal conferences. There have been six conferences in all, not all of them under the auspices of the AACC and the SSBR:

(a) Abidjan, Ivory Coast, 1969. Representatives of the National Conference of Black Churchmen (NCBC) attended the AACC meeting in 1969 and initiated contact between the two groups of theologians. Accounts of this initial encounter were provided by Gayraud Wilmore, one of the NCBC representatives. His account of that meeting in Abidjan is on tape. For an account of NCBC origins and purposes, see Wilmore and Cone, 2, 6, 15–42, 62–64.

(b) Dar es Salaam, Tanzania, 1971. This meeting was between the Tanzanian Council of Churches and the newly established NCBC African commission. For accounts of that meeting, see Priscilla Massie, ed., *Black Faith and Black Solidarity* (New York, Friendship Press, 1973); Cornish Roger, "Pan-Africanism and the Black Church: A Search for Solidarity," *Christian Century* (Nov. 17, 1971) 1345–47; Wilmore and Cone, 447.

(c) Makerere University, Uganda, 1972. This was a consultation between the Department of Religious Studies and the United Presbyterian Church. See Eliewaha E. Mshana, "The Challenge of Black Theology and African Theology," *Africa Theological Journal*, 5 (1972) 18–30.

(d) Union Theological Seminary, New York City, 1973. A consultation was held by the AACC and the SSBR. See Wilmore and Cone, 448.

(e) Legon, Ghana, 1974. Again, the consultation was under the auspices of the AACC and the SSBR. See *The Journal of Religious Thought*, 32/2 (Fall-Winter 1975); James Cone, "Black and African Theologies: A Consultation," *Christianity and Crisis*, 35/3 (March 3, 1975); Gayraud Wilmore, "To Speak With One Voice? The Ghana Consultation on African and Black Theology," *Christian Century* (Feb. 19, 1975).

(f) Accra, Ghana, 1977. The two groups of theologians met under the auspices of the Pan-African Conference of Third World Theologians. See Appiah-Kubi and Torres, 176–86, 196–208. See also Wilmore, "Theological Ferment in the Third World," *Christian Century* (Feb. 17, 1978).

2. By Pan-Africanism I mean generally: (1) a certain historical sense of solidarity between peoples of Africa and the diaspora; (2) the Pan-African movement of the 20th century; and (3) a certain struggle for unanimity within the African continent itself. Members of the black clergy who supported mission in Africa are studied in chap. 1. In regard to the Pan-Africanism of certain contemporary black theologians of Africa and the United States, I refer to Cecil Cone, J. Deotis Roberts, James Cone, Burgess Carr, Desmond Tutu, and Allan Boesak. Their Pan-African views are discussed in chapters 4 and 5.

3. I refer to Cecil Cone and J. Deotis Roberts. Their views are examined in chap. 2.

4. I use the terms "africanization" and "indigenization" synonymously in order to denote the effort of African theologians to make uniquely African the Christianity that came to them by way of colonization. The terms describe the present scope of the African theological focus. Kwesi Dickson's objection to the term "indigenization" must be registered here (*Theology in Africa*, 7–8).

5. See Whitten and Szwed, *Afro-American Anthropology*. The Introduction to this excellent study sets forth the problematics involved in using an appropriate method of analysis vis-à-vis the "creole" culture of black North America.

6. This reflects especially the thinking of James Cone.

7. "Black ministers began in the 1960s to develop a systematic theology of black religion. Although *frequently ahistorical,* the theological writings often reflected trends in the antebellum period" (Berry and Blassingame, 112–13; emphasis added).

8. African traditional religions are neither Christian nor Muslim, but indigenous to sub-Saharan

Africa. Although they have undergone changes over the centuries, reference in this study is made to the traditional religions of the period just prior to colonization. However, inasmuch as these religions are anything but extinct, I refer to them, for the most part, in the present tense.

CHAPTER I

1. Raboteau, *Slave Religion*, provides a fine discussion of the christianization of slaves and the syncretistic nature of slave religion. Chap. 3 should be carefully read. Valuable information on slave religion is provided as well by Genovese, *Roll Jordan Roll*; see esp. book 2. See also Blassingame, *The Slave Community*, chap. 2; Wilmore, *Black Religion and Black Radicalism*, chap. 1.

2. For accounts of the African character of the spirituals and ring shouts, and the distinctiveness of an African tone, pitch, and rhythm, see Miles Mark Fisher, *Negro Slave Songs in the United States* (Secaucus, N.J., Citadel, 1978) 178; Stearns, *Jazz*, 130; Collier, *Jazz*, 16–24; Kaufman and Guckin, *Jazz*, chap. 1, 2, 5. For an introduction to African music, see Nketia, *Music*; Chernoff, *Rhythms*; Bebey, *Music*.

3. But in precisely what way did African traditional religion—vestiges of it—inspire slaves to resist chattelization? It seems plausible that vestiges of a crypto-African traditional religion, escaping slavers' purging, empowered slaves to survive in a way commending resistance to their exploitation. However, the notion of the retention of an African cosmology as comprehensive in the United States as in West Africa is probably more myth than historical fact. For a good discussion of this problematic, see the Introduction to Whitten and Szwed, *Afro-American Anthropology*.

4. For accounts of the various forms of the slaves' "invisible institution," see Blassingame, *Slave Community*, "Americanization of the Slave and Africanization of the South"; Raboteau, 212.

5. See Cecil Cone's account of praise meetings in *Crisis*, 52–53. James Cone (*Liberation*, 58) makes the point that slave religion was not otherworldly.

6. This is especially so for James Cone. See *Black Power*, 97, 101, 131.

7. See Woodson, *History*, "The Independent Church Movement"; Wilmore, *Religion*, "The Black Church Freedom Movement."

8. The view that Richard Allen was an accommodationist is found in Drake, *Redemption*, 31–35. For a more detailed treatment of the AME Church and Richard Allen, see Richardson, *Salvation*.

9. This statement reflects my study of four black theologians: James Cone, Major Jones, J. Deotis Roberts, and Cecil Cone. Their writings are examined in chap. 2, below.

10. See Lowenberg and Bogin, *Women*, "Let Us Make a Mighty Effort and Arise."

11. Henry H. Garnet, moreover, was, with Edward Blyden and Henry M. Turner, fiercely proud of his African ancestry. He was reportedly descended from African royalty, and is buried in Liberia. See Bracey et al., *Nationalism*, "Henry Highland Garnet Describes the Greatness of Africa"; Crummell, *Africa*, "Eulogium on Henry Highland Garnet, D.D." This is a very moving tribute to a great *African*-American.

12. That African theology is a development from this revival of Christianity in Africa does *not* mean that the earliest forms of Christianity in Africa have no relevance to African theologians. "The Confession of Alexandria" of the AACC discloses the relationship African theologians feel to the "fathers of the Early Church in North Africa." See Anderson and Stransky, 132–34.

13. Karl Barth, *Protestant Thought* (New York, Books for Libraries Press, 1971) 16–17.

14. For an account of Olaudah Equiano (Gustavus Vasser), see Edwards, *Travels*.

15. Groves explains: "At the time the first [missionary] societies were organized there were two regions in Africa that particularly invited missionary enterprise: Sierra Leone and the Cape. It was at these two points that the first Protestant plantings were actually made. In due course, they took root and flourished. From Sierra Leone the planting spread along the Guinea Coast, though the hope of striking into the interior of the continent from this vantage ground was not realized. From the Cape the work extended east and north, until finally Livingstone thrust beyond the Zambezi and Central Africa lay at last unveiled" (I, 205).

16. A solid discussion of the founding of Liberia under the auspices of the American Colonization Society is provided by Sanneh, 89–105. See also Groves, I, 290–99; Geiss, 81–82; W. Williams, *Americans*, "Missionary Attitudes toward Emigration and Imperialism"; Buell, *Liberia*; Liebenow, *Liberia*.

17. For accounts of Afro-Americans as oppressors in Liberia, see n. 16, above. On Loft Carey, see Fitts, *Carey*. On Daniel Coker, see Wilmore, 105, 108, 132.

18. These worldviews are discussed in chap. 3, below.

19. See also Delany, *Condition*; Crummell, *Africa*; idem, *Future*.

20. That both men in this period wished to settle in Africa—Crummell actually did so for a period—and that Delany made contact with African chiefs of the Niger in order to settle there and build a Christian "progressive nation in West Africa," suggests their relevance to a historical study of the development of African theology. Obviously, as Wilmore discloses, they have a significant place in black theologians' quest for historical relevance. For more discussion on the activities of Delany and Crummell in Africa, see Lynch, *Blyden;* on Delany, see Delany and Campbell, *Search.*

21. Walter Williams writes: "Crummell's culture-bound position reinforced the ethnocentric belief of Afro-Americans that they were the superior model of civilization which Africans should adopt, but at least it allowed for full acceptance of Africans once they were acculturated" (*Americans*, 121). Sir Richard Burton is, by contrast, described by Robert July as one "who had educated European missionaries to a skepticism over the capacity of the African to digest the benefits of Victorian civilization" (*History*, 340). Thus, while Crummell and Burton were similar in their depreciation of African culture, Crummell differed from Burton in his view that the Africans only needed redemption from their heathen ways. For Crummell, neither the essential equality of Africans with other races nor the myth of African idiocy were issues. See, e.g., Crummell's "The Regeneration of Africa" in his *Africa and America.*

22. Harry Sawyerr, "What is African Theology?" *Africa Theological Journal*, 4 (Aug. 1977) 9.

23. Crowder, *West Africa*, "Background to the Scramble."

24. July, *History*, "The Partition of Africa."

25. Ibid.; see also Sanneh, 169–73.

26. See Groves, vol. 2, for Livingstone's part in opening Africa to the West. See also Forbath, *Congo*, chap. 12–14.

27. See July, 367–68; Crowder, chap. 1–3; Fetter, *Rule*, esp. "Introduction and Historical Summary," and chap. 1.

28. Edward Fashole-Luke, Richard Gray, Adrian Hastings, and Godwin Tasie, eds., *Christianity in Independent Africa* (London, Rex Collings, 1978) 365.

29. Edward Blyden is a fascinating figure. For Pan-Africanists, an assessment of his contribution to Pan-Africanism invites hyperbole: excessive praise of Blyden underscores the immensity of his contribution. But he, like all humans, had his faults, one of which was an enormous ego. Still, in the thought of this very brilliant black man are foreshadowed the views of several of the world's celebrated Pan-Africanists: Marcus Garvey, Casely Hayford, Nmandi Azikiwe, Orishatukeh Faduma, Majola Agbebi, J.E.K. Aggrey, Leopold Senghor, Kwame Nkrumah, and El-Hajj Malik El-Shabazz (Malcolm X). Perhaps the best work on Blyden's life and thought is Hollis R. Lynch's *Edward Wilmot Blyden.* For Blyden's writings, see Hollis R. Lynch, ed., *Black Spokesman: Selected Published Writings of Edward Wilmot Blyden* (London, Frank Case, 1971); and what is considered Blyden's tour de force, *Christianity, Islam, and the Negro Race* (Edinburgh University Press, 1967).

30. See also *Liberia Bulletin*, 11 (Nov. 1897) 40.

31. Blyden could not stand mulattos—some would say that he *hated* them—although he was married to a mulatto. See Lynch, *Patriot,* 38.

32. See John Hope Franklin, *From Slavery to Freedom: A History of Negro Americans*, 5th ed. (New York, Knopf, 1980), chap. 14, esp. pp. 227–50.

33. Ibid., 248.

34. Ibid.

35. Ibid., 251–67.

36. For Turner's concept of divine providence, see W. Williams, 100–101; Wilmore, 122–29. For Blyden's concept of it, see his speech, "The Call of Providence to the Descendants of Africa in America," in Lynch, ed., *Black Spokesman* (n. 29, above).

37. Turner's essay is found in Bracey et al., 154–55. See also J. Cone, *God*, 31; C. Cone, *Crisis*, 65.

38. I refer primarily to James Cone; his views are examined in chap. 2, below.

39. Turner writes: " . . . we are no stickler as to God's color, anyway, but if He has any we would prefer to believe that it is nearer *symbolized* in the blue sky above us and the blue water of the seas and oceans; we certainly protest against God being a white man as against God being white *at all*; *abstract* as this theme must forever remain while we are in the flesh" (in Bracey et al., 155; emphasis added).

40. In other words, researchers of the 19th-century and early 20th-century notions of divine providence, and of the black missiology intrinsically related to emigration, will find two outstanding clergymen supporting both views: Edward Blyden and Henry McNeal Turner. The two, moreover, knew and respected one another. And even Blyden's disdain for light-skinned blacks did not dampen his affection for Turner. Lynch writes: "of [Turner] Blyden noted that despite 'his light

complexion . . . his hair is . . . unmistakably African—his instincts strongly of the race: and he has all the peculiarities of an uncontaminated Eboe' " (Lynch, *Blyden*, 112). Blyden claimed to be of direct Igbo descent (ibid., 3) and, a fortiori, it seems that the depth of his admiration for Turner is revealed in Blyden's attributing to Turner "all the peculiarities of an uncontaminated Eboe" (Igbo/Ibo)—whatever that means.

41. See Fetter, *Rule*, "Introduction and Historical Summary"; Crowder, *West Africa*, "West Africa and the 1914-18 War"; Kwame Nkrumah, *Africa Must Unite* (New York, International Publishers, 1970), Introduction and chap. 1-4. For accounts of events in the U.S.A., see Franklin, *Slavery* (n. 32, above), "Enlarged Dimensions of Racial Conflict"; Berry and Blassingame, 160-70; Woodward, *Career*, chap. 3-4.

42. For an account of the heinousness of Leopold and his butchers, see Nkrumah, *Challenge*, 6-9; Ritchie Calder, *The Agony of the Congo* (London, Gollancz, 1961); Forbath, *Congo*, "The Personal Kingdom of Leopold II"; E. D. Morel, Red Rubber (New York: Negro Universities Press, 1969). For descriptions of lynchings in the U.S.A. and their consequences, see the works by Franklin, Berry and Blassingame, and Woodward in n. 41, above. See as well Tuttle, *Riot*, and esp. the story of a remarkable Afro-American woman, Ida B. Wells, *Crusade*.

43. John A. Garraty and Peter Gay, eds., *The Columbia History of the World* (New York, Harper and Row, 1983) 966-93.

44. See the sources cited in notes 41 and 42, above. See also July, 498-99.

45. Their views on the decrease of radicalism within the black community are discussed in chap. 2, below.

46. See Burkett, chap. 3, esp. pp. 83-84, 88-99. See also Garvey, 33-34.

47. See Wilmore, 145-50; idem, "The Black Messiah: Revising the Color Symbolism of Western Christology," *The Journal of the Interdenominational Theological Center*, 2/1 (Fall 1974).

48. J. Cone, *God*, 124-25 (exposition of the importance of the cross in black theology). For Garvey's views, see Burkett, 53-54, 79-80. Garvey, moreover, held, as does Cone, that Jesus preached a revolutionary message; see Garvey's speech, "Christ the Greatest Reformer," in Garvey, *Philosophy*.

49. See Wilmore, 153-54. Two other sources used by black theologians (e.g., J. Deotis Roberts) when discussing blacks' views of God are Mays, *The Negro's God*, and Thurman, *Jesus and the Disinherited*.

50. See Wilmore, 129; W. Williams, 159; July, 460; Rubin and Weinstein, 77-78; G. Shepperson and T. Price, *Independent Africa* (Edinburgh, The University Press, 1958).

51. See July, 505-6; Rubin and Weinstein, 74; Davenport, 177; Gerhart, 98. For a good summary of African nationalism prior to the post-World War II era, see July, *History*, "Between Two World Wars—Nationalist Frustrations in West Africa."

52. See Rubin and Weinstein, 78; Herskovits, *Human Factor*, 417-18; Ndiokwere, *Prophesy*, "The Emergence of Independent Churches and Prophetic Movements"; Boulaga, *Christianity*, chap. 3; Sanneh, chap. 7.

53. See Hastings, *African Christianity*, "Patterns of Healing," esp. p. 64; idem, *History*, 72-73; Boulaga, 65; Barrett, 31, 116-17, 167, 275.

54. For views that constitute this debate, see Herskovits, *Human Factor*, 422; Sundkler, 48-49; Barrett, 127; Ndiokwere, 22.

55. In general, "Ethiopian" churches show more liturgical continuity with the mission churches, whereas "Zionist" churches are much more influenced by traditional African spirituality. Distinctions made between Ethiopian and Zionist churches, however, tend to muddle issues much more than clarify them. For discussions on this distinction, and the problem it poses, see Sundkler 53-57; Hastings, *History*, 74; Ndiokwere, 28-38; Bosch, *Missiology*, chap. 5.

56. Although Turner discusses Braide's movement as a forerunner of Aladura, he writes in reference to Braide: "The desire for spiritual independence in Africa is not necessarily connected with the rejection of the domination of the white race, as is sometimes suggested" (I, 8). Sanneh, however, writes: "But Braide became something more than the idol of popular devotion: the historical circumstances of his movement cast him in an inevitable political role. He did not need a profound insight into contemporary history to appreciate that European colonialism had begun to transform political relations in Africa. In fact *he preached on the subject of white alien rule*, though his predictions and prescriptions showed an underestimation of the strengths of the new reality" (182-83; emphasis added). Thus, Turner pays little attention to the political ramifications of Braide's sermon on *alien* white rule.

57. For essays on William Wadé Harris, see Bond et al., *Christianity*, chap. I, "The Message as the Medium: The Harrist Churches of the Ivory Coast and Ghana." For a discussion of Kimbangu, see Ndiokwere, 46-50.

58. I refer to John Mbiti, Harry Sawyerr, E. W. Fashole-Luke, and Bolaji Idowu. Idowu, e.g., writes that independency in Nigeria was "symptomatic of the revolt of the spirit of certain Christian Nigerians against the 'unnatural' characteristics of the Church in Nigeria as organized under European leadership. . . . Thus it was that spiritual hunger led to spiritual revolt" (*Church*, 43).

59. Kwesi A. Dickson writes, for instance, " . . . there is a great deal to be learnt from the Independent Churches; furthermore . . . the historic ["mission"] churches have been slow to depart from the received Western forms. . . . *There is no question [that] the Independent Churches [tend] to have a more realistic appreciation of the Spirit and its working in a way that accords with both biblical ideas and African thought"* (*Theology*, 112–13; emphasis added).

60. See Franklin, *Slavery* (n. 32, above), "The Postwar Years"; July, *History*, "Toward Independence."

61. Harvard Sitkoff writes: "Ghana's victorious revolution for independence in 1957 had initiated a wave of freedom movements against [colonialism]. In 1960, a dozen African nations had gained independence. Afro-American students were not unaware; the successful struggles of black Africans both inspired and embarrassed them . . . and . . . James Baldwin jeered: 'All of Africa will be free before we can get a lousy cup of coffee' " (*Struggle*, 83).

62. On Kenyatta, see his *Facing Mt. Kenya*.

63. For an introduction to Senghor's views, see "Negritude: A Humanism of the Twentieth Century," in Cartey and Kilson, *Independent Africa*.

64. For a sampling of their views, see their essays in Cartey and Kilson, *Independent Africa*. For an account of the role of Sékou Touré in the Guinean movement for independence, see Jackson and Rosberg, 208–19. For more on Kaunda, see his *Violence*. On Nyerere, see his *Ujamaa; Development; Crusade*. On Lumumba, see his *Congo My Country* (London, Pall Mall, 1962).

65. See Gerhart, *Power*; Bernard Magubane, *The Political Economy of Race and Class in South Africa* (New York, Monthly Review Press, 1979), chap. 10–11; Davenport, *South Africa*, chap. 18; Benson, *Mandela*.

66. See by Nkrumah, *Ghana*; *Africa Must Unite* (n. 41, above); *Neo-Colonialism: The Last Stage of Imperialism* (New York, International Publishers, 1980). For his notion of African philosophy in relation to what has been called Nkrumaism, see his seminal *Consciencism*. For an account of his support of Lumumba, see Nkrumah, *Challenge*. For an anthology of Nkrumah's political thought, see his *Path*. For his critique of the romantic notion of African socialism, see his *Struggle*.

67. See Rubin and Weinstein, chap. 4–5; Murphy, *History*, chap. 16; July, *History*, "Independent Africa"; Carter and O'Meara, *Southern Africa*; David Martin and Phyllis Johnson, *The Struggle for Zimbabwe* (New York, Monthly Review Press, 1981); Wallerstein, *Africa*.

68. See the references in n. 67, above, esp. Rubin and Weinstein.

69. "The West's needs for raw materials—at a time when much of Asia was lost—had brought an immense expansion in production in many parts of Africa: the Allied need for the copper of Katenga and Northern Rhodesia [Zambia] was the most striking example but not the only one. The uranium for the first atomic bombs came from Africa" (Hastings, *History*, 7).

70. Michael Crowder writes: "Of the four colonial powers that were to occupy . . . Africa, three, Portugal, France, and Britain, had already been installed on the coast [of West Africa] for the whole of the nineteenth century. But prior to 1885, only one had openly demonstrated interest in colonial expansion into the interior of West Africa, and that was France, and even her government was divided over the issue of colonial involvement in Tropical Africa . . . . On the eve of the Berlin Conference . . . the three most important colonial powers in West Africa, Britain, Germany, and France, were *officially* opposed to colonial expansion in West Africa or any other part of Tropical Africa" (*West Africa*, 17). On the process of devolution—the surrender of powers to indigenous authorities by magisterial governments—Wallerstein writes: "The colonial powers—first Britain, then France, then Belgium—decided to move ahead, devolving power upon the nationalist movement as a step (sometimes only implicitly) toward full independence. And so for an interim period, the colonial government and the nationalist movement shared power; there was, in short, a dyarchy" (*Africa*, 60).

71. That the colonial structure remained is the central thesis of Dennis Austin's *Politics in Africa*. From a different perspective, Kwame Nkrumah makes a similar point in his polemics against the West's attempt to balkanize Africa. See his *Africa Must Unite* and *Neo-Colonialism*. Although most newly independent African states remained dependent on the West, Francophone nations that elected to join DeGaulle's French community (*Communauté*) especially retained a neo-colonial relationship. See Rubin and Weinstein, 105. On Sékou Touré's refusal to join the *Communauté*, see Lamb, 221. See also Davidson, *Survive*.

72. For a discussion on the relationship of colonialism and decolonialism to African theology, see Dickson, *Theology*, chap. 3.

73. For an assessment of the impact of this book on African theology, see Hastings, *History*, 63–64, and esp. 117.

74. London, Lutterworth, 1963.

75. The conference stated: "We have rejoiced that since Ibadan many new independent nations have been born in Africa. *We identify ourselves with the aspirations of our peoples toward development of dignity and a mature personality in Christ* and we exhort the Churches on this continent to participate wholeheartedly in the building of the African nation" (*Drumbeats*, 15; emphasis added).

76. See Hastings, *History*, 175–83, 248–57. On the Vapostori, see Bond et al., *Christianity*, 109–35; on the Lumpa Church, see ibid., 137–59; Ndiokwere, 40–45.

77. See the four works by King in the Bibliographic References, below.

78. This comment reflects my study of Afro-American theologians in chap. 2, below.

79. See the seven works by Malcolm X in the Bibliographic References, below. For a fascinating secondary source, see Goldman, *Death*.

80. See Sergio Torres and John Eagleson, eds., *Theology in the Americas* (Maryknoll, N.Y., Orbis, 1976) 177–90.

81. This is an interpretation of Afro-American and African history, an interpretation gleaned from the sources upon which this chapter depends: July, *A History of the African People*; Franklin, *From Slavery to Freedom*; Berry and Blassingame, *Long Memory*; Rubin and Weinstein, *Introduction to African Politics*; Davidson, *The African Genius*; *Let Freedom Come*; *The African Slave Trade*; *Africa in History*; Murphy, *History of African Civilization*; Austin, *Politics in Africa*; Nkrumah, *Africa Must Unite*; Herskovits, *The Human Factor in Changing Africa*; Crowder, *West Africa under Colonial Rule*; Fetter, *Colonial Rule in Africa*.

82. See Hastings, *History*, "Cultural Revolution"; Herskovits, *Human Factor*, "The Search for Values."

83. July, *History*, "In the Heart of Darkness."

84. See Appiah-Kubi and Torres, 204–7. The dynamics of the 1977 meeting in Africa is also recounted in a taped interview I conducted with Gayraud Wilmore and James Cone, July and October 1984. The quote is my own interpretation of the dynamics of that meeting.

CHAPTER II

1. For discussion of these essays, see chap. 4.

2. See Wilmore, chap. 1, 9; Raboteau, chap. 1–3; Sobel, *Trabelin'*; Herskovits, *Myth*; Genovese, *Jordan*; Thompson, *Flash*.

3. Alan Richardson and John Bowden, eds., *The Westminster Dictionary of Christian Theology* (Philadelphia, Westminster, 1983) 324.

4. Ibid., 325.

5. For Barth's yes-and-no typology, see his *The Epistle to the Romans* (New York, Oxford University Press, 1980). See also Cone's, *My Soul Looks Back*, where he writes: "From Barth and others I knew all about the ideological dangers of my procedure. Identifying the gospel with historico-political movements was anathema to anyone who bases his theology on divine revelation. But I purposely intended to be provocative in much the same way that Barth was when he rebelled against liberal theology. As Barth turned liberal theology upside down, I wanted to turn him right-side-up with a focus on the black struggle in particular and oppressed people generally. No longer would I allow an appeal to divine revelation to camouflage God's identification with the human fight for justice. I was angry not with Barth but only with European and North American Barthians who used Barth to justify doing nothing about the struggle for justice. *I have always thought that Barth was closer to me than to them*" (p. 45; emphasis added).

6. Cone, throughout his *Black Theology and Black Power*, asserts that black power is intrinsic to the gospel. On p. 38 he states boldly: "Christianity is not alien to Black Power; it is Black Power."

7. The relationship of neo-orthodoxy to existentialism is revealed in David Tracy's remarks that: " . . . the neo-orthodox continues to insist that the experience of Christian faith shows the radically dialectical and *experiential* relationship now available to every human being who . . . may also be open to *experience* the justifying, salvific power of this faith in the Christian God" (*Blessed Rage for Order* [New York, Seabury, 1979] 28; emphasis added).

8. "Black Power, Black Theology, and the Study of Theology and Ethics," *Theological Education*, 6/3 (1970) 209.

9. I think Walker makes these points throughout his *Appeal*. Two excerpts: "Have not the [white]

Americans the Bible in their hands? Do they believe it? Surely they do not. See how they treat [blacks] in open violation of the Bible!!" And: " . . . I exclaim to my God, 'Lord didst thou make us to be slaves to our brethren, the whites? But when I reflect that God is just, and that millions of my wretched brethren would meet death with glory—yea, more, would plunge into the very mouths of cannons and be torn into particles as minute as the atoms which compose . . . the earth, *in preference to a mere submission to the lash of tyrants*, I am . . . compelled to shrink back into nothingness before *my* maker, and exclaim again, *thy will be done*, O Lord God Almighty' " (p. 28; emphasis added).

10. That "authors produce meaning out of the available system of differences" is taken from Catherine Beasley's *Critical Practice* (New York, Methuen, 1980) 45. According to Beasley, discourse often masquerades itself as normative for all contexts. It is in this sense that Cone's statement about white theologians who "make decisions about the structure and scope of theology" referred me to Beasley. She writes (pp. 45–46): "The role of ideology is to suppress . . . contradictions in the interests of the preservation of the existing social formation, *but* their *presence* insures that it is always possible, with whatever difficulty, to identify them, to recognize ideology for what it is, and to take an active part in transforming it by producing new meanings" (emphasis added). My argument is that new meanings are produced not only from deconstruction of the texts of "white thinker" but also from that of black thinkers such as Garnet and Pennington. The distinction between the two as *forms* of theological discourse, then, allows one to "produce meaning [as in black theology] out of the available system of differences."

11. In *Black Theology and Black Power*, Cone writes that "slave preachers were virtually theologically illiterate, and even to this day few blacks have made any substantial contribution to white theology" (p. 103). But has not the issue been the development of a black theology? And upon what better sources could one rely, in a historical reflection about the antecedents of black theology, than the writings of those whom Carter G. Woodson calls "Preachers of Versatile Genius?" (Woodson, *History*). Clearly, Cone does not confuse slave preachers with preachers such as Garnet. My point here is simply that Cone did not pay enough attention to the thought of the literate black clergy.

12. Richardson and Bowden (n. 3, above), 271.

13. Ibid.

14. Ibid.

15. Ibid., 272.

16. These remarks reflect notes I took in classes held by Prof. Cone. For his views on King, see *God*, 221–22; for Turner, ibid., 61.

17. It seems that Cecil Cone, in talking of an "existential self-understanding as applied to Jesus," is referring to the historiography James Robinson employed in his new quest for the historical Jesus (see Van Harvey, *The Historical and the Believer* [Philadelphia, Westminster, 1966] 13). Cone is correct, then, in implying that the historicity of Jesus was not an issue for the slaves. *Their own* self-understanding of Jesus, however, may be valuable.

18. See also Clifton Johnson, ed., *God Struck Me Dead* (Boston, Pilgrim, 1969).

19. See B.A. Botkin, ed., *Lay My Burden Down: A Folk History of Slavery* (University of Chicago Press, 1973).

20. See C. Cone, *Crisis*, 20, and n. 17, above.

21. Richardson and Bowden (n. 3, above), 444–46.

22. For an account of Gandhi's satyagraha/ahimsa, see Erick Erikson, *Gandhi's Truth* (New York, Norton, 1969). For Martin King's use of these concepts, see John J. Ansbro, *Martin Luther King, Jr.: The Making of a Mind* (Maryknoll, N.Y., Orbis, 1982); see also King, *Freedom*.

23. See Davidson, *Genius* and *Lost Cities*; Lamb, *Africans*; J.B. Webster et al., *History of West Africa* (New York, Praeger, 1972).

24. See Zahan, 46–47; Forde, 233; Herskovits and Herskovits, 16.

25. See Garrarty and Gay (chap. 1, n. 43, above), 516–40, 594.

26. "Black Theology cannot reject the future reality of life after death—grounded in Christ's resurrection—simply because white people have distorted it for their own selfish purposes. The task is redefinition in the light of the liberation of the black community" (Cone, *Liberation*, 147).

27. Major Jones is not included here: he has no published text devoted to the categories that concern me. In his *Christian Ethics for Black Theology*, however, he indicates strongly that he supports efforts to indigenize black theology. Jones asserts, for example, that black awareness has "called forth a new search for some more meaningful redefinitions of links between black people in America and the black peoples of Africa" (pp. 114–15).

28. In his *My Soul Looks Back*, Cone reveals that, upon writing his first book, "it became clear to me that intellectual consciousness should be defined and controlled by black history and culture

and not by standards set in white seminaries and universities" (p. 47). My discussion of Cone reveals, however, that his intellectual awareness was hardly controlled by black history and culture, but indeed by *standards set in white seminaries and universities*. Recall his statement in *A Black Theology of Liberation*: "Since black theologians are trained in white seminaries and white thinkers make decisions about the structure and scope of theology, it is not possible for black religionists to separate themselves immediately from white thought" (p. 117). Clearly, Cone could not in *Black Theology and Black Power* and *A Black Theology of Liberation*.

29. See Fisher, *Songs*; Collier, *Jazz*; Sidran, *Talk*; L. Jones, *Blues People*.

30. See, e.g., Marshall W. Stearns, *The Story of Jazz* (New York, Oxford University Press, 1982) 125.

31. Indeed, African traditional music is always related to and acquires meaning within the matrix of societal functions. See Nketia, *Music*; idem, "The Problem of Meaning in African Music," *Ethnomusicology*, 6 (1962) 1–7; Chernoff, *Rhythm*; Bebey, *Music*.

32. See also Deren, *Horsemen*; Thompson, 163–91; Simpson, 64–71; Whitten and Szwed, 89–99.

33. See Herskovits, *Myth*; Wilmore, *Religion*; Sobel, *Trabelin'*; Hurston, *Church*.

34. See Herskovits, *Myth*, 215; Hurston, 91–94; Simpson, 130–31; Shiela Walker, "African Gods in the Americas: The Black Religious Continuum," *The Black Scholar*, 2/8 (Nov.–Dec. 1980) 33–36.

35. See Kaufman and Guckin, 78–84; Stearns, 99–108; Collier, 35–42; Sidran, 12–13, 36–37; L. Jones, 17–31; Charters, *Blues*.

36. Some studies show that, indeed, the idea of class (or caste) did exist in precolonial Africa. See, e.g., July, *History*; Murphy, *History*; Webster and Boahen, *History*; Davidson, *Slave Trade* and *Genius*; Zahan, *Religion*, pp. 121–25; Fortes and Evans-Pritchard, *Systems*.

37. See July, *History*; Davidson, *Slave Trade*; Webster and Boahen, *History*.

38. Ram Desai, ed., *Christianity in Africa as Seen by the Africans* (Denver, Alan Swallow, 1962) 49.

39. Sawyerr asserts that, although God is supreme, humanity is central to African traditional religion. The human being derives "life and power from God and is capable of producing life by procreation. . . . [Human Beings] can also induce life and power into other elements of creation . . . because [they are] God's vice-regent[s] on earth" (*Evangelism*, 14).

40. This is not to say that one cannot find evidence of africanisms in the United States. For a good discussion of them, see Raboteau, *Slave Religion*, "Death of the Gods"; Tallant, *Voodoo*; Thompson, *Flash*.

41. Alex Haley is one of the few Afro-Americans of the United States who knows the *name* of one of his African ancestors—Kunta Kinte of the Gambia. In his *Roots* (Garden City, N.Y., Doubleday, 1976), Haley refers to him as "the African." His name, Kunta, and his story had been passed down to Haley from generation to generation. For most of us, the names and origins of our African ancestors are unknown.

42. See, e.g., Johnson, *God Struck Me Dead*. In his collection of slave and ex-slave testimonies, the slaves and ex-slaves refer to "Old Moses," "Peter," "Matthew," "Luke," and "John," "father Abraham"; or a slave preacher would say "I am a Hebrew child." The name of Jesus, moreover, is continually on the lips of these slaves and ex-slaves. Although Raboteau reveals the impact of africanisms on black religion (p. 92), and Sobel makes an interesting case for her view that "a quasi-African body of values functioned in almost every African household in America" (p. xxi), the glaring fact remains that black religion of the United States, in its Christian form, is strongly biblical and devoid of elements that would make it *substantially* African. An African cosmology *replete* with divinities, magic, music—ritual symbols—is not at work in the spirituality of black Christians of the United States.

43. Herskovits, in his *Myth of the Negro Past*, attempts such an explanation. But his conclusions on that issue are considered problematic and his methods have been called into question by Afro-American anthropologists. For a sample of their views and disagreements with Herskovits, see Whitten and Szwed, *Afro-American Anthropology*.

44. "The character of the religious milieu, average number of slaves on plantations, and the number of Africans in the slave population were all factors in the survival or loss of African culture. In the United States all these factors tended to inhibit the survival of African culture and religion. It was not possible to maintain the rites of worship, the priesthood, or the 'national' identities which were the vehicles and supports for African theology and cult organization" (Raboteau, 92).

45. Cecil Cone (*Crisis*, 26–28) does give attention to the views of DuBois and Herskovits, and thus states that "most scholars today are reasonably sure that African traditional religion is one of the potent sources of North American black religion" (p. 28). Although issue can be taken with the level of potency, Cone is correct in emphasizing that elements of African traditional religion are

revealed in black religion. There is little evidence, however, to support Cone's very specific claim that the almighty, sovereign God of black religion is a carry-over of the God of traditional Africa. In other words, more anthropological evidence is needed to support that view. And available evidence—the testimonies themselves—reveal a very biblical God.

46. "[Long] contended that history of religion, a discipline more value-free in its approach, was the best tool for examining black religion" (J. Cone, *Soul*, 60). For a sample of Long's views, see his "Perspectives for a Study of Afro-American Religion in the United States," *History of Religion*, 11 (Aug. 1971).

47. Charles Long, "Structural Similarities and Dissimilarities in Black and African Theologies," *Journal of Religious Thought*, 32/2 (Fall-Winter 1975) 10–11.

48. Ibid., 11.

49. Ibid., 11–12.

50. Ibid., 12–13.

51. Ibid., 12–17.

52. See Paul Tillich, *Systematic Theology*, vol. 1 (University of Chicago Press, 1951) 80, 121, 124, 134. See also his discussion of theonomy in his *The Protestant Era* (University of Chicago Press, 1957), "Kairos and Religion and Secular Culture." As Malcolm Diamond explains, moreover, in his *Contemporary Philosophy and Religious Thought* (New York, McGraw-Hill, 1974): "Tillich's analysis allows for the possibility of direct confrontation with being-itself [God] by means of one particular symbol. . . . [For Tillich such a] religious symbol . . . becomes *transparent* to being-itself" (p. 349). A theonomous society, then, is in some sense transparent to the infinite being-itself.

53. In his essay, "Structural Similarities and Dissimilarities in Black and African Theologies," Long refers to Tillich's view that " . . . [Christ] remained *transparent* to the divine mystery until his death which was the final manifestation of his *transparency*" [Tillich, *Systematic Theology*, I, 134). According to Long: "such a Christological statement might . . . critique . . . bearers of modern westernism. What is finite, says Tillich, must be sacrificed for the sake of the infinite [so that the infinite might permeate it]. But the finite in Tillich's system is always first expressed as the *power*, the cultural manifestations of finitude. [Blacks, however,] were shorn of their capacities to be loci of manifestation of finite power on the historical scene" (pp. 19–20). It is in this sense, then, that society was opaque rather than transparent to "the divine mystery" for blacks. Because blacks were powerless in the United States, God revealed God's self to them in spite of the wider American society, which excluded blacks from participation in power.

54. See Long, "Structural Similarities," 13–20; and his "Freedom, Otherness, and Religion: Theologies Opaque," *The Chicago Theological Seminary Register*, 73/1, (Winter 1983).

55. "Freedom," 19–20.

56. Ibid., 17–20.

57. "Structural Similarities," 24.

58. Ibid. That Long is implying that such probing will uncover more substantially the African roots of black religion is borne out in an earlier statement of his in this essay. He writes: "Black[s] . . . feel the sense of a new beginning, but beginnings are not simply futuristic. . . . The integrity of our present and future rests upon a right relationship with our ancestors" (p. 22).

59. Hooks, *Woman*; Davis, *Women*; Wallace, *Macho*; Cade, *Woman*; Hull et al, *Brave*; Gloria Wade-Gayles, *No Crystal Stair: Visions of Race and Sex in Black Women's Fiction* (New York, Pilgrim, 1984).

60. These comments reflect my extensive reading of the writings of black theologians, with a focus on the works on which I have relied in writing chap. 2. See also James Cone, *People*, chap. 6.

61. See Wilmore and Cone, *Theology*, "Black Theology and Black Women"; Jacquelyn Grant, "Black Women and the Church," in Hull, *Brave*.

62. Cone, *Soul*, 123–38, and *People*, chap. 9, "Black Christians and Marxism." See also his *The Black Church and Marxism: What Do They Have to Say to Each Other?* (New York, Institute for Democratic Socialism, 1980).

63. Robert Tucker, ed., *The Marx-Engels Reader* (New York, Norton, 1978) 79.

64. See Nkrumah, *Path*, "Toward Colonial Freedom"; *Neo-Colonialism*; and *Struggle*.

65. See, e.g., Genovese, *Economy*; Eric Williams, *Capitalism and Slavery* (New York, Perigee Books, 1980); Bernard Magubane, *The Political Economy of Race and Class in South Africa* (London and New York, Monthly Review Press, 1979); idem, "Imperialism and the Making of the South African Working Class," *Contemporary Marxism*, 6 (Spring 1983); Ken Luckhardt and Brenda Wall, *Organize . . . Or Starve! The History of the South African Congress of Trade Unions* (New York, International Publishers, 1980).

66. "The approach to a doctrine of man for blacks will need to take . . . Marx quite seriously

. . . as [he] contribute[s] to our deeper understanding of human nature" (Roberts, *Political Theology*, 86).

67. See Cone, Introduction to part 4, "Black Theology and Third World Theologies," in Wilmore and Cone, 445–60; *Soul*, 93–113; *People*, chap. 7, "Black Theology, Black Churches, and the Third World."

68. "Because black and Asian theologians have had few conflicts in our dialogue, we have been able to transport this experience of mutual support to our respective dialogues with Africans and Latin Americans. Why should we fight each other when we have so much to lose in division and so much to gain in unity? *Asians and blacks seem to recognize that point in our theological conversations, and this recognition has enabled us to move to a deeper understanding of each other's struggles*" (Cone, in Fabella and Torres, 244; emphasis added).

CHAPTER III

1. In its "Final Communiqué," the EATWOT Pan-African Conference (1977) stated that the five sources of African theology are: (1) the Bible and Christian tradition; (2) African anthropology; (3) African traditional religion; (4) the African independent churches; (5) other African realities (Appiah-Kubi and Torres, 192–93). I focus on sources 1, 3, and 4.

2. See Kwesi Dickson, "Continuity and Discontinuity between the Old Testament and African Life and Thought" (Appiah-Kubi and Torres, chap. 9).

3. See the discussion of independency in chap. 1, above. In his *African Christianity*, Hastings notes that the Aladura Church "has . . . a seminary" (p. 27). That the church has a seminary implies its possession of an academic theology.

4. For an account of the inappropriateness of the terms "ju-ju" and "fetish," see Parrinder, 15–17. With regard to "primitive" and "animism," see Idowu, *Religion*.

5. See July, *History*, "The Great Migrations"; Murphy, *History*; C. Williams, *Destruction*; Olivia Vlahos, *African Beginnings* (New York, Viking, 1969); Fage and Oliver, *Papers*, "The Prehistoric Origins of African Culture"; Davidson, *Genius*, chap. 1–6; idem, *Lost Cities*, chap. 1–3; Ottenberg, *Cultures*, chap. 1–2.

6. On the Nuer and twins, see the classic text by Evans-Pritchard, *Nuer Religion*, 128–33; for an account of the Igbo infanticide of twins, see Ilogu, 44.

7. Mbiti, *Religions*, 13–14. For Idowu's rejection of Tempels's "vital force," see *African Traditional Religion*, 155–56.

8. In his *Un visage africane de Christianisme*, Mulago writes of Tempels's influence on his work: "*En effect, au cours de notre étude, nous nous sommes assez souvent servi de la même terminologie que cet auteur [Tempels]: vital, accroissement vital, etc.; nous n'avons pas hésité à le citer lorsque ses affirmations s'harmonisaient avec nos vues, et certains pourraient croire que notre travail serait, sous une autre forme, la thèse du missionnaire Franciscain [Tempels]. Pour nous, le plus grand mérite de l'hypothèse du Père Tempels est d'avoir suscité la réaction qu'elle méritait, et d'avoir éveillé les consciences tant africaines qu'occidentales au sens de valeurs cachées, chez les Bantu, sous les apparences de la primitivité* " (p. 156). Mulago, however, refutes Tempels's notion " . . . *que le muntu . . . se fait de l'être*." For Mulago, the *muntu* (human being) is radically dependent on "*l'Etre imparticipé, incréé, . . . transcende toutes les catégories*" (p. 157). For Mulago on *union vitale*, see pp. 115–29.

9. See Mulago, ibid., 115–29.

10. For Mbiti's notion of Zamani, see his *Religions*, "The Concept of Time."

11. Mbiti, "The Concept of Time."

12. See Sawyerr, *Evangelism*, chap. 1; Zahan, *Religion*, chap. 1; Mbiti, *Religions*, chap. 9; Dickson, *Theology*, 47–52.

13. These remarks reflect information given me by Tribal Arts Gallery, Inc., New York City.

14. On Great Zimbabwe, see July, *History*; Murphy, *History*; Fage and Oliver, *Papers*, "The Rhodesian Iron Age."

15. See Danquah, 170–71; Sawyerr, *God*, chap. 2–3; Ilogu, 34–38.

16. See also Idowu, *Religion*, 177. He writes: "there is a cult of the double, by whatever local name it is called, in most places in Africa."

17. Mulago, in his *Visage*, puts it this way: "*Le pacte du sang est . . . le don par excellence, puisqu'il est don de soi, fusion dans l'autre, entrée et réception dans la famille de son ami, entraînant communion de biens et d'intérêts. Il ne peut s'ajouter à l'union naturelle qui est parfaite, mais il limite et s'efforce d'introduire l'ami dans le courant vital qui unit les membres d'une même famille, en lui infusant le principe d'ou découle toute paranté, toute fraternité: le sang. Le pact du sang apparaît donc comme un renforcement de l'individu, de la famille et du clan*" (p. 79).

Blood shed in sacrifice, in addition, is for Africans a potent symbol. As Zahan explains: "African spiritual life is so impregnated with the idea of [sacrifice] that it is practically impossible to find a people on that continent whose religious practices do not include the slaughter of the most diverse victims. It can even be said that sacrifice is the keystone of this religion. It constitutes the supreme 'prayer,' that which could not be renounced without seriously compromising the relationship between man and the Invisible. By sacrifice we mean the flowing blood of slaughtered animals. And it is from the actual blood of animals and human beings who have fallen on innumerable altars that its entire value in Africa derives" (p. 33).

18. See Danquah, *Akan*, chap. 3; Sawyerr, *God*, chap. 2. For more on Akan traditions, see Busia, *Challenge*, chap. 2–3.

19. See Danquah, *Akan*; Sawyerr, *God*, chap. 2; Abraham, *Mind*, chap. 2.

20. On clitoridectomy, see Kenyatta, *Kenya*, chap. 6.

21. See also n. 17, above, and Laye, *Dark Child*. Laye recounts his own circumcision: " . . . the hemorrhage that follows the operation is abundant, very long and disturbing. All that blood lost! I watched my blood flowing away, and my heart contracted. I thought: is my body going to be entirely emptied? And I raised imploring eyes to our healer, the *sema*. 'The blood must flow,' said the *sema*. 'If it did not flow . . . . ' " (p. 125).

22. See also Mbiti, *Religions*, 109; Idowu, *Religion*, 184–89; Ottenberg, 61; Sawyerr, *Evangelism*, 28.

23. Mbiti, *Religions*, chap. 15; Parrinder, chap. 9; Zahan, chap. 6.

24. See also Idowu, *Religion*, 175–76; Sawyerr, *Evangelism*, 12–19; Zahan, 95–109; Davidson, *Genius*, chap. 11; Parrinder, chap. 11. A classic text on witchcraft is Evans-Pritchard, *Witchcraft*. See also Reynolds, *Magic*, and S.F. Nadel, "Witchcraft in Four African Societies" (in Ottenberg, *Cultures*).

25. Mbiti, *Religions*, chap. 16; Idowu, *Religion*, 175–76; Parrinder, chap. 11.

26. Zahan puts it this way: "[From the Africans'] view the individual does not constitute a closed system in opposition in the outside world in order to better secure his own substance and limitations. On the contrary [the African] enters into the surrounding environment, which in turn permeates him. Between the two realities there exists a constant communication, a sort of osmotic exchange, owing to which [Africans] . . . permanently [listen] . . . to the pulse of the world" (p. 9). If Zahan refers to the spiritual reciprocity between the visible and invisible as an osmotic exchange, Parrinder describes it as *Nyama*. He writes "*Nyama* is . . . found in [humans], animals, gods, nature, and things. *Nyama* is not the outward appearance, but the inner essence. . . . [One] thinks at once of electricity, for *Nyama* . . . [is] like an energy or fluid, potent but not moral" (pp. 22–23). To the views of Zahan and Parrinder on the spiritual milieu of traditional Africa I add Mbiti's: "There is a mystical power which causes people to walk on fire, to lie on thorns or nails, to send curses or harm . . . change into animals . . . ; power to make inanimate objects turn into biologically living creatures. . . . African peoples know this and try to apply it in these and many other ways" (*Religions*, 258).

27. Moreover, Idowu explains that Africans have approached the divine in humble submission by way of the ancestors and divinities. Or, Africans have sought "to tap and harness" the energy outside and inside all phenomena, in order "to . . . harness it and make it subserve [their] own end. The principle upon which [the African] works in this case is one of technique, seeking to secure the proper means to the end that he [or she] may have control over . . . elemental forces" (*Religion*, 189).

28. See Mbiti, *Religions*, chap. 14; Davidson, *Genius*, chap. 6–7, 10–16; Idowu, *Religion*, 184–89; Ottenberg, 61; Sawyerr, *Evangelism*, 28; Parrinder, chap. 5.

29. Idowu, *Religion*, 187. His views are echoed by Zahan, 49.

30. Mulago writes of the *cults des ancêtres*: "*Ce monde invisible avec lequel le culte nous met en contact est peuplé par les âmes désincarnées, ancêstres et héros apothéosés, et par le Principe premier et dernier de toute vie. Le culte s'adresse donc aux esprits des ancêtres,—en entendant par ancêtres tous les membres défunts de la famille et du clan,—aux esprits des anciens héros et à Dieu*" (*Visage*, 93).

31. Mbiti, *Concepts*, 45–55; Idowu, *Olodumare*, 71–75; Sawyerr, *God*, 49–51.

32. Idowu, *Olodumare*; Sawyerr, *God*, chap. 3; Murray, 38–39; Simpson, *Religions*; Thompson, *Flash*.

33. Herskovits and Herskovits, *Outline*; Deren, *Horsemen*.

34. This observation reflects a critical reading of the works of Idowu, Mbiti, Mulago, and Pobee. Idowu puts it this way: "It is generally theologically probable that the divinities have no absolute existence—they are in being only in consequence of the being of Deity. All that we have said about the unitary control of the created order by Deity applies here. Because the divinities

derive from Deity, their powers and authorities are meaningless apart from him" (*Religion*, 169). Kwesi Dickson, however, is reluctant to use the terms monotheism or polytheism: "There are no easy solutions to the problem of the relation between God and the gods, and . . . it is much less enlightening than is thought to use such terms as monotheism and polytheism; in a sense they confuse the discussion" (*Theology*, 58). Benjamin C. Ray offers this perspective: "Recent studies suggest that African religions are better understood as involving elements of these schemes [monotheism, polytheism, pantheism] at different theological levels and in different contexts of experience" (*Religions*).

35. See Jahn, Thompson, Chernoff, and Abraham. Benjamin C. Ray explains what he means by "archetypal symbols": "By 'archetypal symbols' I mean sacred images, whether they be gods, ancestors, sacred actions or things, which make up the traditional universe. Such images, enshrined and communicated in myth and ritual, provide a network of symbolic forms, uniting social, ecological, and conceptual elements into locally bounded cultural systems. They give order to experience by framing the world in terms of sacred figures and patterns. Thus encapsulated within local universes of archetypal forms, traditional African thought tends to abolish both time and chance by shaping experience to interrelated moral and ritual patterns" (*Religions*, 17).

36. Noting that Africans have traditionally lived in transition from being to becoming, Zahan writes: "[In] the African concept . . . man is only definable in terms of becoming first of all; he *does not exist* as a human being prior to certain physical transformations or before the performance of rites designed to admit him into adult society as a new member" (p. 9). Focusing on the Dogon, Ray puts it this way: "In ontological terms, being becomes qualified by becoming, essence by existence" (p. 29). In the jacket notes of his *Ritual Cosmos*, Evan M. Zuesse offers this perspective: "In the west we are accustomed to think of religion as centered in the personal quest for salvation or the longing for unchanging Being. Perhaps this is why we have found it so difficult to understand the religions of Africa. These religions are oriented to very different goals: fecundity, prosperity, health, social harmony. . . . African religions . . . are . . . devoted to the sanctification and constant renewal of life. *They are dedicated to Becoming rather than Being*, and seek to sustain a flourishing divine order rather than save the isolated self from it" (emphasis added).

37. Archie Shepp, writing on African-American culture, states: " . . . earliest African pioneers . . . sought, at times, both desperately and resourcefully, to preserve their indigenous cultural heritage and . . . mystify the serious student, for whom the great thematic drama of African religious sensibility vis-à-vis Western scholasticism and rationalism, has been reduced to a hodge-podge of metaphysical compromises" (see Wilmer, *Face*). Zahan puts it this way: "Black Africa has only recently revealed to us its secret thought on the subject taken up in the present work. Even if it is now possible to observe many peoples in the field, *it is nonetheless true that we are often unable to penetrate the meaning of the rites, since we are dependent in large part on the good will and ability of our informants. Unfortunately, many ethnic groups still refuse to participate in a collaboration of this type* (p. 2; emphasis added).

38. Kwesi Dickson puts it this way: "For many African theologians, theologizing has meant presupposing the traditional Western doctrinal statements but giving them what amounts to a thin veneer of traditional cultural coating. [This is] a basically unsatisfactory procedure" (*Theology*, 4). Aylward Shorter has written on this tension between adaptation and incarnation: *African Christian Theology—Adaptation or Incarnation?* According to Shorter, the issue of adaptation or incarnation " . . . was the question asked by the Bishops of Africa and Madagascar at the 1974 Roman synod" (p. 3). Shorter writes, moreover, " . . . the Bishops repudiated 'theology of adaptation' in no uncertain terms and opted for what they called 'the theology of incarnation.' " For further discussion of the tension between adaptation and a more critical africanization, see Ngindu Mushete's "The History of Theology in Africa: From Polemics to Critical Irenics" (in Appiah-Kubi and Torres, chap. 3, esp. pp. 27–30). F. Eboussi Boulaga, however, implies that African theology now is no more than adaptation, even though African theologians claim to reject adaptation: ". . . it is taken for granted that when Christianity learns to speak to their 'soul,' [Third World] peoples will hasten to embrace it into a language in accord with their sensibilities and culture. This is the notion at the origin of the discourse on the necessity of the indigenization of Christianity, of its incarnation in new cultures. This discourse, these programs are usually reducible to a criticism of what is referred to as Western Christianity. Rarely do they sketch the form to be substituted for this Western Christianity, and when they do, the sketch consists mostly of a disquisition on local curiosities, folklore, or peculiarities of lifestyle that have indeed disappeared or are barely surviving" (*Christianity*, 57).

39. Dickson puts it this way: "The quest for an African theology assumes that there is much more to be done than is implied by indigenization which, by its very nature does not encourage original thinking and analysis; African theology is meant to involve a sustained articulation of faith

which would bear the marks of an original African experience" (*Theology*, 120). "Thus it is essential that African Christians should be in a position to express in a vital way what Christ means to them, and to do so in and through a cultural medium that makes original thinking possible" (ibid., 4–5). It seems, then, that Dickson equates indigenization with adaptation. Shorter, on the other hand, in his *African Christian Theology* equates adaptation with an uncritical syncretism.

A word must be said about Mulago's early use of *le principe de l'adaptation*. Mulago writes: "*L'adaptation n'est rien d'autre que cette présentation du message chrétian par son aspect le plus en harmonie avec les aspirations du peuple à gagner au Christ*" (*Visage*, 30). Although Mulago's remarks here appear to commend an africanization that serves the goals of Western christianization, Mulago also says: "*La tactique missionare, l'adaptation n'est point une tactique de 'propagandiste,' n'est pas un stratgème, mais une fidélité à la mission de l'Eglise, qui n'est autre que le prolongement de l'Incarnation du Verbe, l'adaptation de Dieu à l'homme. Ce qui guide l'apôtre n'est pas d'abord un intérêt de propagande; c'est la logique de sa foi* (p. 31). Here, then, Mulago seems in agreement with Dickson and the bishops of the synod of 1974. Perhaps Mulago's *principe de l'adptation* translates into "principle of incarnation."

40. *Journal of the American Academy of Religion*, 44/2 (June 1976) 275–87.

41. Dickson, however, takes issue with Awolalu here: "That there is a sense of sin against God in Africa has been documented. . . . However, the view that all offenses are finally against God is to be seen in the context of the attempt to respond to the Western typing of African religion, which response has led to the creation of such expressions as 'diffused monotheism'; for not all offenses are in fact consciously believed to be against God" (*Theology*, 67).

42. "This 'primitive high god' is a product of ignorance and prejudice. There are too many stay-at-home investigators on the job, while those who go out into the field often find it difficult to leave behind at home their own preconceived notions" (Idowu, in ibid., 19).

43. For Idowu's provisional rejection of the notion of ancestor worship, see his *African Traditional Religion*, 178–89. For the views of Jomo Kenyatta on this issue, see his *Facing Mt. Kenya*, 253–58.

44. Mbiti, "Some African Concepts of Christology," in Samartha, *Faiths*.

45. Mbiti, "Our Savior as an African Experience," in Lindars and Smalley, *Christ*.

46. See Sawyerr, *Evangelism*; Danquah, *Akan*. For Pobee's discussion of this Akan anthropology, see his *African Theology*, 49.

47. "But if there is a future to the Kingdom, it . . . cannot be divorced from its present effectiveness. This is where Dodd's contribution of 'Realized Eschatology' becomes so crucial, even if not sufficient" (Mbiti, *Eschatology*, 42).

48. See, e.g., Dickson and Ellingworth, *Revelation*; Appiah-Kubi and Torres, *Theology*.

49. See, e.g., Cutrufelli, *Women*; El Dareer, *Woman*; Obbo, *Women*; Abdalla, *Sisters*.

50. These remarks were made during my trip to South Africa in August 1982. The woman is the wife of a professor at the Federal Theological Seminary.

51. Moyo, "The Quest for African Christian Theology and the Problem of the Relationship between Faith and Culture—The Hermeneutical Perspective," *African Theological Journal*, 12/2 (1983).

52. A penetrating, critical analysis of the South African homelands is provided in Roger Southall's *South Africa's Transkei*. Other sources of information: Gerhart, *Power*; Davenport, *South Africa*; Fredrickson, *Supremacy*.

53. Supportive of this judgment is my own eyewitness account. Having traveled throughout South Africa, having visited the homelands of KwaZulu and Baphuthatswana, having lived in Soweto for a week, I can testify to the fact of black deprivation maintained by Pretoria.

54. On the Freedom Charter, a liberal document, see Gerhart, 94–95, 98, 118, 146–47; Davenport, 279–80.

55. Hountondji, 33–37; Okere, *Philosophy*, chap. 1; Wiredu, *Philosophy*, Introduction and chap. 1–3.

CHAPTER IV

1. See Introduction, n. 1, b, d, e, and f.

2. First published in *Worldview*, Aug. 1974. Reprinted in Wilmore and Cone, 477–91.

3. This remark reflect interviews I conducted with Gayraud Wilmore, New York Theological Seminary, and with James Cone, UTS, New York City, in 1984.

4. On the Legon conference, and reports on its value and scope, see *The Journal of Religious Thought*, 32/2 (Fall-Winter 1975).

5. Mbiti published his essay in *Worldview* just four months prior to the Legon consultation (Dec.

29-31, 1974). Thus, it was quite contemporaneous with the essays given in Legon. In fact, Desmond Tutu's essay, "Black Theology/African Theology—Soul Mates or Antagonists?," was written in response to Mbiti.

6. See n. 4, above.

7. *African Theological Journal*, 4 (Aug. 1971).

8. See J.J. Maguet, "The Problem of Tutsi Domination," in Ottenberg, *Cultures*; Lamb, *Africans*, 12–13.

9. Michel Kayoya, *My Father's Footprints* (Nairobi, East African Publishing House, 1973) 95.

10. That Kayoya supported the africanization of Christianity is clear throughout his *My Father's Footprints*. Much of his theology retains traditional Burundi concepts.

11. The affinity between Cone and Kayoya is found in their commitments to justice in the form of the liberation of the oppressed. That there is no *formal* connection between them, however, must be stressed.

12. For Cone's views on the "cheapness" of reconciliation without complete liberation, see his *God of the Oppressed*. For Bonhoeffer's views on "cheap grace," see his *The Cost of Discipleship* (New York, Macmillan, 1979).

13. That Fashole-Luke implies that black South Africans depend too heavily on the theology of James Cone is borne out by a footnote on the following page of the "Quest" essay: "For the American perspective on Black Theology, which has to some extent influenced theologians in the Republic of South Africa, see James Cone, *Black Theology and Black Power*...[and] *A Black Theology of Liberation*" (p. 75). Fashole-Luke does not say outright that black South Africans depend too heavily on Cone's works, but his suggestion that they adopt "the theological insights of their white oppressors" seems contrary to what Cone stresses: *no reconciliation prior to complete liberation*. It seems, then, that Fashole-Luke believes that should black South Africans adopt the theology of their oppressors rather than that of Cone, black theology in South Africa would become a "genuine relevant Christian" theology. "Genuine relevant" theology for Fashole-Luke undermines the significance of race.

It is well known that Cone's theology has strongly influenced black theology in South Africa. Gerhart puts it this way: "Coming to South Africa later in time but affecting black thinking as much or more than writings from Africa were works by black Americans, including . . . the writings of James Cone . . . on black theology" (*Power*, 275). See also Basil Moore: "The term 'Black Theology' was coined in the United States where it is to a large extent a theological response by black theologians to the emergence of black power. This is best exemplified in James Cone's earlier work *Black Theology and Black Power*" ("Challenge," 1).

14. See J.H.P. Serfontein, *Apartheid, Change, and the NG Kerk* (Emmarentia, S. Africa, Taurus, 1982), chap. 3; Marjorie Hope and James Young, *The South African Churches in a Revolutionary Situation* (Maryknoll, N.Y., Orbis, 1981) 30–31.

15. (Capetown, Methodist Publishing House, n.d.) 23.

16. I refer to the incident at Sharpville in 1960. Reportedly, more than 67 blacks were shot in the back while fleeing police. The blacks were protesting the pass laws. In 1976 more than 600 school children were murdered by police in Soweto. They were protesting the use of Afrikaans as the principal medium of instruction. See Gerhart, 1–2; Mzimela, 172.

17. See Mzimela, *Apartheid*; Benson, *Mandela*; Donald Woods, *Biko* (New York, Paddington, 1978); Luckhart and Wall, *Organize*; Millard Arnold, *Steve Biko: Black Consciousness in South Africa* (New York, Vintage, 1979); The Report of the Study Commission on U.S. Policy toward Southern Africa, *South Africa: Time Running Out* (University of California Press, 1981).

18. See Hope and Young (n. 14, above), 77.

19. This judgment emerges from intense study of Prof. Cone's work and close association with him during the course of my theological education.

20. Black theologians whom I have in mind here are James Cone, J. Deotis Roberts, and Cecil Cone.

21. See also Rubin and Weinstein, 168–79; Austin, *Politics*.

22. See *Africa*, 149 (Jan. 1984); ibid., 150 (Feb. 1984); *Africa Now*, 36 (April 1984); ibid., 39 (July 1984); *West Africa*, 3464 (Jan. 9, 1984); ibid., 3476 (April 2, 1984).

23. Assembly Secretariat, *The Struggle Continues: Official Report, Third Assembly, AIP, Africa Conference of Churches* (Nairobi, AACC, 1975) 77.

24. "As an African, one has an academic interest in Black Theology, just as one is interested in the 'water buffalo theology' of southeast Asia" (Mbiti, in Wilmore and Cone, 481).

25. First published in *The Journal of Religious Thought*, 32/2 (Fall-Winter 1975) 25–33; reprinted in Wilmore and Cone, 483–91.

26. See Carty and Kilson, *Independent Africa*, 179–92; Nkrumah, *Consciencism*, 78–79; Alex Quaison-Sackey, *Africa Unbound* (New York, Praeger, 1963), chap. 2.

27. See Eberhard Bethge, *Dietrich Bonhoeffer* (New York, Harper & Row, 1977), "The Confessing Church in the War"; Eberhard Bush, *Karl Barth* (Philadelphia, Fortress, 1976) 226.

28. See Serfontein (n. 14, above), chap. 3–4.

29. See Tutu, *Wilderness*; idem, "Letter to the Prime Minister," *South African Outlook*, 106/1262 (July 1976) 102–4.

30. First published in *Pro Veritate* (S. Africa), Jan. 15 and Feb. 15, 1972. Reprinted in Wilmore and Cone, 463–76.

31. Providing background to this consultation, Cornish Rogers writes that in 1970, "in an attempt to be of use to African nations, the African commission of NCBC established a Pan-African Skill Project. This sought to link the technical needs of maldeveloped black African nations by recruiting black applicants for two-year tours of service to an African government" ("Pan-Africanism and the Black Church," *Christian Century* [Nov. 17, 1971] 1345).

32. *Struggle Continues*, 77.

33. On the australopithecines, see Murray, 44–45.

CHAPTER V

1. See Jesse Mugambi, "Liberation and Theology," in *WSCF Dossier No. 5* (June 1974) 41–42; Kofi Appiah-Kubi, "Jesus Christ—Some Christological Aspects from African Perspectives," in John Mbiti, ed., *African and Asian Contributions to Contemporary Theology* (Celigny, Switzerland, WCC Bossey Ecumenical Institute, 1977).

2. Notwithstanding the affinity between the theologies of Cone, Carr, and Tutu, African theology differs considerably from black theology today. My examination of the histories from which both theologies emerged, and of texts representative of those histories, have made this clear. Thus, African theology, as defined by Mbiti, Fashole-Luke, and Sawyerr, is as a distant cousin to black theology, especially that of James Cone.

3. Catherine Belsey, in her *Critical Practice*, writes: " . . . recent work . . . has put in question not only some of the specific assumptions of common sense, some of the beliefs which appear *obvious* and *natural, but the authority of the concept of common sense itself, the collective and timeless wisdom whose unquestioned presence seems to be the source and guarantee of everything we take for granted . . . . In other words, it is argued that what seems 'obvious' and 'natural' are not given but produced in a specific society by the ways in which that society talks and thinks about itself and its experience*" (pp. 2–3; emphasis added). My point here, then, is that nothing commends the view that black and African theologians are *obviously* and *naturally* siblings now and for all time. The view that they are siblings, to allude to Belsey, is *produced*; it is not simply *given*. It must be produced, moreover, by scholars sharing similar assumptions, ideologies, hopes, and dreams. It would be ludicrous, then, to assert that Mbiti and Cone are siblings, *ipso facto*. Belsey, furthermore, writes: "Ideology is *inscribed in* discourse in the sense that it is literally written or spoken *in it;* it is not a separate element which exists independently in some free-floating realm of 'ideas' and is subsequently embodied in words, but a way of thinking, speaking, experiencing" (p. 5). In other words, the view that the theologians are siblings has neither a priori status nor is it the inevitability of some logocentrism destined to bear itself out in the text. It is, *merely*, "a way of thinking, speaking, experiencing." It is, then, subject to endless revision.

4. Peter Gay, *The Enlightenment: An Interpretation. The Rise of Modern Paganism* (New York, Norton, 1966) 201.

5. For a discussion of philosophical theology, see Friedrich Schleiermacher, *Brief Outline on the Study of Theology* (Atlanta, John Knox Press, 1977) 19–40; John Macquarrie, *Principles of Christian Theology*, 2nd ed. (New York, Scribner's, 1977) 43–58; David Tracy, *The Analogical Imagination* (New York, Crossroad, 1981) 57–59.

6. See Geiss, *Movement*, chap. 6–9; Esedebe, *Pan-Africanism*, chap. 1; Drake, *Redemption*; Colin Legum, *Pan-Africanism* (New York, Praeger, 1965), chap. 1; W. Williams, *Americans*; Wilmore, *Religion*, chap. 5; Padmore, *Pan-Africanism*.

7. See Geiss, chap. 7; Esedebe, chap. 1.

8. See Geiss, chap. 5; Drake, *Redemption*, "Ethiopianism and Religious-Political Movements"; Esedebe, chap. 1; Davidson Nichol, *Africanus Horton* (London, Longmans, 1969); Sanneh, chap. 7.

9. See Geiss, chap. 12; Esedebe, chap. 2–4; Legum, chap. 11; M'buyinga, chap. 1.

10. See Geiss, chap. 20; Esedebe, chap. 5; Legum, chap. 4–8; M'buyinga, chap. 5; Rubin and Weinstein, chap. 10.

11. For the views of Blyden, see Lynch, *Blyden* and *Black Spokesman* (chap. 1, n. 29, above). For Nkrumah, see his *Ghana* and *Consciencism*. For the views of Crummell, see his *Africa and America* and *The Future of Africa*; see as well Casely Hayford, *Ethiopia Unbound: Studies in Race Emancipation*, 2nd ed., with a new Introduction by F. Nnabuenyi Ugonna (London, Frank Cass, 1969). For the views of Turner, see his "God is a Negro," in Bracey et al., *Nationalism*. See also by DuBois, *The World and Africa*, and *The Autobiography of W.E.B. DuBois* (New York, International Publishers, 1968).

12. Geiss writes: "Pan-Africanism as an ideology of emancipation maintained the principle that all men and all races are equal and therefore should enjoy equal rights. The claim to equal rights was formulated in the course of a polemic against all . . . who postulated that the white races were superior and the coloured races inferior, i.e., against all theories on racial superiority" (p. 96). However, Geiss also discloses what he perceives as an "irrational-racist tendency" in Pan-Africanism (p. 102). But he claims that it was the exception rather than the rule. Still, one can find certain notions of black superiority in Pan-Africanism. Martin Delaney, for instance, in his *The Condition, Elevation, Emigration, and Destiny of the Colored People of the United States*, writes that "colored people can and do stand warm climates better than whites; and find an answer fully to the point in the fact, that they also stand *all other* climates, cold, temperate, and modified, that white people can stand; therefore, according to our oppressor's own showing, we are a *superior race*, being endowed with properties fitting us for *all parts* of the earth, while they are only adapted to *certain* parts" (p. 202).

For an additional example of the notion of black superiority, see Aptheker, *History*, "Afro-American Superiority: A Neglected Theme in the Literature."

Bibliographical References

AACC. *The Church in Changing Africa; Report of the All-Africa Church Conference*. New York, International Missionary Council, 1959.

———. *The Drumbeats from Kampala*. London, Lutterworth, 1963.

———. *Engagement: Abidjan '69*. Nairobi, 1970.

———. *The Struggle Continues*. Nairobi, 1970.

Abdalla, Raqiya Haji Dualeh. *Sisters in Affliction: Circumcision and Infibulation of Women in Africa*. London, Zed Press, 1982.

Abraham, W.E. *The Mind of Africa*. University of Chicago Press, 1962.

Abrahams, Roger, ed. *African Folktales*. New York, Pantheon, 1983.

Anderson, Gerald H., and Stransky, Thomas F., eds. *Mission Trends No. 3: Third World Theologies*. New York, Paulist, 1976.

Appiah-Kubi, Kofi, and Torres, Sergio eds., *African Theology en Route*. Maryknoll, N.Y., Orbis, 1979.

Apter, David. *Ghana in Transition*, 2nd ed. Princeton, Princeton University Press, 1972.

Aptheker, Herbert. *Afro-American History: The Modern Era*. New York, Citadel, 1971.

———. *To Be Free*. New York, International Publishers, 1969.

Austin, Dennis. *Politics in Africa*, 2nd ed. Hanover, University Press of New England, 1984.

Ayandele, E. A. *Holy Johnson, Pioneer of African Nationalism 1836-1917*. New York, Humanities Press, 1970.

Barongo, Yolamu, ed. *Political Science in Africa: A Critical Review*. London, Zed Press, 1983.

Barrett, David B. *Schism and Renewal in Africa: An Analysis of Six Thousand Contemporary Religious Movements*. Nairobi, Oxford University Press, 1968.

Bascom, William. *Ifa Divination: Communication Between Gods and Men in West Africa*. Bloomington, Indiana University Press, 1969.

Bastide, Roger. *The African Religions of Brazil*. Baltimore: Johns Hopkins University Press, 1978.

Bebey, Francis. *African Music: A People's Art*. Westport, Ct., Lawrence Hill, 1980.

Belsey, Catherine. *Critical Practice*. New York, Methuem, 1970.

Ben-Jochannan, Yosef. *Black Man of the Nile and His Family*. New York, Alkebu-lan Books Associates, 1973.

Bennett, Lerone. *Before the Mayflower*. Baltimore, Penguin, 1978.

Benson, Mary. *Nelson Mandela*. London, Panaf Books, 1980.

Berry, M. F., and Blassingame, John. *Long Memory*. New York, Oxford University Press, 1982.

Blassingame, John W. *The Slave Community: Plantation Life in the Ante-Bellum South*. 2nd ed. New York, Oxford University Press, 1979.

Blyden, Edward. *Christianity, Islam, and the Negro Race*. London, Edinburgh University Press, 1967.

Boesak, Allan. *Black and Reformed: Apartheid, Liberation, and the Calvinist Tradition*. Maryknoll, N.Y., Orbis, 1984.

———. *Farewell to Innocence: A Socio-Ethical Study on Black Theology and Black Power*. Maryknoll, N.Y., Orbis 1976.

Bond, George; Johnson, Walton; and Walker, Sheila S., eds. *African Christianity: Patterns of Religious Continuity*. New York, Academic Press, 1979.

Bosch, David J., comp. *Missiology and Science of Religion B.D. III*. Pretoria, University of South Africa, 1973.

Botkin, B. A., ed. *Lay My Burden Down*. University of Chicago Press, 1973.

Boulaga, F. Eboussi, *Christianity Without Fetishes: An African Critique and Recapture of Christianity*. Maryknoll, N.Y., Orbis, 1985.

Bracy, J., Meier, A., and Rudwick, E., eds. *Black Nationalism in America*. Indianapolis, Bobbs-Merrill, 1970.

Bruce, Calvin E., and Jones, William, eds. *Black Theology II*. Lewisburg, Pa., Bucknell University Press; London, Associated University Presses, 1978.

Buell, Raymond Leslie. *Liberia: A Century of Survival, 1847–1947*. Philadelphia, University of Pennsylvania Press and The University Museum, 1947.

Burkett, Randall K. *Garveyism as a Religious Movement*. Metuchen, N.J., Scarecrow Press, 1978.

Busia, K.A. *The Challenge of Africa*. New York, Praeger, 1964.

Cade, Toni, ed. *The Black Woman*. New York, New American Library, 1970.

Carter, Gwendolen, and O'Meara, Patrick, eds. *Southern Africa: The Continuing Crisis*. Indiana University Press, 1982.

Cartey, Wilfred, and Kilson, Martin, eds. *The Africa Reader: Colonial Africa*. New York, Vintage, 1970.

——. *The Africa Reader: Independent Africa*. New York, Vintage, 1970.

Charters, Samuel. *The Roots of the Blues: An African Search*. New York, Perigee Books, 1981.

Chernoff, John Miller. *African Rhythm and African Sensibility*. University of Chicago Press, 1979.

Cleage, Albert B., Jr. *The Black Messiah*. New York, Sheed and Ward, 1969.

Cole, Bill. *John Coltrane*. New York, Schirmer, 1976.

Collier, James Lincoln. *The Making of Jazz: A Comprehensive History*. New York, Dell, 1978.

Cone, Cecil. *The Identity Crisis in Black Theology*. Nashville, AMEC, 1975.

Cone, James. *Black Theology and Black Power*. New York, Seabury, 1969.

——. *A Black Theology of Liberation*. Philadelphia, Lippincott, 1970.

——. *God of the Oppressed*. New York, Seabury, 1975.

——. *For My People: Black Theology and the Black Church*. Maryknoll, N.Y., Orbis, 1984.

——. *My Soul Looks Back*. Nashville, Abingdon, 1982; reprint ed., Maryknoll, N.Y. Orbis, 1986.

——. *The Spirituals and the Blues*. New York, Seabury, 1972.

Crowder, Michael. *West Africa under Colonial Rule*. Evanston, Northwestern University Press, 1968.

Crummell, Alexander. *Africa and America*. New York, Negro Universities Press, 1969.

——. *The Future of Africa*. New York, Scribner, 1862.

Cutrufelli, Maria Rosa. *Women of Africa: Roots of Oppression*. London, Zed Press, 1983.

Danquah, J. B. *The Akan Doctrine of God*. London, Frank Cass, 1966.

Davenport, T.R.H. *South Africa: A Modern History*, 2nd ed. Buffalo, University of Toronto Press, 1980.

Davidson, Basil. *Africa in History*. New York, Collier, 1974.

——. *The African Genius*. Boston, Little, Brown, 1969.

——. *The African Slave Trade*. Boston, Little, Brown, 1980.

——. *Can Africa Survive? Arguments against Growth without Development*. Boston, Little, Brown, 1974.

——. *A History of West Africa*. Garden City, N.Y., Doubleday, Anchor Books, 1966.

——. *Let Freedom Come: Africa in Modern History*. Boston, Little, Brown, 1978.

——. *The Lost Cities of Africa*. Boston, Little, Brown, 1970.

Davis, Angela Y. *Women, Race, and Class*. New York, Random House, 1983.

Davis, David B. *The Problem of Slavery in Western Culture*. Cornell University Press, 1966.

Delany, Martin. *The Condition, Elevation, Emigration, and Destiny of the Colored People of the United States*. New York, Arno Press and the New York Times, 1968.

——, and Campbell, Robert. *Search for a Place. Black Separatism and Africa, 1860*. University of Michigan Press, 1969.

DeLusignan, Guy. *French-Speaking Africa since Independence*. New York, Praeger, 1969.

Deren, Maya. *Divine Horsemen: The Living Gods of Haiti*. New York, Thames and Hudson, 1953; reprint ed., New York, McPherson, 1970.

Dickson, Kwesi. *Theology in Africa*. Maryknoll, N.Y., Orbis, 1984.

——, and Ellingworth, P., eds. *Biblical Revelation and African Beliefs*. Maryknoll, N.Y., Orbis, 1969.

Diop, Cheikh Anta. *The African Origin of Civilization: Myth or Reality?* Westport, Ct., Lawrence Hill, 1974.

Drake, St. Clair. *The Redemption of Africa and Black Religion*. New York, Third World Press, 1977.

DuBois, W.E.B. *On the Importance of Africa in World History*. New York, Black Liberation Press, 1978.

——. *The Negro*. New York, Oxford University Press, 1972.

——. *The Negro Church*. Atlanta University Press, 1903.

——. *The Seventh Son: The Thought and Writings of W.E.B. DuBois*, 2 vols. Julius Lester, ed. New York, Random House, 1971.

——. *The Souls of Black Folk*. New York, New American Library, 1969.

——. *The World and Africa*. New York: International Publishers, 1965.

Dudley, Billy. *An Introduction to Nigerian Government and Politics*. Indiana University Press, 1982.

Duffy, James. *Portugal in Africa*. London, Penguin, 1962.

Edwards, Paul, ed. *Equiano's Travels*. London, Heinemann, 1977.

El Dareer, Asma. *Woman, Why Do You Weep? Circumcision and Its Consequences*. London, Zed Press, 1982.

Ellison, Ralph. *Shadow and Act*. New York, Random House, 1972.

Esedebe, P. Olisanwuche. *Pan-Africanism: The Idea and Movement, 1776–1963*. Washington, D.C., Howard University Press, 1982.

Evans-Pritchard, Edward E. *Nuer Religion*. New York, Oxford University Press, 1974.

——. *Witchcraft, Oracles, and Magic among the Azande*. Oxford, Clarendon, 1983.

Fabella, Virginia, and Torres, Sergio, eds. *Irruption of the Third World: Challenge to Theology*. Maryknoll, N.Y., Orbis, 1983.

Fage, J.D., and Oliver, R.A., eds. *Papers in African Prehistory*. New York, Cambridge University Press, 1970.

Fanon, Frantz. *The Wretched of the Earth*. New York, Grove, 1968.

Fauset, Arthur H. *Black Gods of the Metropolis*. University of Pennsylvania Press, 1971.

Fetter, Bruce, ed. *Colonial Rule in Africa: Readings from Primary Sources*. University of Wisconsin Press, 1979.

Fisher, Miles Mark. *Negro Slave Songs in the United States*. Secaucus, N.J., Citadel, 1978.

Fitch, Bob, and Oppenheimer, Mary. *Ghana: End of an Illusion*. New York, Monthly Review Press, 1966.

Fitts, Leroy. *Loft Carey: First Black Missionary to Africa*. Valley Forge, Judson, 1982.

Foner, Philip, S. *American Socialism and Black Americans*. Westport, Ct., Greenwood Press, 1977.

Forbath, Peter. *The River Congo*. New York, Dutton, 1977.

Forde, Daryll, ed. *African Worlds: Studies in the Cosmological Ideas and Social Values of African Peoples*. Oxford, Oxford University Press, 1976.

Fortes, M. and Evans-Pritchard, E. E., eds. *African Political Systems*. New York, Oxford University Press, 1969.

Frazier, E. Franklin. *The Negro Church in America*. New York, Schocken, 1978.

Fredrickson, George. *White Supremacy: A Comparative Study in American and South African History*. New York, Oxford University Press, 1981.

Friedland, William, and Rosberg, Carl. *African Socialism*. Stanford, Stanford University Press, 1964.

Garvey, Marcus. *Philosophy and Opinions of Marcus Garvey*. Compiled by Amy J. Garvey. Totowa, N.J., Frank Cass, 1967 reprinted, New York, Atheneum, 1969.

Gayle, Addison. *The Black Aesthetic*. Garden City, N.Y., Doubleday, 1971.

Geiss, Imanuel. *The Pan-African Movement: A History of Pan-Africanism in America, Europe, and Africa*. New York, African Publishing Co., 1974.

Genovese, Eugene. *The Political Economy of Slavery*. New York, Random House, 1967.

——. *Roll Jordan Roll*. New York, Vintage, 1976.

Gerhart, Gail. *Black Power in South Africa: The Evolution of an Ideology*. University of California Press, 1979.

Gillespie, Dizzy, with Al Frazer. *To Be Or Not To Bop*. Garden City, N.Y., Doubleday, 1979.

Glasswell, M., and Fashole-Luke, E.W., eds. *New Testament Christianity for Africa and the World*. London, SPCK, 1974.

Glaze, Anita. *Art and Death in a Senufo Village*. Bloomington Indiana University Press, 1981.

Goldman, Peter. *The Death and Life of Malcolm X*, 2nd ed. University of Illinois Press, 1979.

Groves, Charles Pelham. *The Planting of Christianity in Africa*, 4 vols. London, Lutterworth, 1948–64.

Guillot, René. *Guillot's African Folktales*. New York, Franklin Watts, 1965.

Harding, Vincent. *There Is a River: The Black Struggle for Freedom in America.* New York: Harcourt, Brace, Jovanovich, 1981.

Harris, Sheldon. *Paul Cuffe, Black America, and the African Return.* New York, Simon and Schuster, 1972.

Harrison, Paul Carter. *The Drama of Nommo.* New York, Grove, 1972.

Hastings, Adrian. *African Christianity.* New York, Seabury, 1976.

——. *A History of African Christianity, 1950–1975.* New York, Cambridge University Press, 1979.

Herskovits, Melville. *Dahomey: An Ancient West African Kingdom*, vol. 2. Evanston, Northwestern University Press, 1967.

——. *The Human Factor in Changing Africa.* New York, Random House, 1962.

——. *The Myth of the Negro Past.* Boston, Beacon, 1958.

——, and Herskovits, Francis L. *An Outline of Dahomean Religious Belief.* Milwood: Kraus, 1976.

Hodgkin, Thomas. *Nationalism in Colonial Africa.* New York, New York University Press, 1957.

Hodgson, Janet. *Ntsikana's 'Great Hymn': A Xhosa Expression of Christianity in the Early 19th Century Eastern Cape.* University of Cape Town, 1980.

Hooks, Bell. *Ain't I a Woman: Black Women and Feminism.* Boston, South End Press, 1981.

Horton, James Africanus. *West African Countries and Peoples.* Edinburgh University Press, 1969.

Hountondji, Paulin, J. *African Philosophy: Myth or Reality.* Indiana University Press, 1983.

Huet, Michel. *The Dance, Art, and Ritual of Africa.* Introduction by Jean Laude, text by Jean-Louis Paudrat. New York, Pantheon, 1978.

Hull, Gloria T.; Scott, Patricia Bell; and Smith, Barbara, eds. *But Some of Us Are Brave.* Old Westbury, N.Y., Feminist Press, 1982.

Hurston, Zora Neale. *The Sanctified Church.* Berkeley, Turtle Island, 1983.

Idowu, E. Bolaji. *African Traditional Religion: A Definition.* Maryknoll, N.Y., Orbis, 1975.

. *Olodumare: God in Yoruba Beliefs.* London, Oxford University Press, 1962.

——. *Towards an Indigenous Church.* Oxford University Press, 1965.

Ilogu, Edmund. *Christianity and Igbo Culture.* New York, NOK Publishers, L.F.D., 1974.

Isichei, Elizabeth. *A History of Nigeria.* New York, Longman, 1984.

Jackson, Henry. *From the Congo to Soweto: U.S. Foreign Policy toward Africa since 1960.* New York, Quill, 1984.

Jackson, Robert, and Rosberg, Carl, eds. *Personal Rule in Black Africa.* University of California Press, 1982.

Jahn, Janheinz. *Muntu: The New African Culture.* New York, Grove, 1961.

James, George. *Stolen Legacy.* New York, Philosophical Library, 1976.

Johnson, Clifton, et al., eds. *God Struck Me Dead.* Philadelphia, United Church Press, 1969.

Jones, Leroi. *Black Music.* New York, Quill, 1967.

——. *Blues People.* New York, Morrow, 1963.

Jones, Major. *Black Awareness.* Nashville, Abingdon, 1971.

——. *Christian Ethics for Black Theology.* Nashville, Abingdon, 1974.

Jones, William. *Is God a White Racist?* Garden City, N.Y., Anchor, 1973.

July, Robert. *A History of the African People*, 3rd ed. New York, Scribner's, 1980.

Kagame, Alexis. *La philosophie bantu-rwandaise de l'Etre.* Brussels, Académie Royale des Sciences Coloniales, 1955.

Kaufman, Fredrick, and Guckin, John P. *The African Roots of Jazz.* New York, Alfred Publ., 1979.

Kaunda, Kenneth David. *Kaunda on Violence.* Colin Morris, ed. London, Sphere Books, 1982.

Kayoya, Michel. *My Father's Footprints.* Nairobi, East African Publishing House, 1973.

Keil, Charles. *Urban Blues.* Chicago, University of Chicago Press, 1970.

Kenyatta, Jomo. *Facing Mt. Kenya.* New York, Random House, 1965.

King, Martin Luther, Jr. *Strength to Love.* Philadelphia, Fortress, 1981.

——. *Stride toward Freedom.* New York, Harper & Row, 1958.

——. *Where Do We Go From Here: Chaos or Community.* Boston, Beacon, 1968.

——. *Why We Can't Wait.* New York, New American Library, 1964.

Kirwen, Michael C. *African Widows.* Maryknoll, N.Y., Orbis, 1979.

Lamb, David. *The Africans.* New York, Random House, 1982.

Lawson, E. Thomas. *Religions of Africa.* New York, Harper & Row, 1984.

Laye, Camara. *The Dark Child.* New York: Farrar, Straus, and Giroux, 1978.

Legum, Colin. *Pan-Africanism*. New York, Praegar, 1965.

Liebenow, Gus. *Liberia: The Evolution of Privilege*. Cornell University Press, 1969.

Lincoln, C. Eric. *The Black Church since Frazier*. New York, Schocken, 1978.

Lindars, B., and Smalley, S., eds. *Christ and Spirit in the New Testament*. Cambridge University Press, 1973.

Litwack, Leon F. *Been in the Storm So Long*. New York, Knopf, 1979.

Locke, Alain, ed. *The New Negro*. New York, Atheneum, 1969.

Lowenberg, Bert James, and Bogin, Ruth, eds. *Black Women in Nineteenth-Century American Life*. Pennsylvania State University Press, 1981.

Luckhardt, Ken, and Wall, Brenda. *Organize . . . or Starve! The History of the South African Congress of Trade Unions*. New York, International Publishers, 1980.

Lynch, Hollis. *Edward Wilmot Blyden: Pan-Negro Patriot*. New York, Oxford University Press, 1970.

———. *Black Spokesman: Selected Published Writings of Edward Wilmot Blyden*. London, Frank Cass, 1971.

Magubane, Bernard. *The Political Economy of Race and Class in South Africa*. New York, Monthly Review Press, 1979.

Mamdani, Mahmood. *Imperialism and Fascism in Uganda*. Trenton, Africa World Press, 1984.

Marable, Manning. *Blackwater: Historical Studies in Race, Class Consciousness, and Revolution*. Dayton, Ohio, Black Praxis Press, 1981.

Mays, Benjamin. *The Negro's God*. Boston, Chapman & Grimes, 1938; reprint ed., Westport, Ct., Greenwood, 1969.

Mbiti, John S. *African Religions and Philosophy*. New York, Doubleday, 1970.

———. *Concepts of God in Africa*. London: SPCK, 1979.

———. *Introduction to African Religion*. New York, Praeger, 1975.

———. *New Testament Eschatology in an African Background*. Oxford: Oxford University Press, 1971.

M'buyinga, Elenga. *Pan-Africanism or Neo-Colonialism: The Bankruptcy of the O.A.U.* London, Zed Press, 1982.

Mezu, S. Okechukwu. *The Philosophy of Pan-Africanism*. Georgetown University Press, 1965.

Milingo, E. *The World in Between: Christian Healing and the Struggle for Spiritual Survival*. Maryknoll, N.Y., Orbis, 1984.

Monti, Franco. *African Masks*. New York, Paul Hamlyn, 1969.

Moore, Basil, ed. *The Challenge of Black Theology in South Africa*. Atlanta, John Knox Press, 1974.

Morel, E. D., *Red Rubber: The Story of the Rubber Slave Trade Flourishing on the Congo in the year of Grace 1906*. Negro University Press, 1969.

Mulago, Vincent. *Un visage africaine du Christianisme*. Paris, Présence Africaine, 1962.

———, et al. *Des prêtres noirs s'interrogent*. Paris: Les Editions du C. E. R. F.

Murphy, E. Jefferson. *History of African Civilization*. New York, Dell, 1972.

Murray, Jocelyn, ed. *Cultural Atlas of Africa*. New York, Facts on File Publications, 1981.

Mushete, Ngindu, ed. *Combats pour un Christianisme africain: Mélanges en l'honneur du Professeur V. Mulago*. Kinshasa, Faculté de Théologie Catholique, 1981.

Muzorewa, Gwinyai H. *The Origins and Developments of African Theology*. Maryknoll, N.Y., Orbis, 1985.

Mzimela, Sipo. *Apartheid: South African Naziism*. New York, Vantage, 1983.

Ndiokwere, Nathaniel, I. *Prophecy and Revolution*. London, SPCK, 1981.

Nelson, Hart M. *Black Church in the Sixties*. University Press of Kentucky, 1975.

Newman, Dorothy et al., *Protest, Politics, and Prosperity*. New York, Pantheon, 1978.

Nketia, J. H. Kwabena. *The Music of Africa*. New York, Norton, 1974.

Nkrumah, Kwame. *Africa Must Unite*. New York, International Publishers, 1970.

———. *Challenge of the Congo*. New York, International Publishers, 1967.

———. *Class Struggle in Africa*. London: Panaf Books, 1981.

———. *Consciencism*. New York, Monthly Review Press, 1970.

———. *Ghana: The Autobiography of Kwame Nkrumah*. New York, International Publishers, 1981.

———. *Neo-Colonialism: The Last Stage of Imperialism*. New York, International Publishers, 1965 reprinted, London, Panaf Books, 1981.

———. *Revolutionary Path*. London, Panaf Books, 1980.

Nyerere, Julius. *Crusade for Liberation*. New York, Oxford University Press, 1978.
———. *Man and Development*. New York, Oxford University Press, 1974.
———. *Ujamaa—Essays on Socialism*. New York, Oxford University Press, 1968.
Obbo, Christine. *African Women: Their Struggle for Economic Independence*. London, Zed Press, 1980.
Okere, Theophilus. *African Philosophy: A Historico-Hermeneutical Investigation of the Conditions of Its Possibility*. New York, University Press of America, 1983.
Oliver, Roland, ed. *The Middle Age of African History*. New York, Cambridge University Press, 1981.
———. and Fagan, Brian. *Africa in the Iron Age c. 500 B.C. to A.D. 1400*. New York, Cambridge University Press, 1975.
Omer-Cooper, J.D. *The Zulu Aftermath: A Nineteenth-Century Revolution in Bantu Africa*. Burnt Mill, Longman Group, 1980.
Ottaway, David and Marina. *Afro-Communism*. New York, Africana Publ. Co. 1981.
Ottenberg, Simon and Phoebe, eds. *Cultures and Societies of Africa*. New York, Random House, 1960.
Padmore, George. *Pan-Africanism or Communism?* New York, Roy Publishers, n.d.
Parrinder, Geoffrey. *African Traditional Religion*, 3rd ed. London, Sheldon Press; 1974; New York, Harper & Row, 1976.
Pobee, John S. *Toward an African Theology*. Nashville, Abingdon, 1979.
Quarles, Benjamin. *Black Abolitionist*. New York, Oxford University Press, 1975.
———. *The Negro in the Making of America*. New York, Collier, 1969.
Raboteau, Albert. *Slave Religion*. New York, Oxford University Press, 1980.
Radcliffe-Brown, A.R., and Forde, Daryll, eds. *African Systems of Kinship and Marriage*. New York, Oxford University Press, 1965.
Radin, Paul, ed. *African Folktales*. New York, Schocken, 1983.
Ranger, T. O., and Kimambo, I. N., eds. *The Historical Study of African Religion*. Nairobi, Heineman, 1972.
Rattray, Robert. *Religion and Art in Ashanti*. London, Oxford University Press, 1959.
———. *Tribes of the Ashanti Hinterland*, vol. 1. Oxford, Clarendon, 1932.
Ray, Benjamin C. *African Religions: Symbol, Ritual, and Community*. Englewood Cliffs, N.J., Prentice-Hall, 1976.
Reynolds, Barrie. *Magic, Divination and Witchcraft among the Barotse of Northern Rhodesia*. Berkeley, University of California Press, 1963.
Richardson, Harry. *Dark Salvation*. Garden City, N.Y., Anchor, 1976.
Riefenstahl, Leni. *The Last of the Nuba*. New York, Harper & Row, 1973.
Roberts, J. Deotis. *A Black Political Theology*. Philadelphia, Westminster, 1974.
———. *Black Theology Today: Liberation and Contextualization*. Lewiston, Pa., Edwin Mellen Press, 1984.
———. *Liberation and Reconciliation: A Black Theology*. Philadelphia, Westminster, 1971.
———. *Roots of a Black Future*. Philadelphia, Westminster, 1980.
Rodney, Walter. *How Europe Underdeveloped Africa*. Dar es Salaam, Tanzania Publishing House, 1972.
Rosberg, Carl G., and Nottingham, John. *The Myth of Mau Mau: Nationalism in Kenya*. New York, Meridian, 1970.
Rubin, Leslie, and Weinstein, Brian. *Introduction to African Politics*, 2nd ed. New York: Holt, Rinehart, and Winston, 1977.
Ruchames, Louis. *Racial Thought in America*. University of Massachusetts Press, 1969.
Samartha, S. J. ed. *Living Faiths and Ultimate Goals: Salvation and World Religions*. Maryknoll, N.Y., Orbis, 1975.
Sanneh, Lamin. *West African Christianity: The Religious Impact*. Maryknoll, N.Y., Orbis, 1983.
Sawyerr, Harry. *Creative Evangelism: Towards a New Christian Encounter with Africa*. London, Lutterworth, 1968.
———. *God: Ancestor or Creator? Aspects of Traditional Belief in Ghana, Nigeria, and Sierra Leone*. London, Longman, 1970.
Shorter, Aylward. *African Christian Spirituality*. Maryknoll, N.Y., Orbis, 1980.
———. *African Christian Theology*. Maryknoll, N.Y., Orbis, 1977.
Sidran, Ben. *Black Talk*. New York, DaCapo Press, 1981.
Simpkins, Cuthbert Ormond. *Coltrane: A Biography*. Philadelphia, Hendon House, 1975.

Simpson, George Eaton. *Black Religions in the New World*. New York, Columbia University Press, 1978.

Sitkoff, Harvard. *The Struggle for Black Equality 1954–1980*. New York, Hill and Wang, 1981.

Sobel, Mechal. *Trabelin' On: The Slave Journey to an Afro-Baptist Faith*. Westport, Ct., Greenwood, 1979.

Southall, Roger. *South Africa's Transkei*. New York, Monthly Review Press, 1983.

Stamp, Kenneth. *The Peculiar Institution: Slavery in the Ante-Bellum South*. New York, Random House, 1956.

Stearns, Marshall W. *The Story of Jazz*. New York, Oxford University Press, 1982.

Sundkler, Bengt, G.M. *Bantu Prophets in South Africa*, 2nd ed. New York, Oxford University Press, 1961.

Sweet, Leonard. *Black Images of America 1784–1870*. New York, Norton, 1976.

Tallant, Robert. *Voodoo in New Orleans*. New York, Collier, 1962.

Tempels, Placide. *Bantu Philosophy*. Paris, Présence Africaine, 1959.

Thompson, Robert Farris. *Flash of the Spirit*. New York, Random House, 1984.

Thurman, Howard. *Jesus and the Disinherited*. Nashville, Abingdon-Cokesbury, 1949.

Turner, Harold W. *History of an African Independent Church: The Church of the Lord (Aladura)*, 2 vols. Oxford, Clarendon Press, 1967.

Tuttle, William. *Race Riot: Chicago in the Red Summer of 1919*. New York, Atheneum, 1972.

Tutu, Desmond. *Crying in the Wilderness*. John Webster, ed. Grand Rapids, Eerdmans, 1982.

———. *Hope and Suffering*. Mothobi Mutloatse, comp.; John Webster, ed. Grand Rapids, Eerdmans, 1984.

Wade-Gayles, Gloria. *No Crystal Stair: Visions of Race and Sex in Black Women's Fiction*. New York, Pilgrim Press, 1984.

Walker, David. *Appeal to the Coloured Citizens of the World*. New York, Hill and Wang, 1965.

Wallace, Michelle. *Black Macho and the Myth of the Super-Woman*. New York, Warner Books, 1980.

Wallerstein, Immanuel. *Africa; The Politics of Independence*. New York, Random House, 1969.

Warren, Robert P. *Who Speaks for the Negro?* New York, Random House, 1965.

Washington, Joseph. *Black Religion*. Boston, Beacon, 1964.

Webster, J.B., and Boahen, A.A. *History of West Africa: The Revolutionary Years—1815 to Independence*. New York, Praeger, 1972.

Wells, Ida B. *Crusade for Justice*. Alfreda M. Duster, ed. University of Chicago Press, 1970.

West, Cornel. *Prophesy Deliverance!* Philadelphia, Westminster, 1982.

West, Richard. *Back to Africa: A History of Sierra Leone and Liberia*. New York: Holt, Rinehart, and Winston, 1970.

Whitten, Norman and Szwed, John, eds. *Afro-American Anthropology: Contemporary Perspectives*. New York, Free Press, 1970.

Williams, Chancellor. *The Destruction of Black Civilization*. Chicago, Third World Press, 1976.

Williams, Walter. *Black Americans and the Evangelization of Africa 1877–1900*. University of Wisconsin Press, 1982.

Wilmer, Valerie. *The Face of Black Music*. New York, DaCapo Press, 1976.

———. *As Serious As Your Life*. Westport, Ct., Lawrence Hill, 1981.

Wilmore, Gayraud. *Black Religion and Black Radicalism*, 2nd ed. Maryknoll, N.Y., Orbis, 1983.

Wilmore, Gayraud, and Cone, James H. *Black Theology: A Documentary History, 1966–1979*. Maryknoll, N.Y., Orbis, 1979.

Wiredu, Kwasi. *Philosophy and an African Culture*. New York, Cambridge University Press, 1980.

Woodson, Carter G. *The History of the Negro Church*. Washington, D.C., Associated Publishers, 1972.

Woodward, Vann G. *The Strange Career of Jim Crow*, 2nd rev. ed. New York, Oxford University Press, 1966.

X, Malcolm. *The Autobiography of Malcolm X*. As told to Alex Haley. New York, Ballantine, 1981.

———. *By Any Means Necessary*. New York, Pathfinder Press, 1980.

———. *The End of White World Supremacy: Four Speeches by Malcolm X*. Imam Benjamin Karim, ed. New York, Seaver Books, 1971.

———. *Malcolm X on Afro-American History*. New York, Pathfinder Press, 1979.

———. *Malcolm X Speaks*. George Breitman, ed. New York, Grove, 1966.

———. *Malcolm X Talks to Young People*. New York, Pathfinder Press, 1982.

————. *Two Speeches by Malcolm X*. New York, Pathfinder Press, 1972.

Zahan, Dominique. *The Religion, Spirituality, and Thought of Traditional Africa*. Chicago, University of Chicago Press, 1979.

Zuesse, Evan M. *Ritual Cosmos: The Sanctification of Life in African Religions*. Ohio University Press, 1979.

Index

Compiled by James Sullivan